LET ME TELL YOU A STORY

LET ME TELL YOU A STORY

A Memoir of a Wartime Childhood

Renata Calverley

WINDSOR
PARAGON

First published 2013
by Bloomsbury
This Large Print edition published 2013
by AudioGO Ltd
by arrangement with
Bloomsbury Publishing Plc

Hardcover   ISBN: 978 1 4713 2416 1
Softcover   ISBN: 978 1 4713 2417 8

British Library Cataloguing in Publication Data available

Printed and bound in Great Britain by
MPG Books Group Limited

I dedicate this book to my husband, Bruce,
my daughters, Sarah and Kay,
and the rest of my family

CHAPTER ONE

September 1939. 10,
Jagiellońska Street, Przemyśl

'Wake up, Renata! wake up!' Mamusia's voice was urgent.

I turned over and started to pull the covers over my head. I didn't want to get up. I wanted my mother to go away and leave me alone. But Mamusia was already wrapping me up in her quilt. She lifted me out of bed and began stumbling along the long narrow corridor, past the kitchen and the bathroom and out of the apartment towards the stairwell. She hugged me tighter as we hurried down the two flights of stairs, past the big front door and on down towards the basement. Half awake now, I clung to her. I was afraid she would drop me on the hard floor. She had never run down the stone steps before. Hadn't she always told me never to run down the stairs?

You must always walk carefully, Renata, and hold the banister rail.

She had told me this over and over again even though the rail was well above my head and walking downstairs, holding on, was most uncomfortable. But tonight was different.

In the distance I could hear the sound of thunder—big, loud crashes raging around us. It must be a bad storm, I thought, if we had to leave our home in the middle of the night and shelter in that dark, smelly basement. When we reached the cellar beneath our apartment block,

1

our neighbours were already huddled together, wrapped in blankets, talking in low voices. Through the half-light I could see Babcia, my grandmother, amongst the ghostly faces but I couldn't find my father.

'Where's Tatuś?' I asked.

'Darling, he's somewhere in Europe still, with the Polish Army,' Mamusia said, sighing deeply.

'Why?' I asked.

'Because there's a war on. As I told you before.'

I clutched Rabbit tightly inside my quilted cocoon.

She placed me gently on the ground and stood up, turning her attention to our neighbours' urgent whispers. No one had explained to me what war was. I pulled her quilt closer around me, tucking it back under my feet where its folds were letting in the cold autumnal air. I buried my face in its softness and surrounded myself with the recognisable smell of my mother. In the flicker of candlelight Mamusia's quilt came alive. The familiar peacocks, embroidered with the multicoloured threads that I liked to pull when Mamusia wasn't looking, spread out like huge, colourful fans in hundreds of blues; their emerald-green eyes had all turned and were watching me.

It reminded me of the story of the giant with a hundred eyes who guarded the gates of a mysterious place called the Underworld. People went there when they died—or had it been the giant who guarded a cow that belonged to a goddess and she had put each of his hundred eyes on the tail of her favourite bird, the peacock? I yawned. I couldn't remember—I would have to ask Mamusia

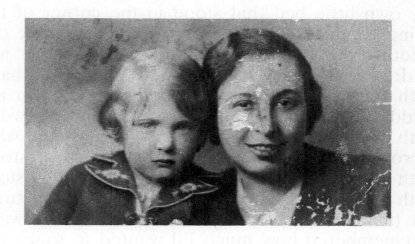

Renata and her Mamusia, Tosia, before the
outbreak of the Second World War

to tell me the story again. I wanted to hear all her
wonderful stories again. The ones she told whilst
getting ready to go out when I would sit at the foot
of her bed on her dark blue velvet chaise longue,
watching her.

'Do I look nice?' she always asked me.

I would look at her smiling lips, her big brown
eyes surrounded by a mass of shiny dark hair.

'Oh, yes. You look beautiful,' I'd answer every
time, as she finished putting on her make-up and
straightening her hair, because she was. Mamusia
was the most beautiful mother in the whole wide
world.

In the flickering candlelight I felt myself being
hushed back to sleep by the murmuring voices. I
didn't resist because the peacocks were watching
the darkness, protecting me from the crashes of
thunder that raged outside.

3

When I awoke the next morning, I was back in my own little bed that stood in the corner of the living room. I looked round, trying to work out whether the events of last night were real or just a dream. The heavy table and matching chairs with their lion-paw feet were still standing in the middle of the room. The large sideboard crowded with silver ornaments still leaned against the wall. Across the room, the blue-and-white stove stood with its head touching the ceiling. I loved that stove with its heat and shiny tiles; some had little pictures on them of the countryside, others had flowers. I remembered how much I'd wanted to touch the people with their funny pointed hats and strange clumsy shoes that Mamusia called clogs. I loved sitting near the stove with Mamusia while she told me stories and we ate bowls of wild strawberries and sour cream. Then came the moment when finally Babcia and Mamusia were out of the room at the same time and I ran over to touch those magical scenes. But the stove was hot and burned my fingers. I stuck my finger in my mouth to stop myself from crying. I never touched the stove again but I never stopped looking at the pictures.

The smell of Babcia's cooking drifted through from the kitchen. It made me feel hungry so I called out to my grandmother. But it was Mamusia who appeared in her bedroom doorway, the one between my bed and the stove. She smiled at me.

'My little darling is awake,' she said, lifting me out of bed, hugging me tight and planting a kiss on the top of my head. 'It's time for breakfast, sweetheart.'

She didn't say anything about last night. The storm had passed and everything was just the same

4

as before. It must just have been a bad dream.

*   *   *

But things weren't the same as before. Mamusia and Babcia were the same, our house and the things we did every day remained the same. Mamusia still went out most days to her work. I would be left at home with Babcia and Marynia, my nanny. Marynia still took me out for my afternoon walk, even though my cousin Zazula didn't accompany us any more. Yet *something* had changed. I didn't know what.

At first it was little things, Mamusia and Babcia no longer laughed quite as much. They would often go quiet when I walked into the room and then start whispering when I left. Mamusia wrote a letter to my father every day. To begin with he used to write back, and Mamusia would lift me up and together we would sit at her writing desk. She would open the thin grubby envelopes and read aloud Tatuś's news, repeating his words once, twice, even three times. Then she would take her own thick cream paper from a small drawer in the front of the desk, pick up her black pen and write a reply. I would watch as her fingers guided the ink across the page leaving its trail of black loops, dots and squiggles that I could not understand. But now she would leave me playing with my toys and sit alone at her desk with a big frown on her face. She wrote letter after letter.

In the beginning I wanted to help. I would leave my toys and go to her at her desk.

'Are you writing to Tatuś?' I would ask and try to climb on to her lap.

5

'Yes. Now go and play with Rabbit,' she would say, stroking my hair and then gently pushing me away. 'I need to concentrate and get this letter in the post.'

After trying to climb up on to her lap a few times I gave up. It was always better not to disturb my mother when she was concentrating. Yet although she wrote lots and lots of letters on her lovely cream paper, she hardly ever received one of Tatuś's grey, grubby ones in reply. More often than not, her cream envelopes were returned unopened.

Great-aunt Zuzia, Babcia's sister, didn't change. She still came to visit. I always knew when she was on her way to see us because I could hear the *clickety-clack* of her shoes with the long, thin heels in the street below. I would stand on tiptoe on the balcony outside my parents' bedroom and peer over the railings in between the hundreds of pots brimming with flowers. I couldn't wait for Aunt Zuzia to come. I'd watch her walking along the pavement until she was swallowed by the door of our apartment block. Then I would run to our front door and sit on the top stone step and wait for her. I could hear her as she climbed the stairs, *clickety-clack*, to our apartment. I loved the visits from Aunt Zuzia.

Aunt Zuzia was *always* happy and laughing, smothering me with kisses and presents. She brought me pretty things like the special grown-up outfits I loved best. She and her husband, Great-uncle Julek, didn't have any daughters, only two sons, my cousins Fredzio and Jerzyk. They were much older than me. Aunt Zuzia always wore the most beautiful clothes, bright colours— reds and blues, yellows and pinks. Her shoes were

6

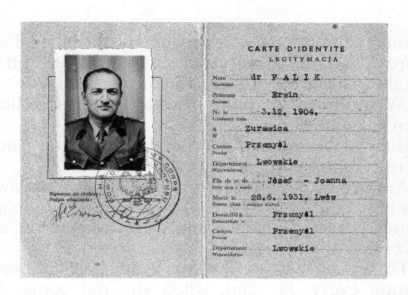

The identity card belonging to Renata's father, Dr Erwin
Falik, when he joined the Polish army as a physician

so elegant with their high heels, bows and buckles.
Babcia used to sigh and say, 'She's as colourful as
a butterfly.' She did look like a butterfly and when
I grew up, I wanted to look like my happy Aunt
Zuzia.

One day, while carrying me up the stairs to our
apartment, whispering and giggling, she slipped
and fell. One of the heels of her scarlet peep-toe
sandals came off. We sat there on the stairs and
stared at the broken shoe. We were stunned and
dismayed. I thought she'd be so cross but when I
caught her eye she burst out laughing. We laughed
and laughed. Then Aunt Zuzia pulled herself up
and tried to walk but she went *loppity-lop* on one
side and kept falling over.

7

I could *not* understand why life wasn't normal any more. What had the storm done to our lives? I tried to talk to Mamusia but she didn't understand.

'What storm, darling?' she said as if she didn't even remember.

Babcia just shook her head. 'Run along now, there's a good girl, and play with your toys.'

And where was Tatuś? He had never been away this long before. Every day I wished he would come home because Mamusia now always looked sad and never had any time to play.

Then came the week when Aunt Zuzia stopped visiting every day and, when she did come, she brought with her grumpy Great-uncle Julek instead of exciting presents.

'Why is Uncle Julek always so miserable?' I asked Babcia.

'There is a war on,' Babcia explained. 'Your uncle has a lot of sick people to look after. He has to work long hours in the hospital and not in his own clinic any more. The hospital stays open all day and night. That's why he's so tired.'

This war was beginning to get on my nerves. I asked Mamusia again and again what it was. She always said that it was when men were fighting each other but whenever I peeped out of the window I never saw any men fighting. She never said why the war had made my father disappear or my beautiful happy Aunt Zuzia almost as grumpy as Uncle Julek. She was always crying now and talking about Cousin Jerzyk as if he was dead and as for Uncle Julek, well, he never smiled and became grumpier with every visit.

Other relatives, those who had often come to our house too, stopped visiting altogether; Cousin Fredzio and his beautiful wife Frederika from Lwów, Aunt Adela, the wife of Mamusia's brother Uncle Cesio, and their daughter, my cousin Zazula. Tatuś's parents from the country never visited and I soon forgot what they looked like. The grown-ups now spent their time talking in low, serious voices about boring things I still did not understand like *war* and *Germans*, whoever *they* might be.

Then one day even Aunt Zuzia and Uncle Julek stopped coming and the apartment seemed very empty. I felt lonely and sad. Even my nanny, Marynia, no longer came to pick me up and take me for our daily walks in the park. I missed the laughter, the love, feeling safe. I could not understand what had happened but I knew that the nice things had gone and they weren't coming back and no one would tell me why.

Renata on the balcony of Jagiellońska Street, 1938

'Wake up, Renata! Wake up!'

I woke up without protest, listening for the thunder. I grabbed Rabbit and followed Mamusia along the hallway. She didn't say anything. Babcia came out of her bedroom next to mine and the three of us made our way down the steps to the basement, together with everyone else in the apartment block. Another storm was raging outside and I was tired. I just wanted to go back to sleep. But I knew that I mustn't argue and must do as I was told. Mamusia had that look on her face—she was concentrating. A little while later, wrapped in her blue peacock quilt, I fell asleep on the cold, hard cellar floor.

This time when I woke up we were still in the basement. The thunder hadn't stopped.

'Why are we still here?' I asked Mamusia. I was scared, I didn't know what was going on.

'Oh, my darling, I didn't realise that you were awake.' Mamusia pulled me towards her. 'The Germans are bombing the city.' Mamusia groped for my hand in the darkness and held it tight. We huddled closer together in that cold, dank basement for what seemed like forever. Then at last the thunder stopped and, one by one, everyone left the basement and went back upstairs.

Our apartment was filled with smoke. It smelt horrid and made me choke. I rushed down the hallway, through the living room, past my bed and on into Mamusia's room to look out of the window.

'Mamusia!' I cried. 'The balcony is broken and Babcia's flowers are all over the street. There is a bed down there too. What's happened? Where is everyone? The street is empty!'

The balcony was hanging off the wall and I didn't dare go out. The railing had broken and now Babcia's pots full of beautiful flowers that had filled the balcony had gone. I looked out onto the street. I didn't recognise the view. The tall stone houses were dirty and their balconies had collapsed. Their flowers and flowerpots sat on the pavement with mounds of earth, tables and chairs. The street below, which was usually full of people, was empty. The smell of burning was worse than inside.

Mamusia didn't answer my questions. Instead she picked me up and held me close. I could feel her tears wet on my cheeks. Then after a while, she said, 'Don't worry, darling, at least we are safe.'

'Safe from what?' I stared at her. 'The thunder?'

'Safe from the bombs and the soldiers fighting. That's why we had to go into the basement so that we wouldn't get hurt. It doesn't matter about our things, as long as you and me and Babcia are safe. It's all over for now.'

At last I was beginning to understand what was happening—there was no thunder, just the bombs that the men were using to fight each other. But these fights were worse than those I had with Cousin Zazula, these man-fights meant breaking things that weren't theirs and hurting people they didn't know. Suddenly I realised that maybe Cousin Jerzyk really was dead after all. I looked over Mamusia's head and saw plumes of smoke blotting out the summer sun and the view of the River San and the mountains beyond.

Babcia was wandering through the rooms of the apartment, as if she were walking and sleeping at

11

the same time, leaving a trail of footprints in the dust that also filled the air and was now settling on the stove, the furniture, on the Persian rugs that covered the wooden floors, the silver on the sideboard, the writing paper on Mamusia's little desk. Even the pictures that now hung crookedly on the walls.

We both just stood and stared.

Then suddenly Mamusia looked at me and said brightly, 'Don't worry, it is nothing that a little bit of cleaning can't put to rights.' She patted her skirts and turned towards the broom cupboard and began to make a start.

*   *   *

A few days later, Mamusia came back from a visit to town looking worried and carrying something in her hand. Babcia met her at the door and took her into the kitchen. Usually I wasn't allowed in the kitchen in case I hurt myself—my grandmother was the boss of that room and she was the cook. But that afternoon I followed and sat with them at the small table.

'Uncle Julek has told me that we mustn't go out of our front door without wearing one of these,' Mamusia said.

She opened up her hand and showed us three yellow six-pointed stars. Looking at them in the dim light of the kitchen, I thought they looked quite pretty, just like stars fallen from heaven on a clear night, except that the colour was not quite right and the points were too short. I wouldn't mind having to wear one of those.

'Why? Why us?' said Babcia.

'All of us,' Mamusia replied, 'all of us . . . Jews. Julek says we have no choice. Gestapo orders.'

'What does it mean?' Babcia asked. 'Why only us?'

I felt glad that I wasn't the only one who didn't understand.

'We have to wear it,' Mamusia said quietly. 'Julek was insistent and he should know now that he is on the committee that liaises with the Gestapo. It'll only be for a while, until the war is over.'

War.

There was that word again. So war meant more than soldiers fighting and breaking things that weren't theirs, it also meant soldiers killing each other and we, who didn't want to fight, having to wear pretty little stars so that they wouldn't hurt us by mistake. Pretty stars to keep us safe. I liked that idea. I felt very grown-up now that I knew what Mamusia and Babcia were talking about.

But then Babcia spoilt it by saying, 'I don't like this. I don't like this at all.'

*   *   *

The next day Mamusia went off to work as usual. She made sure that the yellow star wouldn't fall off the arm of her coat before opening the apartment door. I went back to playing with my toys. In the living room I had lots of toys, soft toys of every description, spinning tops and of course dolls—all in pretty dresses. My special doll was Baby Doll dressed in a long white nightdress with lace around the neck and sleeves. She lay in her very own pram.

'Oh you and Baby Doll,' Mamusia always

laughed. 'The day Tatuś and I gave you that pram, you would *not* let go of it. Even when you were asleep, you held on to it firmly through the railings of your cot—all night. We couldn't prise your fingers off it for fear of waking you.'

I loved Baby Doll but Rabbit was my favourite. He had a blue coat, red shoes and stripy trousers. He had to go everywhere with me. I could not bear to be away from him day or night. Whenever I felt scared, Rabbit was with me. He hugged me when I was sad. He dried my tears when I was crying. He *always* listened to me and he never looked cross. I loved to suck his floppy brown ears and tell him all my secrets, like touching the stove. He *never* once told anybody else.

I put Rabbit on the floor and was trying to get my spinning top to go. It was bright red and stood upright on one leg. It had a handle that I had to pump up and down to make it spin. But I wasn't very good at the pumping and I couldn't get it to spin.

'Babcia,' I called out as usual. 'Please spin my spinning top for me.'

Babcia never complained. Out she came, wiping her hands on a tea towel, her kind eyes smiling. She lowered herself on to the floor beside me. Once settled, she pumped its handle up and down and then away my spinning top spun across the room in a flash of colours. We watched it gradually slow and wobble before toppling onto its side. I crawled after it on my hands and knees.

Babcia sat on the floor, smiling, saying, 'Quick! Catch the top, Renata.'

When I had, I handed it back and Babcia pumped the handle and sent it spinning across the room all over again.

Mamusia had not been gone long when she reappeared at the front door. It was strange to see her home so early and Babcia heaved herself onto her knees and then slowly stood up leaning on one of the chairs and went to the door.

'What is it?' I heard her ask.

Mamusia closed the front door and began to take off her coat.

'They don't want me any more,' she said. 'I am no longer allowed to work at the university. I am no longer required.'

I saw the yellow star on the arm of her coat before she let it fall onto the chair beside her.

'I don't know how we will survive without my salary. None of the money from Erwin has reached us. We should have done what they advised us to do—given up our religion and we could all have gone with him to . . .' She never finished her sentence, only looked at Babcia guiltily before saying, 'I shall have to find some other work.'

Days passed and my mother was out from early morning until late at night. I saw little of her and, when I did, she had no energy left to play with me. I would sit in her lap, my head on her chest, listen to the steady beating of her heart and wish things would go back to how they were before. Then one evening she returned with news.

'At last,' she said, 'Julek has managed to find me some work in the hospital. It's only menial work but at least there will be a little bit of money coming in.'

I was so happy because Babcia and Mamusia were smiling again.

Then I noticed changes inside our apartment. The beautiful things that had filled our house were

15

gradually disappearing. One morning I woke to find the large silver teapot on the sideboard, opposite my cot, was missing. I lay in my bed staring at the empty space.

At first I thought that Babcia must have put all the beautiful things in our apartment away, out of my reach, like she'd always threatened to do. She didn't like me touching the ornaments, running my fingers along their smooth surfaces. But I liked to stare at my reflection in the polished silver and make faces. I loved looking into the faces of the little porcelain ladies that Babcia so treasured. The prettiest things were in my grandmother's bedroom, which was like an Aladdin's cave. Her 'jewel', as she called it, was a large ornate box full of chocolates and sweets, just for me.

'But, Mamusia, where has it gone?' I asked when she came into the room. 'Has someone taken it?'

'No, my love. I had to sell it.'

Now I knew what had really happened to Mamusia's beautiful things.

*   *   *

Just before New Year, Aunt Zuzia made a surprise visit to our apartment. We hadn't seen her for ages and I was overjoyed to see her. But my smile froze when I saw that her feet were bare; she was shaking like a leaf.

'They've been to our house and taken my clothes, and my furs,' she cried. 'I was too frightened to stay in our apartment on my own waiting for Julek to return. So I decided to come here.' She sat down on the chair by the door and nervously pressed her little yellow star. 'You'll never believe this! On my

16

way here, they demanded my boots. What are they doing—what on earth is happening?'

'Who are they?' I asked. Now I was really frightened. Someone was stealing people's clothes and boots.

No one answered my question.

Mamusia put her arms around Aunt Zuzia and then went to fetch a bowl of warm water for Aunt Zuzia's frozen feet. Babcia disappeared into her room and I could hear her rummaging through her wardrobe. When she returned, Babcia was holding a pair of shoes and some clean stockings in her hand.

'Here, take these.' She gave Aunt Zuzia a pair of worn brown shoes. 'The soles are still good. They are a bit small for me so they should fit you. I won't be needing them.'

Aunt Zuzia took the shoes and reached forward and gave Babcia a big hug. As Aunt Zuzia sat quietly with her feet in the bowl of warm water I tried to work out who 'they' were and what 'they' would want with Aunt Zuzia's clothes.

'Ah, that's better, I can feel my toes again.' Aunt Zuzia sighed. 'I hope I don't get chilblains.' She dried her feet, put on Babcia's shoes and stockings and made ready to leave.

'I must go,' she said as she pulled on a brown coat that I hadn't seen before. 'I must get back to Julek. He doesn't know what has happened and he'll think I've deserted him.' She gave a funny sort of laugh that sounded more like a sob and quickly kissed the top of my head. Then she squeezed Babcia's hand.

I looked at her strange clothes, the old coat, clumpy brown shoes and thick stockings. She

17

looked more like a brown moth than a colourful butterfly. It was then that I knew that something was terribly wrong.

CHAPTER TWO

June 1942–September 1943. Przemyśl Ghetto

The loud bang made me jump. I'd been playing on the floor with my toys. I ran over to the open window in my parents' bedroom just ahead of Babcia, leaned over the broken railings and peered down into the street below.

I grabbed Babcia's hand.

'Did you see it?' I asked excitedly, pulling at her sleeve and jumping up and down.

'Calm down, my darling.' Babcia tried to move herself between me and the window.

But I could already see people gathering on the street below.

'There's going to be another one,' I yelled. 'Let me see!'

Babcia took no notice of my cries and pulled me away from the window and back into the room.

'But I wanted to see the fireworks,' I shouted. 'I haven't seen any for ages.'

Babcia let go of my arm and returned to the window. 'Stay where you are,' she ordered before drawing the curtains and blocking out the summer sunshine.

'But, Babcia!' I cried, unable to understand why she didn't want me to see these wonderful things.

'But nothing.'

She drew me towards her and led me to the big sofa that stood in front of the blue-and-white-tiled stove. She picked up a large book of fairy tales from the small table at the end of my bed, sat down and made herself comfortable.

'Well,' she said, looking up at me. 'Do you want a story?'

It was earlier than usual for my favourite part of the day but I wasn't going to complain. I climbed on to the sofa and together in the dim light of the living room we left the apartment and began our journey into the land of magic. Babcia's soft voice wove its way through the tales that I knew by heart but, even so, each time I heard them I discovered new and exciting words, and the pictures in my head became more real. I drank in everything and soon forgot that down in the street below and up into the market square beyond the fireworks were still going off, and I wasn't at the window enjoying them.

Mamusia returned that evening after I'd gone to bed. I heard the front door open and quietly shut, silence and then gentle footsteps cross the wooden floor only to become too soft for me to hear once she reached the Persian rug outside the kitchen. Then I could hear Babcia's voice sounding scared but I couldn't hear what she was saying. Mamusia's replies were calm and unhurried. I caught a few of the words, strange words I hadn't heard before. Then Mamusia was repeating, louder, what she had said, as if Babcia couldn't understand, 'The synagogue has been destroyed.'

Why were my mother and grandmother so worried about the *synagogue*? We had never been there even though it was only just down the road.

19

Then as she opened the kitchen door I heard her say, 'We need to pack. We need to be ready. It could happen at any time.'

I lay in my bed staring at the ceiling.

We are going to leave this place, I thought. Tatuś must be on his way home and he is going to take us away with him. Why else would we be going? We wouldn't be going without Tatuś.

I tried to remember what my father looked like. I could see his dark eyes and the gentle, loving smile as his face came towards me. He was bending over to pick me up and then, holding me high in the air above his head, he was throwing me up towards the ceiling and I was flying and laughing with joy. Just like a bird, I thought, as I spied my yellow canary, Tomek, in his cage at the end of my bed. Then Tatuś's hands were firmly back around my waist catching me, not letting me fall. Safe. Secure. Oh, I love my Tatuś, I thought sleepily, and drifted off to sleep.

But it wasn't my father who banged loudly on the door very early the following morning. I sat up in my bed and watched two soldiers in grey-green uniforms burst in and fill up the narrow hallway. They were carrying guns.

How rude, I thought, as Mamusia came out from her bedroom fully dressed. I watched her cross the living room and go down the hall. I wanted Mamusia to say something, to tell them to go away, but she looked at the two men as if she had been expecting them. The tall one spoke first, barking at Mamusia, and then when Babcia appeared at her bedroom doorway he laughed a horrid laugh and said, 'I'll give you five minutes to get ready. Maximum.'

Then he turned and strode out towards the stairwell, his feet loud on the polished floor. The smaller one stood where he was, watching Mamusia and Babcia gather together their bags and put on their coats, saying nothing. Mamusia came over to me carrying my coat and dress and shoes.

'Come on, darling, put these on,' she said softly.

I could see her hands shaking as she tried to help me with first my dress and then my shoes. She put them on the wrong way round and we had to start all over again.

'Where are we going, Mamusia?' I whispered, afraid of the reply.

My mother didn't look at me. She helped me into my coat, searching for an answer she didn't have.

'And Rabbit? What about Rabbit?' I panicked as the tall soldier came back into the apartment.

'Hurry up!' he barked. 'We have to go.'

Mamusia scanned the room quickly and seeing no sign of Rabbit picked up Baby Doll and pushed her into my arms.

'Here, take your doll,' she said in a voice I didn't recognise.

'But Rab—What about Tomek? Who'll feed him?' I asked, forgetting Rabbit for a moment, as I caught sight of the canary at the end of my bed.

Mamusia looked at the soldiers who were getting impatient.

'Can we bring the bird?' she stammered.

The tall soldier laughed his cold laugh. 'Take what you want. You're leaving now.' His smile disappeared as he raised his gun.

We made our way, the two soldiers pushing us from behind, out of our empty apartment and down the two flights of worn steps and onto the street below where there were more soldiers waiting. I had never been outside so early in the morning, and I hung back, frightened of what was hiding in the shadows. But Mamusia gently pulled my arm and led the way forward. The canary cage bumped against my leg as we were hurried along the street, Babcia's stockinged legs kept pace with mine. I wasn't aware of where we were going or in which direction we were heading. My view was blocked by the river of legs all following the same course, all carrying suitcases and bundles of belongings. I noticed everyone was wearing their yellow stars and no one said a word. Perhaps the sky really had fallen and Chicken Licken was right, after all.

We hadn't gone far when we were directed towards an open doorway. We made our way inside and a soldier pointed his gun towards a second door that was not quite shut. Babcia led the way, gripping her small battered suitcase so hard that the veins stood out like blue worms on the back of her hand. Then Mamusia and I stepped into the room together, holding hands tightly. The German soldier followed with his gun held out in front of him.

The room smelt horrible, like boiled cabbage mixed with the same smell as that of the fruit seller who, sucking on his cigarette, came out from behind his stall to give me a treat whenever Aunt Zuzia and I visited the market. The room was cold and small, blotchy brown in colour with paper curling off the walls. There was only one small, dirty window smeared with finger marks, and newspaper was stuck over much of the glass. It couldn't let in much of the morning light and so the room was dark even though the summer sun was rising outside. The floor was bare and the floorboards grimy. It couldn't have been cleaned for ages.

I glanced at Mamusia, terrified. What were we doing here? I wanted to go home *now*. Mamusia said nothing, she was taking it all in too, the chipped sink in the corner with its dripping tap, the piles of furniture and the empty light sockets dangling from the ceiling tangled up with thick, grey cobwebs and a huge, scary spider with long hairy legs.

The room was so crowded with furniture that it was difficult for Mamusia to find us a space. We had so little with us. At home all our things had finally disappeared and there was so much space to play. But this room was not just for us, there were several people here already. Men and women dressed in ragged clothes were sitting on the iron beds shoved together so that they were almost touching. They did not move or smile, they just watched us silently, each one wearing their yellow star on the left arm. As soon as we were inside, the soldier turned and left, and we heard the door being locked behind him. Still no one spoke but everyone was looking at us. There was no room to move and nowhere to escape.

Mamusia squeezed between the narrow beds, some of which were covered with rags and bits of clothing and others by itchy-looking grey blankets. She found three empty beds for us and, shaking, sat down on one, placing Tomek in his cage on the bed beside her. She looked very shocked. She looked like I felt. We said nothing.

The people remained silent; no one moved. In the middle of the room stood a large metal bucket that stank and steamed—this I later realised was

23

our only toilet.

'Why are we here?' I asked. 'I want to go home. I want Tatuś. And I'm hungry.' Wailing, I turned and clung to Babcia who, like Mamusia, had so far not uttered a word. She took me in her arms and hugged me tightly.

'You know there is a war on,' Mamusia replied. 'Things are always different in a war. We have to live here for now, in this ghetto.'

There it was, something else this war was responsible for. And what was a *ghetto*? Why wouldn't anyone explain to me what it all meant? But I just nodded, I was too tired and didn't feel that I could ask her *again*. I longed to be back at home in my cosy bed with Rabbit and all my other friendly toys around me.

That first night as I lay down to sleep, Mamusia one side and Babcia on the other, the blankets prickled my body and made me itch. Mamusia took me into her bed, held me tight trying to reassure me but I knew that she too longed for our cosy, familiar feather quilts and soft, comfortable beds. Oh, to be able to snuggle down under the covers as I had done every night, and screw my eyes up tight and imagine I was invisible. Then, and only then, would I be able to hide from the monsters that lurked in the shadows. They wouldn't be able to see me and I could fall asleep—safe and warm. But here on this hard, smelly bed, I knew there was no escape. In this room full of shadows, the monsters were everywhere and with every passing moment I could feel them drawing closer until one night I knew they would come out of the shadows and get me. I held on to Mamusia tightly and vowed never to let her go.

24

Soon after we came to stay in the ghetto my mother stopped laughing and her smiles never reached her eyes. She and Babcia were never in the room at the same time. As soon as Mamusia returned, Babcia went out.

'Where are you going?' I asked Mamusia one day as she was preparing to leave me yet again in that dark room.

'You ask me that every day, my darling,' she replied, 'and every day I try to explain to you that I have to go to work, in a factory.'

This word *factory* meant nothing to me. All I wanted was for things to be as they'd always been. I missed the comforting arms of Marynia, my beautiful Aunt Zuzia and Cousin Zazula—where was she? And why did Babcia, who had always been at home to keep me company, now have to go to the factory too?

My rumbling stomach made me think, yet again, of food. I thought about food all the time. I longed for Babcia's *bigos*—a mixture of sausage, meat, *sauerkraut* and spices—and her scrumptious red *borscz* soup that turned a beautiful pale pink with the blob of sour cream that I stirred in with my spoon. I couldn't understand why Babcia had stopped making these delicious things. Wouldn't it cheer us up if we had just one tasty thing to eat? All we'd had to eat since we arrived in this room was slices of sour bread and watery cabbage soup.

I wasn't allowed to go outside and inside there was nowhere to run and play—no children, only Sophie but she was a lot older than me and had to go to work with the grown-ups. I had to keep quiet all day so passed the time in our room eating what

25

little food I was given, talking to Baby Doll (which was not nearly as good as talking to Rabbit) or telling her stories that Mamusia and Babcia used to tell me before we came here. Often I would speak to my little Tomek whose cheeps, like Mamusia's smiles, had almost vanished. I would repeat the strange words I'd heard that day, hoping the meaning would pop into my head, as I watched Babcia moving slowly round the room trying to clean the place—an impossible job.

During the day Babcia was exhausted, having worked all night in the factory. She would often doze in the afternoon and when she fell asleep, facing me, I would study the strong features on her handsome face and let the feeling of utter love wash over me. Her grey-white hair was always drawn tightly back into a bun and she still looked kind, especially when she slept. Yet the furrows on her face were deeper now and from time to time she would frown in her sleep.

The best times were when Babcia was in a more contented mood and she would tell me fairy tales about magic lands which made us forget the horrible room we were in. At other times she recounted stories of my parents, and of Aunt Zuzia or Aunt Adela, while sitting on the end of her bed rocking me in her arms.

The other people in the room were strange and bad-tempered. I tried to stay out of their way as much as possible. To amuse myself, I pulled at the loose strips of wallpaper. Underneath were patches of pinkish-coloured wall, which were so much prettier than the patchy brown covering it, even though they felt wet to the touch. One evening Sophie's mother, an old woman in a headscarf,

26

looked up from her bed and saw me pulling off a long ribbon.

'You wicked child!' she screamed at me, then turned to Mamusia. 'Just look at what your wicked child is doing.'

'Be quiet, you'll frighten her. She wasn't doing anything wrong,' Mamusia replied, trying to calm her down.

'Nothing wrong? *Nothing wrong?*' the woman spat, her eyes like slits and her dark, stained teeth showing through her parted lips.

'The wallpaper was coming off anyway,' my mother replied, doing her best to stick up for me. 'And look, the colour underneath is so much prettier. It's not her fault we are here. She's just a child who should be outside playing in the sunshine, not cooped up in this filthy pigsty. Just leave her alone.'

Mamusia's voice got louder and louder until the woman didn't say another word. She gave us a nasty look and turned her back. From then on Mamusia and the woman didn't speak to one another even though their beds were close together. Life was so miserable.

Mamusia was now constantly unhappy. One minute she would seem not to notice me at all and the next she would be smothering me with kisses as if her life depended upon it. She and Babcia looked sad and worried and would talk together in hushed whispers. Then I began to see Babcia cry. This upset and frightened me terribly and I had to turn to my mother for comfort.

And so I lived in a state of unease—so many puzzling things had happened to change our lives. These new and unpleasant feelings that I didn't understand and the fear of the unknown made me feel heavy and tired and frightened. Then one night as I lay in bed trying to sleep another thought went flashing through my mind: My father had left us and hadn't come back; what if the same thing happened to my mother? I would have no parents, no one to look after me except Babcia but she was old. The fear of this made my heart beat fast and left me cold and sweating. I couldn't imagine anything worse than to lose both my parents. I felt sick and giddy. I was tormented by nightmares that night in which I was lost in a crowd, searching and searching for my parents. By the time I woke up I still hadn't found them.

The days turned into weeks and still we couldn't sleep properly. So many strange noises filled the quietness at night and not just from the other people in the room. Sometimes at night I would hear the rumble of lorries that Sophie's old mother would call a *purge*.

'The lorries are back,' she would call from the dirty window. 'Soldiers and dogs coming to take the next batch.'

'The next batch of what?' I asked.

'Batches of women, men, children. Old or young. Doesn't matter any more,' she replied before someone told her to be quiet.

I would hear the sounds of the engines starting up and the rumble of the lorries driving away.

'So this is what it is to be a Jew,' someone said, 'to be taken away in the middle of the night without being allowed to say goodbye.'

'But where do they take them?' another voice asked.

'Relocated to work camps, so they say,' replied

28

the first. 'They don't come back, not now. They just disappear. Tell me what crime I have committed so that I can ask for forgiveness and let God be my judge, not these Nazis. What crime is there in being Jewish?'

Still I didn't understand. I understood the ghetto was a place where those who didn't want to fight were sent to live and work until the war was over, but these new strange words, *Nazi, crime, purge*, I would repeat over and over again in my head as I lay on my bed trying to find ways to stop being so bored. By listening to the others, I learned quickly. Without knowing, I was learning how to survive.

'Just as if we were playing hide and seek,' Babcia said.

'German soldiers don't like small children,' Mamusia told me. 'They will take you away if they find you and I might never see you again.' She said enough to frighten me and it had the desired effect. Every time a soldier came into the room, I leapt out of sight—lay on the floor, like a sleeping lion, and didn't move a muscle until he left.

*   *   *

One early afternoon Babcia and I had the room to ourselves. Everyone else was at work. Babcia was busy washing clothes in the chipped sink in the corner and I was sitting on my bed hugging Baby Doll, and watching my yellow canary hopping about in his cage. That day, for once, Tomek was chirping away merrily and dropping crumbs everywhere. I loved that canary and spent hours and hours talking to him. The little bird seemed to listen and watch, turning sideways with one black boot-button eye turned towards me. He was my special pet, a reminder of home and all things normal. But today I was feeling so disappointed that I had brought Baby Doll with me rather than Rabbit. I was remembering back to that awful night, Mamusia telling me what to do, what to take in that voice I hadn't recognised. I had seen Rabbit lying on the floor under my bed after Mamusia had pushed Baby Doll into my hands. I had urged Mamusia to get him. 'But there won't be space,' Mamusia had explained. 'We will be sharing a room with a lot of other people and they will have things to bring too. You have to choose.' But I didn't choose. Baby Doll had been chosen for me and Rabbit was forgotten. I wondered if I would ever see him again. I missed him so much. I wanted to tell Rabbit everything. He would know what to do.

Babcia had finished the washing and was draping underwear over the back of a chair and allowing the water to drip onto the bare floorboards.

'Time for your bath, darling,' she said. 'The water is still warm, so you will enjoy it.'

She had carefully saved the water from the washing and poured it into a large enamel basin. I hated baths here. The water was never warm enough and there was no room to splash about and no yellow ducks to float like I used to do. Babcia undressed me quickly and stood me shivering in the basin. She briskly rubbed the lukewarm water over me with a sponge, and then wrapped me in a towel. This was the worst bit. Babcia rubbed and towelled so hard that it hurt and left my skin all tingling and hot. I loved Babcia, but not when she was rubbing me dry with a towel. Next she dressed me in a vest, then pyjamas and finally a sweater over the top to keep me warm. She carried me over to the table and put a bowl of soup and a small piece of bread in front of me. I looked at the soup, angry at being rubbed so hard and frustrated at having to eat that horrible soup, yet again.

I thought back to happier times when, in the evenings, I would sit on the deep sofa in front of the stove snuggled up to Mamusia and sometimes with Babcia too. Mamusia would tell me stories about the people in the pictures on the stove or read to me from my collection of books. I remembered the long summer afternoons when we would sit side by side, eating bowls of wild strawberries with sour cream and sugar or *makowiec*, a delicious cake filled with poppy seeds. There were the cold winter afternoons when we warmed ourselves with bowls of hot soup that Babcia had made from the mushrooms we had collected on our walks, followed by warm pastries fresh from the oven or a slice of creamy cheesecake.

'Don't want soup,' I said. 'I want milk and cake.'

'There isn't any,' said Babcia, sounding tired. 'Eat what you're given.'

I looked into those sweet, kind eyes now dulled by fatigue and worry. With frustration growing inside me, I shouted, '*No*,' and tears welled up in my eyes. Everything became blurry as I began to cry.

Babcia slapped me hard on the leg.

No one had ever smacked me before. I screamed. This was followed by another slap. Suddenly realising what she had done, Babcia picked me up and held me close.

'My darling, my precious,' she murmured in my ear. 'I am so sorry,' and she kissed my smarting leg.

31

I felt her tears on my cheek and realised she was crying too before she wiped her own eyes and kissed my leg again and again. My weeping continued, but it was no longer for myself but because I had made Babcia so angry and unhappy. Then after a while Babcia put me down, sat beside me and patiently spooned the soup into my mouth. We said nothing as I ate obediently; swallowing every mouthful of that tasteless, grey water.

By the time I had finished it was almost dark and there were sounds of activity outside on the street. A factory hooter blared in the distance and voices could be heard. I knew Mamusia would be home soon but then it would be Babcia's turn to put on her coat and scarf, kiss us both and go out. She would be back in the room in the morning when I woke, but then Mamusia would be gone again.

The door opened and a gust of icy wind swept through the room. Mamusia came in and stood in the doorway pulling off her headscarf. With a cry of delight, I jumped across from bed to bed to reach her. She scooped me up in a huge hug. She then set me down and turned to kiss her own mother who was already in her coat and adjusting the yellow star on her sleeve.

'They're due again tomorrow,' I heard Mamusia say.

'Are you sure?' Babcia asked.

'So they say.'

'You mustn't go in. I will say you're sick.'

'Do you think that'll make the slightest difference? If I don't turn up I will be severely punished. It's better to go in and just pray.'

Babcia laughed. 'Praying doesn't make any difference. I stopped praying long ago. How can there be a God who allows *this* to happen?'

Although I didn't understand their words, I felt frightened. Was Mamusia going to leave me like Tatuś? What about Babcia? Who was going to look after me? Would I lose both my parents *and* Babcia? I stared at them wide-eyed and began shaking like a leaf. Mamusia suddenly looked down at me and, turning away from Babcia, smiled.

'I have a treat for you, my darling,' she said, 'but it's our little secret.'

'What? Are we going home? Are we going to see Tatuś? Marynia?'

'No, not yet,' she said. 'But I have something for you. Look.'

She put her hand into her pocket and pulled out a lump of black bread and a small piece of sausage. I stretched out my hands to take it, but my grandmother pulled me back.

'No, Renata. You've had supper. This is for your mother. She's hungry and she must eat to keep up her strength. Do you understand?' she added, looking straight at Mamusia as she pulled on her coat.

'Yes, Mother, I understand,' Mamusia said, kissing Babcia on the cheek as she stepped out into the darkness.

Mamusia closed the door quickly and turned back to smile at me. 'Don't worry, darling, I'll share it with you,' she said and sat down on a bed. 'Let's eat it before the others get back. Now remember this is our little secret.'

I looked lovingly at my mother. Sausage. I hadn't tasted anything like that for ages. My mouth began to water. Yet as I looked into her smiling face I noticed once again that her eyes had stopped shining. They didn't sparkle any more and she always looked sad, even when she smiled. When I hugged her now I could feel her bones sticking out and her hair that used to be so full and shiny was all flat and always pulled back tightly into a bun.

We sat close together on the bed and Mamusia took a small bite from the hunk of bread, but instead of tasting the sausage she put it to her nose and smelt it. Then she took another small nibble of the bread and again smelt the sausage, breathing in deeply to savour it fully. She looked down at me and smiled.

'Have you had some bread with your soup?' she asked.

'Yes,' I replied, 'but I want some sausage, because I'm still hungry and I hate that bread.' I stretched out my hand. Mamusia looked at the sausage and inhaled its smell one last time then handed it to me.

'Enjoy it, my darling,' she said softly.

I snatched the morsel from her and crammed it into my mouth and gobbled it up greedily.

'That was lovely,' I said when the last scrap was gone. 'Can I have some more?'

'There isn't any more,' Mamusia said, stroking my hair.

I pushed her hand away angrily and began to cry. 'I want to go home. I want my Tatuś,' I wept.

The door of the room opened and two women and a man shuffled in. Both of the women were draped in shapeless grey clothes and wore headscarves. The man had a black cap on his head and the tattered remains of a suit. All of them had a yellow star on their sleeve. No one smiled. No one spoke. They just sat down silently on their beds.

34

A moment later the door opened again and a few more people came in. In front was the one I was most scared of, Sophie's mother. She was the one who had shouted at me and called me wicked. Now she collapsed on a bed sobbing loudly.

'She's gone! She's gone!' she wailed, tears running down her wrinkled face.

Forgetting that they weren't friends, Mamusia knelt beside her and put her arms around her. She said nothing. No one said anything. They just listened to the tearful wails of the old woman.

'They came to the factory this afternoon. They just arrived. No warning. They just pointed at people and took them. No warning, no explanation, no time to say goodbye. They just shoved them into trucks. They took my Sophie. My only child. I shall never see her again. Why didn't they take me? I'm old and useless. I'll never see her again.' Her sobbing filled the room.

'Where have they taken Sophie?' I whispered to Mamusia, but Mamusia didn't reply.

A man who looked like a skeleton finally broke the silence.

'Those lorries were going to Auschwitz. I heard one of the Nazis say so. It will be all of us sooner or later. We will all die.'

'A typically spineless male remark!' retorted Janka, a youngish woman with curly black hair and an apron tightly tied round her middle. 'This is no way to survive. We've got to hang on to hope, not just give in. That's what those animals want. They want to break our spirit. Well, they're not going to break mine if I can help it.'

I clung to my mother.

'Remember the child,' Janka said to the room at

35

large. 'She's terrified, poor little mite.'

They turned their blank eyes to me and no one said a word.

*   *   *

As I lay in my bed with my mother beside me, hating the prickly blankets, I tried to make sense of the words and conversations I had heard. I listened to the strange noises coming from the grown-ups around me and found it unfair that the adults could lie in bed making all sorts of grunts and groans and whistles when they were supposed to be asleep and sometimes they would even talk or cry out. Their beds would always creak when they turned over or shifted position. But no one would say anything to *them*. Yet if I awoke from a frightening dream and cried out, everyone woke up and was only too ready to tell me off, calling me 'bad' and 'a nuisance'.

Every night I would worry about something. That night I was worried by the crying of the old woman and Sophie who had been taken away. I hoped and prayed with all my heart that nobody would separate me from Mamusia and Babcia. What had happened to Sophie? Why was Mamusia so upset that evening? Why were all the grown-ups so quiet and troubled when they were usually so grumpy and full of complaints? I stretched out my hand in the dark and felt the humped shape of my mother in the next bed. I felt safe. Mamusia was there, right next to me. She rolled over and lay on her side facing me and I could feel her warm breath on my face.

The next night, I woke from a bad dream. I sat up and crawled to the foot of my bed. By the light

36

of the flickering candle, left burning in case anyone needed to use the bucket at night, I could just make out Mamusia in the bed next to me. Perched on a small wooden table at the foot of the bed was the bird cage covered with a grubby old towel so that little Tomek would sleep too and not disturb anyone. I lifted a corner of the towel and peered at my little yellow bird, sitting on his perch with feathers all fluffed up and his head tucked under one wing. Comforted, I blew him a little kiss, then crawled back under the blanket and was soon fast asleep.

I dreamt that I was at home, in my parents' sunlit bedroom with the blue peacock quilt lying across the bed. I dreamt that Sophie was standing there with her flat brown hair, dirty dress and stockings with holes at the knee. She was talking to one of the peacocks who was nodding and pointing the way with his head. Sophie was staring at the peacock, fascinated by the colours and smiling. I hadn't seen Sophie smile before. Then suddenly, she stepped backwards and disappeared down a big black hole and all I could hear was her screams.

I woke with a start. There was something heavy on my feet, weighing me down. Terrified, I sat up and saw a still, black shape at the foot of my bed. Suddenly the shape lunged forward and leapt into the air. It leapt at the cage and my small yellow canary. The cage toppled off the table and crashed to the floor. The little door swung open and as quick as a flash the cat's paw was inside. Tomek stood no chance, although he fluttered around the cage desperately trying to escape the claws. The hysterical flapping sound of his pathetic wings was followed by a heavy silence. And there was the cat,

37

back on my bed, eating Tomek, with his limp little body dangling out of its mouth. Tiny yellow feathers fluttered like confetti onto the grey blanket. Bursting into loud, agonised wails I tried to grab the cat, which dropped the remains of my beloved canary on the bed and returned silently into the shadows. Beds were creaking; figures were heaving themselves out of sleep into sitting positions.

'Shut that noise up!' a woman's voice snapped.

'Stop that brat howling,' someone else snarled from the darkness. 'The soldiers will be in to shoot us all before you know it.'

'She's upset,' Mamusia said, hugging me close, explaining to the room at large. 'That cat has just eaten her pet canary and she loved him so much.'

'Who cares about a bird when people are dying of starvation? People are being murdered by the Germans? Think of my Sophie. It'll be us sooner or later!' shrieked the old woman. 'What about Hannah?'

There were grunts of agreement from around the room as everyone settled back in bed and soon silence fell.

I'd heard about Hannah that evening after Babcia had left. Mamusia wasn't yet back to distract me. I'd heard how the Nazis had visited the factory without warning. A terror-stricken silence had fallen as everyone stood by helpless and afraid, watching the latest 'chosen' being prodded, beaten and brutalised as they were hustled off to the waiting lorries. That day Mamusia had been spared. They had targeted the old and infirm. Thank goodness Babcia didn't work the day shift.

'Tosia will tell you,' one woman began. 'She was standing next to Esther. Esther made the mistake

38

of trying to shield her mother from the soldiers by standing in front of her,' continued the woman. 'But when she moved in front of Hannah, one of the young soldiers saw the old lady, grabbed her and pushed her with the butt of his rifle.

'Then when Hannah turned round and held out her arms to her daughter, he just kicked her in the back,' another voice interrupted.

'Esther could do nothing but simply stand and watch. She couldn't even say goodbye.'

'Hannah was pushed out of the door and into the waiting lorry.'

'Nothing new there,' came the gruff voice of a man. 'Shan't see her again. She'll be dead before the day's out.'

'Hopefully,' said another. 'Poor Esther. Poor Hannah. Such a lovely woman.'

'But long after the last of the lorries had driven away,' the first voice continued, 'Esther had just stood there still as a statue, white as a ghost, tearless. In shock, probably. She didn't go back to work and guess what, the soldiers just ignored her.'

'Then she broke down, fell to the floor crying and pleading to the darkness to be taken too. They didn't, of course. Just left her there. Animals. It would have been the kindest thing to do.'

Mamusia didn't know that I knew this story. I had already heard others like it. As my mind turned from Hannah, to Sophie, to Tomek and back again I cried inconsolably in Mamusia's arms. I couldn't understand what was happening or why, yet I understood enough to feel the worry and torment and I was terrified. Gradually, in the warmth and comfort of Mamusia's hold, my eyelids became heavier and heavier until at last I fell asleep, soothed by the knowledge that Mamusia was there to protect me.

* * *

That night must have seemed endless for Mamusia. She had spent a sleepless night holding me tight. She must have been glad when the room turning its usual grey meant that it was the morning. Activity of any sort was better than the nightmares that came at night and played tricks with your mind. She tried to get out of bed without waking me, but I stirred as soon as she moved. I remembered immediately that something terrible had happened. I looked to where my canary's cage had stood and burst into tears again. This woke the others and the grumbles of the day began. The smell from the communal bucket grew worse as the occupants of the room took turns to use it, one after another.

The factory hooter sounded and the men and women in the room began to tie their headscarves and put on the ragged remains of their coats. Even though the room was stuffy it was bitterly cold and the sound of rain outside added to the misery.

I was still crying and holding on tightly to Mamusia as she tried to get dressed and pull on her armband with its yellow star with one hand. She kept glancing anxiously at the outer door and I realised that Babcia hadn't yet returned from the night shift.

'Where is Babcia?' I sobbed. I desperately wanted to tell Babcia about Tomek and the horrible black cat. She would understand; she would comfort me. I pushed away the piece of bread Mamusia offered me.

40

'I don't want it,' I said through my tears.

'There's nothing else, darling,' Mamusia said. 'You must eat.'

The factory hooter sounded again. Still the people from the night shift hadn't appeared.

The old woman wailed, 'Another purge. They must be there again.'

The silence outside confirmed the thoughts of all the people in the room.

My mother sat rocking me in her arms, saying nothing. I could feel her shaking. She knew she should be going, but was totally unable to release me and leave me on my own.

Then without warning the door burst open and a German soldier in a heavy overcoat holding a gun in his hands rushed in bringing with him the howling, cold wind.

'Everyone to work. *Now!*' he yelled. 'Stir yourselves, you filthy pigs, before I shoot the lot of you!'

Everyone began to move slowly forward towards the open door through which the wind howled with its biting cold.

Without thinking or being told to do so, as the door opened, I'd automatically jumped out of Mamusia's arms and lain on the floor out of sight between our beds. Mamusia tried to remain calm. I knew she would have to leave me and I prayed that Babcia would turn up quickly. Why hadn't Babcia come back? What was happening? Would Mamusia leave me alone? My mother made a great effort to sound casual and unconcerned as she bent down, pretending to pick something up.

'I must go. Don't move, my precious. Babcia will be here soon to look after you and I will be back

41

this evening,' she whispered. 'Perhaps I may even have another piece of sausage.'

It was too dangerous to kiss me so she moved towards the door after the others and shuffled through without a backward glance.

The soldier waited until the room was empty and with a final glance around he too left, banging the door behind him. He didn't notice the little golden-haired girl lying on the floor between two of the beds.

I lay on the draughty wooden floorboards, just as my mother had told me to do, but still my grandmother didn't return. This was the first time I had been totally alone in the room. I felt cold and very frightened. I stayed where I was, watching the door and hugging Baby Doll, drifting off to sleep and then suddenly waking as the cold and fear gripped me again and again. I was too young to measure time in minutes or hours but, as my stomach growled, I counted the meals I knew I was missing. Breakfast. Lunch. Supper. Hungrier and hungrier.

Eventually, shivering with cold, I walked round the room in search of food. All I could find was a small piece of very dry bread that I swallowed greedily and felt even emptier than before. I returned to the space between the two beds and the empty feeling in my stomach turned to pain, which made me cry. I couldn't balance on the bucket without help, so in the end a warm puddle spread where I sat and eventually I fell asleep.

* * *

I awoke to a room that was completely dark. A

whole day had passed and Babcia hadn't returned. I climbed into Mamusia's bed and crouched under the grey blanket, comforted in part by the familiar smell of my mother.

At last the door opened and the old woman and Janka hurried in.

'Where is she?' Janka said. Then she called out, 'Renata, where are you? Are you here?'

I came out from under the blanket shaking and clutching Baby Doll, my last link with my old life. 'Where is my Mamusia and my Babcia?'

Janka burst into tears, picked me up and hugged me tight, rocking back and forth and crying.

'I want Mamusia!' I wailed, trying to push her away. 'I want my Babcia and I want my canary. I want to go home and I want sausage.'

'Your mummy and granny have had to go away for a little while,' Janka said, releasing her grip a little. 'They asked me to look after you until they come back. You'll be all right with me. I will give you something to eat and you can sleep with me in my bed tonight.' She looked at me kindly.

'I want my Mamusia. I want my Babcia.'

'How are we going to cope with the brat?' the old woman snarled.

I looked at her through my tears. Her face was that of a wicked witch—a walnut covered in wrinkles with a nasty expression. Just like the witch in 'Hansel and Gretel'. She stood well away from me, but leaned forward as if she wanted to snatch me.

'They'll find her and then we'll *all* be dead.'

'I seem to remember a different story from you when your Sophie was taken away. You were only too glad of sympathy. Have some pity for the child

43

and just remember how kind her mother was to you,' Janka spat at her with venom in her voice.

The old woman wiped her eyes and spoke in a slightly softer voice. 'That's all very well but how are you going to cope with that burden round your neck? Don't expect any help from me—or anyone else for that matter. The sooner they catch the brat the better for us all. What's the point of trying to keep her alive now, with no one left to look after her? All the other children have gone. It's only a matter of time.'

'Her mother may come back. Don't be so heartless.' Janka tried to cover my ears.

'Don't make me laugh! Does anyone *ever* come back? Do you think they are taken away for a little *holiday*?' the old woman snarled. 'Grow up, girl; it may be your turn sooner than you think and don't expect me to look after that child if you are taken.'

'You are a hard-hearted old woman. I don't expect anything from you. You're not human. You're just as bad as those German pigs. Don't bother to speak to me again. Just keep out of my way or you'll be sorry.'

I could sense that Janka was very angry, but couldn't really follow what the argument was about.

'When will Mamusia and Babcia come?' I sobbed. 'Who will put me and Baby Doll to bed? I'm so sleepy.'

'I will.' Janka tried to smile and gave me another hug. 'I promised your Mamusia that I would look after you and I will.' Janka looked me in the eyes and wiped my tears away. 'She asked me to give you a big hug from her and to tell you to be a good girl until she gets back. She will try to be back as soon as she can and so will your Babcia.'

'Where have they gone and why didn't they take me with them?' I asked, wanting the answers that no one was prepared to give.

'They've gone away with a lot of other people from the factory in a big lorry,' explained Janka.

'But why didn't they come home and say they were going?' I demanded.

'They weren't allowed to. The Germans were in a hurry and made them leave straight away.'

Janka's voice broke and she wiped her nose on her sleeve.

'*Where* have they gone?' I pleaded.

'I don't know.'

'Tell the child the truth,' said Piotr, the skeleton man who had come in while all this was going on. He stood dabbing at his brow with a filthy handkerchief. 'She'll have to know sooner or later.' Then he turned to me. 'Your mother and grandmother were taken off to Szebnie in a purge. That's what the Nazis said. They will never come back. You'll never see them again. Even if you go there yourself—which you probably will. *If* you live that long.'

His strange, mad laugh filled the room but changed to a yelp of pain as Janka turned and hit him so hard across the mouth that blood spewed out between the gaps in his teeth.

That was September 1943 and I was nearly six. It was the last time I ever saw my Mamusia and Babcia.

One day soon after Mamusia and Babcia disappeared out of my life, panic set in once more. An order had gone out saying that everyone left in the ghetto had to be counted and moved. Piotr turned on Janka and, pointing a dirty finger at me,

45

Mamusia and Renata, 1939

hissed, 'What did I tell you? Her time has come.
All the other children in the ghetto have gone. How
will you hide her now? And if we are going to be
moved how are you going to look after her?'

Janka, looking very pale and worried, drew me
to her and for once couldn't fire off an answer to
Piotr.

'You'll just have to stay here, Renata,' she said.
'Hide like you always do and don't come out for
anyone. No one knows you are here any more so
they won't be looking for you. I will try and come
back for you.'

Piotr snorted but a look from Janka silenced

46

him. I could tell in the way she spoke that she too knew that, if chosen, she wouldn't be able to come back to find me. We sat silently on the bed together holding on to each other and not saying a word. I was too frightened to cry and Janka was too tired or too worried to tell me that everything would be all right. I could feel the faceless monster from the dark shadows creeping ever closer.

From somewhere outside we heard noises. Barking orders broke the stillness inside the room. Gun butts pounded on doors. Men and women began shouting and crying. More orders. Scuffling feet. Muffled sobs. Doors banging. Automatically I dropped to the floor, my heart pounding in my chest, my head filling with blood making me dizzy and sending stars flashing in front of my eyes. Janka stood up shielding me from view and I manoeuvred myself under the bed and lay frozen on the floor. The door to our room burst open and soldiers entered.

'Everyone out!' one of them ordered. *'Now!'*

I could see Janka's feet in her dirty brown shoes with the heels so worn they were almost gone, moving slowly towards the door making the dust and dirt rise into the air and swirl around and around. I squeezed my eyes shut, trying to block out the noise of heavy boots on the wooden boards. Then the room went quiet and I heard nothing but the pounding of the blood in my ears and the beating of my heart in my chest. Then softly, slowly, I heard another sound—footsteps. Booted feet carefully moving this way and that around the beds, stopping and starting as if looking for something— someone. I willed myself to disappear but instead opened my eyes and then I saw them—black boots

47

standing within a few inches of my face. I can't remember what happened next but I was aware of a hand grabbing my hair and pulling me out from under the bed. I kicked and struggled but the grip was tightening. I was yanked from my hiding place and finally saw it, that terrifying monster from the shadows that had kept me company every night patiently waiting and watching for the right moment.

The time had come.

I couldn't make a sound. I tried to kick out and wriggle free but he threw me out through the door and into the glaring daylight. Panic-stricken and half blinded I stumbled along in front of this giant of a man with the barrel of a gun poking my back between my shoulder blades. I searched the blank, staring faces, desperately trying to find Janka, but could see no one. Without warning the soldier pushed me onto the ground with his gun. I looked up into the face of the monster towering above me. He looked down and stopped. Hesitated. Seconds passed that felt like hours.

'What do we do with this one, Oberleutnant Schwam-mberger?' he barked.

The SS camp officer turned round, his eyes found me kneeling on the ground. No one made a sound. I caught a slight intake of breath. His polished boots came towards me covered with dust and squeaking slightly, then stopped. I looked up at him, and with the bright daylight dancing behind his peaked head, I could only see a black shadow where his face should have been.

He said nothing then bent down and pulled me up by one arm, shouting, 'Here, take your blonde changeling. She's yours!' He threw me into a small

48

group of men and women and into Janka's arms.

Janka pulled me behind her and tried to hide me with her skirt. I glimpsed the blank faces of a large group of thin men and women dressed in rags standing opposite us—so different from the smart uniformed soldiers and the beautifully dressed people from the town watching us through the fence as if we were one of the street shows Aunt Zuzia and I liked to watch before the war. Suddenly all the noises began to flow away. I became icy cold and started trembling as waves of sickness rose in my throat. I grabbed onto the back of Janka's skirt with both hands as if my whole life depended upon it and my legs gave way beneath me.

*　　　*　　　*

I returned to the ghetto with Janka and the small group of Jews that hadn't been taken away at gun-point. As the noise of fireworks filled the air that afternoon, I no longer wished I could watch, but simply longed for Mamusia and Babcia to return. I no longer cared that I was dirty and hungry and never went outside. I just wanted my mother and grandmother more than I had ever wanted anything in my life. But they didn't come. No one came.

In those days and weeks after they were taken from me, as time passed and with no one to shelter me from the events outside the room, my understanding of the situation began to grow and soon made me old beyond my years. I slowly realised that what old Piotr had said was right— perhaps I really would never see my mother or grandmother again. But I did have a father still, somewhere, fighting to save us. One day he would return. He had to—I just had to be patient.

CHAPTER THREE

September 1943. Przemyśl Ghetto

First my father, and now my mother and grandmother had vanished from my life. Alone in the room, my thoughts turned more and more to happier times and to Marynia, the nanny I adored. Babcia told me that Marynia had lost her own baby at the same time that I came into the world. I often wondered how she had come to lose her baby and was very pleased that she hadn't lost me and had enough milk for me. She had cared for me and loved me since the day I was born. She'd been my second mother.

I remembered my daily walks in the park, often with Cousin Zazula, and how we would laugh as we clutched my so-called treat. Poor Aunt Žuzia, she so loved taking me to the morning market and every time she would insist on buying me a special treat—a slice of melon.

'It'll make you grow into a big healthy girl,' Aunt Zuzia always said.

I loved my Aunt Zuzia but I hated melon. Every day, after my aunt had brought me home and said goodbye to Babcia, Marynia and I used to wrap up the offending slice and take it with us on our daily walk in the park. We buried every single piece in a flower bed beside the greenhouse.

'Our little secret,' Marynia would say, putting a

50

finger to her lips and looking serious for a moment. 'It will help the flowers grow.'

We never told Aunt Zuzia what we did with the melon because Marynia said that she would be cross. Even though I never breathed a word about what we did, I still found it hard to imagine Aunt Zuzia being cross. Now I found my mouth watering at the thought of those juicy melon slices.

Babcia had told me that Marynia wasn't a Jew and she didn't have to live in the ghetto. New questions formed in my mind: Where was she now? Did she still think of me? Did she still love me?

Renata, aged one and a half, with Marynia in the park

As the days turned into weeks, we continued to follow the same daily routine but, even though there were fewer people in our room now, there was still not enough food to go round. In turn the adults became less and less tolerant. Food was always the topic of conversation, especially when the weekly food delivery arrived for the soldiers inside the ghetto wall.

'He came again today,' Piotr snarled. 'Him and his horse. They had eggs, fresh vegetables and meat. I saw him unloading it all. All bright and cheerful he was too as if he didn't know what was going on here.'

Once a week a cartload of provisions arrived in the ghetto, the cart pulled by an old grey mare and driven by a short, middle-aged Polish man. We all knew when it was delivery day, the sound of the horse's hooves could be heard clip-clopping along the empty cobbled streets. The cart was loaded with luxuries for the Nazis but nothing for us. We were left to exist on the same black bread, watery cabbage soup and sometimes if we were lucky a bowl of coarse porridge.

Nothing came or went through the ghetto gates without someone noticing and the word spreading. We were all thirsty for news, always wanting to hear even the smallest piece of information, but no one more so than me. I was the only one who never left the room and so I relied on the conversations of the other people to help relieve my boredom. Everyone was familiar with the routine: the cart would arrive at the entrance to the ghetto; the driver would produce his papers, exchange banter and conversation with the guard on duty who would open the gates and in he rode. The Pole would deliver the provisions to the appointed German officer and return the way he'd come. Jusiek drove the cart. He was popular with the Nazi guards and would cheerfully engage in friendly conversation, always ready for a laugh. Anyone passing would try their hardest to hear what he was saying.

It was no secret that Jusiek was willing to do things for the soldiers, and in exchange for small amounts of money smuggle in extra bottles of alcohol and cigarettes. No one asked him where he managed to get these goods. No one wanted to know. He was so popular, in fact, that sometimes he brought his wife along for the ride, and she too was allowed through the gates of the ghetto to help him deliver and unload his goods.

Janka said his wife was a large, round woman, brown-haired and, like her husband, smiley and cheerful. She wore big old-fashioned skirts and an apron tied around her large waist. She talked to everyone, even the Jewish women going to or from the factory. Since she was nothing other than cheerful, friendly and kind, people began to relax in her presence and talk more openly to her. In this way they were able to gather snippets of information from her about what was happening outside the ghetto. Snippets that would later pass through all the occupied rooms of the ghetto, repeated and reinterpreted every which way you like.

It was late one afternoon and Janka and I were alone in the room. She had just returned from the factory and was sitting with her swollen feet in a bowl of water while I sat beside her with my fingers dabbling in the water. The door opened and a figure entered the room. On hearing the door I

53

dived off the bed on to the floor. From my hiding place I recognised the bulk of the person standing in the doorway.

'Marynia!' I shrieked, rushing to the door and flinging myself into my nurse's arms.

Marynia scooped me up and hugged and kissed me. Both she and I were laughing and crying, hugging and kissing.

'Let me look at you, my sweetheart,' Marynia said. 'How pale and thin you are, you poor little crumb. But things will be better now, I promise. I will look after you. Don't you worry.'

By now Janka had taken her feet out of the bowl and had padded across the room leaving wet footprints behind in the dirt. She approached us, glaring at the stranger with suspicion and resentment.

'Who are you and what are you doing here?' she demanded, not recognising Jusiek's wife.

'My name is Marynia. I was Renata's wet nurse before the war broke out, then her nanny. I've known her all her life,' she said, smiling at me. She turned back to Janka. 'As soon as I heard what had happened to her mother and grandmother, I decided I must do something to save my little one.' She paused. 'Who are *you*?'

Janka looked down at me clinging to Marynia's skirt.

'I'm Janka. I have been caring for Renata since they took her mother away. I promised Tosia I would look after her and I will for as long as I survive.'

'Thank God for you,' said Marynia softly. 'There can't be many who would have taken such a risk for a small child.' Marynia stopped and looked at

54

Janka for a long time. 'They would have shot you if they'd found her.'

'They did find her,' Janka replied. 'But for some reason they have let her be—that golden hair and those blue eyes, no doubt.'

Before Marynia could ask any further questions Janka started firing questions at Marynia.

'You're not Jewish? What are you doing here? What can you do to help?'

Not listening to what was being said, I clung on to my beloved nanny. I knew that everything would be all right. Marynia had come to take me home. Perhaps Tatuś was waiting outside. Perhaps the people who told me I would never see Mamusia and Babcia again had been wrong. Perhaps, right now, they were at home sitting in the warm, cosy living room around the big table piled with food and all my toys on the floor just where I'd left them—even Rabbit.

Then Marynia knelt down on the floor, so close to me that our faces were nearly touching. I could feel her breath and hear the urgency in her voice.

'Listen, my precious,' she said. 'You must listen very carefully and do exactly what Janka and I tell you. This is not a game and if you don't do exactly what we say things could go very wrong. Do you understand?'

I looked at Janka. Her face, so worn and thin, was now smiling—I had never seen her smile like this, she looked so pretty. She nodded at me. I looked back into Marynia's familiar face. Although her eyes were earnest, she was smiling too.

'In a few minutes,' Marynia explained slowly, 'we're going to play a game. We're going to leave this room together. You and me. No one will see you because you will be hidden under my skirt. I am so fat now that no one will notice an extra bulge.' Marynia made a face that made me want to giggle. 'You won't be able to see where you are going because it will be very dark under my skirt. But I will lead you. You just walk when I walk, and stop when I stop. Won't that be fun?'

'Are we playing blind man's buff like we used to?' I asked.

'N . . . yes, sort of,' Marynia agreed. 'Only this really is a very important sort of blind man's buff, with a bit of hide and seek as well,' she added with a wink. 'We won't have far to walk until I stop and start climbing into a cart. And that will be the difficult bit. You must do exactly what I do. You mustn't make the smallest sound, even if it hurts and even if you hear voices. We must make sure, you and I, that not one little bit of you sticks out from anywhere under my skirt. Everyone must think it's just me climbing into that cart and making a real mess of it because I'm so big.'

'Why are we getting in a cart?'

'To get you out of the ghetto without anyone knowing. Do you remember Jusiek, my husband?'

'Yes.' But I wasn't sure if I did.

'Well, he's going to drive us out of the ghetto. How would you like that?'

'Oh, that sounds wonderful. Where will we drive? Are we going straight home?'

Before Marynia could answer, Janka shook her head and said, 'You're crazy. You'll never get away with it. The Germans are far too clever. They'll see through your silly trick. You're not taking the child and risking her life on a hare-brained scheme like that. She's staying here with me. I promised her

56

mother.'

'How long will it be before there's another purge and they take you away?' Marynia looked at her. 'What will become of the child then? Do you think I would risk *her* life? She's like my own. I only wish I could help you too, but we would never get away with it. It's the only chance she has and we have to try.'

Janka nodded slowly. 'I will pack her things.'

'Forget about her things.'

'Baby Doll?' I cried.

'Remember what I told you,' Marynia said sternly. 'There's no room for Baby Doll under my skirt. She will have to stay behind to look after Janka and I will try to get you another one when we get out of here.'

Marynia stretched out her hand to Janka who had begun to cry. Tears rolled down her cheeks.

'You are a good woman, Marynia,' she said, wiping her eyes on the corner of her skirt. 'Thank you for everything you've done and may you both get out safely. God bless you.'

Janka bent down to kiss me for the last time. She hugged me tight and then stood up, put on her shoes and walked out of the room and into the fading afternoon light without another word or a backward glance.

I never saw or heard of Janka again.

'Right,' said Marynia, hoisting up her thick serge skirt. 'In you go, just between my legs, and when I move, you move. We're doing a kind of dance. Ready? Now remember, not a sound, whatever happens, until I tell you that you can speak. This is the biggest game of our life and we're going to win.'

It was dark and hot and smelly under those

57

heavy skirts, but because I had lived in the ghetto it didn't worry me. I knew that I must obey Marynia. Marynia was always right. It felt good to be with her again, safe and secure. I stood between her legs and held on to her, ready to move when she was.

I felt Marynia step slowly forward and I moved too. It was hard but I concentrated with all my might on moving my feet when she did. We walked and moved, out into the street. Then I heard the deep, muffled voice of a German soldier.

'Well, if it isn't the good Jusiek's comely wife. What have you brought us today to ease our lot?'

Marynia's feet stopped.

'I've left the deliveries over there, like they told me to, and anyway there's nothing wrong with *your* lot,' she replied, laughing. 'You lead the life of princes.'

'Well, we need to, dealing with these dirty Jewish pigs—may they rot in hell.'

'May they indeed,' Marynia agreed and began to move slowly forward.

'Without being too personal, you've put on some weight since I saw you last,' said the German soldier as we waddled past. 'We obviously pay you too much and you live too well. I shall have a word with the Kommandant.'

'If you do, no more vodka.' Marynia laughed, putting her hands on her stomach—the top of my head. 'I must be on my way to help Jusiek unload. See you next time.'

We continued walking, passing several German soldiers who all knew her and obviously liked her. To each and every one she paused to chat and, every so often, she would pat the front of her bulging dress as if to smooth it down. These pats reassured me and in spite of everything I felt safe.

At last Marynia stopped.

'So, here we are,' she said very loudly. 'I don't feel well, Jusiek. You're going to have to help me climb into the back of the cart where there's room to lie down. I can hardly lift my legs today.'

'You're too fat,' Jusiek grumbled. 'I've done enough lifting for one day without having to heave you on board as well.' I could hear his footsteps coming round the side of the cart. 'Come on then. One two three—up you go!' he instructed as he pushed Marynia up the steps and into the back of the cart.

Somehow we both managed the climb without any bit of me peeping out from under her skirt. Marynia spread her skirts around her and perched on a bale of straw in the bottom of the cart. She then clutched her stomach and bent over.

'Slip under the straw,' she hissed. 'I will cover you over and sit beside you. Remember, don't move an inch.'

I wriggled down and lay in a little bundle on the floor and Marynia covered me with straw. Jusiek clambered into the driving seat, flicked his whip and the ancient horse set off for home at its usual slow plod.

As always the cart had to stop at the exit. Jusiek showed their papers and exchanged friendly banter with the guards.

'*Auf Wiedersehen*. See you next week,' Jusiek and Marynia called out as the cart jolted forward and the sound of the horse's hooves on the cobbles rang out once more.

We moved slowly through the gates, back into the world beyond the ghetto.

59

It wasn't until the cart pulled into the yard that Marynia bent down again and whispered, 'There, Renata, you are safe. You can come out now, but be very quiet. We don't want the neighbours to know you are here. You have been such a good girl.'

But I didn't stir and in a panic Marynia pulled aside the straw. There she found me curled up, fast asleep, sleeping like a baby.

* * *

Later that night after I had been tucked up in bed under a feather quilt I could hear Jusiek and Marynia arguing next door.

'I had to rescue Renata. I had to get her out of there. You know I did . . .'

'You are so bloody stupid,' Jusiek replied. 'So am I for going along with it. I must be mad. You're risking *our* necks for a Jew child.'

'It isn't *any* Jew child,' she cried. 'It is my little Renata. She's like my own. Just think if it had been—but Jusiek cut her off.

'Now that you've got her here, what exactly do you propose to do with her?'

'She can stay—for a bit.'

'She can stay here until tomorrow morning and not a minute longer. I'm not going to endanger my job and our lives for some Jew child. I've given in to you this far, but no further. Your stupid sentimentality will get us both into trouble and even if you think you have some sort of debt to pay, just you remember that *I* haven't. I always said you were daft over that child. You always put your job and that child before me. Well, now you haven't got a

60

job and if you want me to stick around, you'll do as I say. I'm making good money and you're not going to spoil it. D'you understand?'

'Perfectly,' Marynia responded in an icy voice.

CHAPTER FOUR

October 1943. Somewhere in Przemyśl

To my relief I didn't leave Marynia's house the following day. I was used to amusing myself. Now I did it in the hope that Jusiek would change his mind and let me stay. But my relief was short-lived. It was early one morning soon after I had arrived when Marynia came into the sitting room where I was playing with my new doll. Marynia had kept her promise and given me a small, rosy-cheeked rag doll dressed in a brown cotton dress and a white apron to replace Baby Doll. She had given it to me at breakfast.

Marynia sat beside me on the floor and told me of the surprise she had arranged. 'We are going to visit your Aunt Adela and your cousin Zazula,' she said, her eyes shining.

I couldn't believe it.

It had been such a long time since I had last seen Zazula and I never imagined she was so near by. I was so excited (and a little nervous) to think that I would see her again, especially as I now had my new doll to show her.

Zazula was my favourite cousin. She was four years older than me, the sister I never had. We used to play with our dolls, either at her house or mine, share treats and outings, go on visits together to the country to visit Tatuś's relatives. We loved chasing each other across the lawns of the town's parks with Marynia in tow, sharing our secret of buried water-melon slices and competing to finish our ice creams first. The age difference had never bothered us—she was the boss on account of her years and I was quite happy (most of the time) to agree to her plans, whether it be the day for a dolls' tea party or time to draw pictures or read a book. Being older, Zazula usually got her own way so it was easier to agree with her but sometimes it had made me cry from frustration.

'Yesterday I visited your aunt. She told me that she made a promise to your mother,' Marynia continued. 'If something ever happened to your mother, Aunt Adela would look after you and likewise your mother would look after Zazula if something happened to Aunt Adela.'

'What's happened to Mamusia?' I heard myself asking. 'Won't she come back and get me?'

'No, darling,' Marynia said. 'She won't be coming back, but your father will. You just have to be patient.'

So old Piotr had been right after all. I had secretly hoped that he had said such hateful things because he was angry and cruel, just like Cinderella's stepmother, but now that Marynia had said I would never see Mamusia again I felt sick and dizzy. I pushed the feelings of misery back down inside me. I couldn't let Marynia see how upset I was because I was sure that Jusiek would want to send me away even sooner. So instead I asked, 'Where is Zazula? Is she far from here?'

Marynia laughed. 'No, not far, they are still in

Przemyśl. We will go there today.'

Later that morning we set out. I was clutching my doll in one hand and with the other holding tightly onto Marynia's coat. It was bitterly cold and Marynia had wrapped me up well in lots of scarves and stuffed my hands into a pair of old gloves which were far too big for me. We walked quickly and soon Marynia was panting and out of breath.

'Are you tired?' I asked.

'No, sweetheart,' replied Marynia. 'I get out of breath sometimes. It's nothing to worry about.'

We seemed to walk for ever along empty streets that I didn't recognise. Every so often we passed groups of armed soldiers and Marynia's hand would reach for mine and hold it tight. As we passed one group of soldiers one of them stared at us. Marynia tried to hurry by as if she hadn't noticed.

'Papers!' the soldier demanded, his gaze moving from Marynia to me and back again.

Marynia said nothing but fumbled in her bag and drew out some crumpled sheets and handed them to the soldier. Then she began talking, explaining in her jovial, rambling way that she and her daughter were going to visit an elderly relative.

'Can't leave her too long on her own,' she said, 'not in weather like this. Who knows what might happen with no one looking out for her. Don't want her getting sick, that would be the last straw. My daughter's a good girl, always likes to see her aunt. Helps with the cleaning too. Makes my life a little easier, I must say.'

The soldier said nothing but glanced again at Marynia and then briefly at me clutching on to Marynia's coat before handing her documents back and gesticulating with his head for us to be on our way. We walked further on down the street before turning into a small alleyway that led between two buildings and out on to another road lined with houses.

We stopped in front of a tall apartment house and Marynia rang the bell. An old man answered and after a short mumbled exchange that I couldn't hear he led us slowly up several flights of stone steps and left us outside a closed wooden door.

Marynia knocked three times and then three times again very quickly. After a short pause, bolts were pulled back from the inside and the door was opened just a crack. Then after a moment it was flung wide. Before I knew what had happened, I found myself in my aunt's arms and someone grabbing my arm and dragging me inside. It was a delighted Zazula. She hadn't changed very much; she was a little taller perhaps but her dark straight hair and heavy fringe still framed her pale face out of which her deep brown eyes shone.

'I'm so glad you've come,' Zazula exclaimed. 'We can play hospitals and mummies and daddies together. It's been so boring playing alone all the time.'

I was so happy. At last I was with people I loved and with whom I felt safe. So it was a great shock when Marynia bent down to kiss me goodbye.

'Where are you going, Marynia?' I cried. 'I thought I was going to stay with you for ever until Mamusia or Tatuś come back. Or at least Tatuś, because you said Mamusia will never come back. But I want you to wait here till my father comes to get me.'

'I can't stay, my precious,' Marynia explained, slowly kneeling down in front of me. 'I have to go

64

back to look after Jusiek. But you are a lucky girl to be with your aunty and your cousin and I'll visit you whenever I can. I promise. I really promise. And you know I never break a promise.'

She placed the doll in my hands and turned away as she stood up.

She was crying when she left and so was I. Nothing stayed the same, people were either coming or going and I was so tired of trying to work out what was happening. Zazula saw that I was upset and brought a picture book to show me, and I soon cheered up when Aunt Adela offered me a piece of bread and jam.

'I'm glad you've come to live with us,' Zazula told me again. 'It'll be fun to have someone to play with, even if you are still a baby.'

Zazula would never let me forget that she was *four* years older. How I wished then that I was ten too. It seemed to me that to be ten was properly old and clever and thoroughly grown-up. I couldn't wait to get there.

*　　　*　　　*

I was very happy to be with my cousin and aunt even though we never went out. Each day a lady called Teodora visited us in the apartment carrying a basket covered with a cloth. Inside the basket was bread, milk, a few vegetables and sometimes even a few eggs or a very small piece of meat. It was the best food I had tasted for a very long time, but there was never quite enough and we were always hungry. Zazula kept talking about how much she missed sweets and chocolate, but I didn't know what she meant. It had been so long since I had eaten them.

65

Aunt Adela was always worried until Teodora appeared. When she arrived, Teodora would join Aunt Adela and they would sit in the corner of the room on hard-backed chairs and talk in hushed voices. Sometimes Teodora stayed a long time and other times she left without speaking a word.

'She's our only contact with the outside world,' Aunt Adela explained. 'She tells us what is going on in Przemyśl and the rest of Poland, and gives news of our friends.'

We couldn't leave the apartment and knew that we had to keep quiet at all times. Zazula and I played games and this made life much more fun than the ghetto. Of course there were times when we got on each other's nerves.

'Leave me, alone,' I'd whisper, and then I'd wish that I was as grown-up and as clever as my cousin. Then I would win the next game of snap and some of the arguments.

Aunt Adela spent many hours each day telling us stories. Some made me sad, like the ones she told us about my parents, which only made me miss them more, but others made me dream about the wonderful time we would have when we could all live happily ever after. Then there were the stories, some of which I remember Babcia having told me, about princes and princesses, giants, fairies and witches that came from two large books, *Grimm's Fairy Tales*, and another by Hans Christian Andersen. These stories were exciting and scary and we spent hours re-enacting them. Perhaps it wasn't surprising that I'd begun to suffer from terrible nightmares about dragons who breathed fire and monsters in grey-green uniforms, trying to devour me.

I would lie in bed at night and look into the shadows in a desperate search to find the monsters hidden there before they found me. It wasn't enough any more to simply put my head under the covers, close my eyes tightly and imagine I was invisible. The outside world now came into the safety of my bed so that I no longer felt safe anywhere. To try and calm my fears I took to repeating words over and over again, new words I had heard, strange words I couldn't pronounce, and slowly my fears would subside and I would drift off to sleep.

But these were the horrors of real life as well as of my imagination. Often we would hear thunder rumbling around, sometimes far away and at other times much nearer.

'Silly, that's not thunder,' said Zazula. 'They're bombs. Houses being bombed. That's why there's so much smoke.'

From then on I knew that each crash must mean that more people were dead or badly hurt. When I asked what the fireworks were, Zazula looked worried and whispered, 'Those are the shots from soldiers' guns. They are shooting people who aren't doing what they are told and sometimes they are shooting people like us who are hiding from them.'

Whenever we heard these noises our heads would jerk up from what we were doing and our eyes would search for Aunt Adela. As the terror mounted, Zazula then I would leap from our chairs and cling to my aunt for safety. When we heard them at night, it was the signal for everyone in the apartment block to descend the stone stairs to the cellar. We would drop whatever we were doing and go to Aunt Adela who would wrap scarves round our heads and rugs round our shoulders and lead us by the hand to join the other residents clutching pillows and blankets, desperate to reach the cellar beneath the house. No one gave us a second glance.

The cellar was pitch black, musty and damp. The air was so cold that it hurt. It seemed to get under our clothes, and into our bones. Everyone huddled together in the bowels of the earth, seeking warmth and companionship, waiting for the bangs and crashes to end.

Eventually someone would light a candle and people would start to talk in low voices, trying not to draw attention to themselves. Their outlines flickered across the cellar walls, shadows that were huge and even more frightening than the dark, driving me back into the land of witches and monsters. They were out there in the darkness, waiting and watching for a chance to get me. Silent screams would fill my lungs and head and, as I tried to squash the fear inside me and fight the desperate urge to escape the cellar, I would reach out for my aunt's hand and squeeze it tight.

One evening the three of us were sitting at the table. At Zazula's request, Aunt Adela was telling us a story about how she had met Zazula's father.

'Your father was Renata's mother's, your Aunt Tosia's, brother,' said Aunt Adela. 'Cesio, your father, was a student at university because he wanted to become a lawyer so that he could help people. Anyway, one evening I went to a wonderful party. There were so many people; some were Jewish, others Catholic but that didn't matter because we were all friends and all loved dancing and having fun. The ladies were wearing beautiful dresses and their hair was pinned up. The men wore suits and were very good-looking. I was so excited to be there. I'd been looking forward to this party for weeks. Then I saw him across the room, sitting there on his own watching all the men and women dancing. He was so handsome I couldn't take my eyes off him.'

Aunt Adela paused for a moment, smiling quietly as she remembered.

'I knew then that he was the one. He turned and looked straight at me, and before I knew it he was standing in front of me asking me to dance. From that moment on we were never out of each other's sight for long. He was so clever and full of fun and laughter—just like his sister, your mother, Renata.' Aunt Adela stroked my hair. 'I fell in love with him and he with me and so, of course, we wanted to get married. But our family was rich. Your grandfather, Zazula, owned part of a gold mine, had many houses both here in Poland and in a faraway city called London in a country called England. But Cesio was just a poor student. I thought my father would be angry and not let me marry him but he saw how much we loved each other, how hard Cesio worked and what a good lawyer he would be so he finally agreed.'

Zazula sat entranced as she listened to the fairy-tale story of her mother and her father.

'Where is Uncle Cesio now?' I asked. I had never asked before because I had just assumed that he had gone away to fight the Germans like my father.

Aunt Adela looked at her hands. 'He was killed just after the war started.'

Suddenly the thunder started. We jumped up and automatically followed the routine, bundling ourselves up in scarves and rugs and making our

69

way along with the neighbours down into the cellar. Only that night it was different; the crashes were closer and louder than before; the walls of the cellar and the ground where I sat shook.

'They are bombing very close tonight,' someone said.

At that moment there was a huge, almighty boom and the candle went out. I felt as if I was being lifted up into the air and thrown down again very violently. The crashing went on, and on, and so did the shaking. Then there came the sound of falling and smashing above us. The ceiling seemed to explode and enormous pieces of plaster and wood fell through the huge gaps above our heads and rained down on top of us. The blackness became clouded with dust and I heard screams. My throat tightened as my own cries fought to be let out to join the terrible confusion and noise. The debris kept falling. I couldn't understand what it was or where it was all coming from until I detected the outline of a chair as it came hurtling crazily through the black hole, which had once been the ceiling.

In terror I screamed my aunt's name over and over again, but there was no reply. Then I heard Zazula's voice through the darkness.

'Renata, where are you?'

'I'm here!' I cried, crawling in the dirt, groping in the darkness for my cousin. Zazula appeared beside me.

'Hold on to me and we'll find Mummy.' We clung to each other and cried together but no one came. Not for a long time.

That night my nightmares became real. My night terrors that stopped me from sleeping were nothing

70

compared with this. The noise, the smell and the dusty air only made me think that things could not get any worse. In the dark Zazula and I managed to find our way out of the cellar and up on to the street. The apartment block had been opened up like a doll's house and all around lay piles of rubble. There were a lot of people lying on the ground moaning and more people busy digging a man out of one of the piles of rubble. He screamed as they freed him, his leg was twisted—it looked as if it had been put on the wrong way round—and blood oozed on to the ground. No one took the slightest bit of notice of us standing there, not knowing what to do or where to go. Then through the dust and the rubble we saw Aunt Adela, unhurt but ashen-faced and badly shaken.

'Renata! Zazula!' she cried, running towards us.

She pulled us to her and hugged first Zazula and then me.

'Oh no,' Aunt Adela said. 'Look.'

Zazula and I followed her gaze up to our apartment block. It had vanished—at least the front of it had. From where we were standing we could see into the rooms, all the way up. Beds and chairs hanging over the edges of what had once been floors. As we watched, a bath with its clawed feet clinging to the remains of what had once been the bathroom fell out of an upstairs room, hitting the ground and shattering into a hundred pieces. We realised that there was no apartment. No hiding place. We were out on the street with nowhere to go and no possessions. I had lost a second doll—she had been left behind in the flat when the bombing had started.

'We must go back and get my dolly,' I said,

turning to my aunt.

'Don't be silly, darling. We can't. It's not safe.'

'But we must. She'll be frightened and ever so hungry.' I grabbed Zazula's arm. 'We must, mustn't we, Zazula? You know how lonely she will be.'

All I could think about was my doll, the one Marynia had given me to replace Baby Doll whom I'd had to leave in the ghetto.

'We can't get up to our apartment and that's that. We must find somewhere else to go,' said my aunt.

We stood there in the darkness. All we had were the clothes in which we were standing. It was then, with the loss of Marynia's doll, that I finally began to understand the seriousness of what was happening around me.

*   *   *

The next few days blurred into a jumble of confusion and continuing sadness over my lost doll. Aunt Adela managed to find somewhere for us to sleep and someone who would give us food. But we couldn't stay in any place for long.

'No, we can't stay here again tonight,' my aunt would explain to us when I began to complain about having to move yet again. 'It's just too dangerous for them to help us any longer.'

'Mummy's friends are risking their lives helping us,' Zazula said. 'We are lucky that they help us even for a day or so, otherwise we would end up in the ghetto where you were.'

I shuddered at the thought of being sent back there and vowed never to complain again. Aunt Adela no longer told us stories; she was either

72

angry and impatient, or in tears. Occasionally she even smacked us if we didn't instantly obey her. Then came the day when we found ourselves in a small cramped attic space above a kitchen dresser. Zazula and I had to climb a wooden ladder and crawl through a small trapdoor.

'I can't breathe, Zazula,' I complained. 'Where are you?' I reached for her hand.

Zazula and I were pushed in there on at least two occasions.

'Stay still and don't make a sound,' Aunt Adela ordered us.

With no room to move, and the pins and needles in my legs and pains in my arms getting worse, I could feel my panic rising. We could hear scrabbling and squeaks and then something ran over my body with hard, scratchy little feet. Just in time I remembered not to cry out but when it scrambled over Zazula, she let out a high-pitched scream. Later, when we were allowed out, no one said a word. Aunt Adela stood and watched tight-lipped as the man in whose house we were hiding and whose name we didn't know dealt with us.

'You first.' He pointed at Zazula.

He put her, and then me, across his knee, lifted our skirts, pulled down our knickers and slapped us hard several times to remind us that we must never again make a noise, whatever happened, when we were hiding. It was our first beating.

'The pain you have now is nothing, *nothing*, compared with the pain you will feel if the Nazis find you,' he explained angrily as we stood in front of him crying and shaking and rubbing our backsides. 'If you ever dare to make a noise again, I will use a belt on you.'

Aunt Adela refused to comfort us.

'You both deserved to be punished. Our friend is risking *his* life and that of his family by hiding us. Go to bed. I'm so cross with you both.'

Crouching under the blankets with a bit of sheet stuffed in my mouth to make sure I didn't make a sound and get another beating, I cried myself to sleep. It wasn't the pain that made me cry. I simply couldn't understand why I should have been punished for the noise Zazula had made. But we had learned our lesson. We had learned to accept whatever hiding place was available without complaint, and to never, ever make a noise.

CHAPTER FIVE

October–November 1943

As the long hours became days and the days turned into weeks, Aunt Adela, Zazula and I moved from one house to another, spending no more than a few nights with any one family.

'Why don't *they* have to hide?' I said, as we prepared to make yet another move.

'Because the Nazis don't want to kill *them*.'

'But why do they want to kill us?'

'Because we're different,' said Zazula, losing patience. 'We are Jews and the Nazis don't like Jews. I told you, it's to do with our brown hair and brown eyes. Mummy's friends are Catholic.'

She turned her back on me as if to signal that I'd asked enough questions. It didn't put me off. I asked the same questions every few days and yet I still didn't understand what the problem was. Didn't I have blonde hair and blue eyes? Surely Zazula must have noticed? Why then did I have to hide? I was too afraid of saying anything to Zazula for fear of making her angry.

The shifting rooms, hiding places and families began to blur together. Perhaps there were only a few families that passed us between them. Perhaps there were lots of families with whom we stayed— I don't know. But then we arrived at Mrs Posadzka's.

Mrs Posadzka was a widow and was delighted, but obviously worried, to see us. She bustled us quickly into her tall, thin house and declared, 'You can stay here with me. Marynia told me you needed somewhere to stay and I have an empty room. You must keep quiet though and only use the toilet when no one is around. Nobody knows that you are staying here—you must be quiet as mice. But I suspect you girls are good at being mice by now, aren't you?'

I liked Mrs Posadzka, she was younger than Babcia but older than my mother, short with brown wavy hair and soft skin. When she wasn't in a rush she would tell us stories, not like the ones in the books that were destroyed in the apartment, but stories about people we knew.

'I know your father,' she said one day. 'He was a chest doctor at the Military Red Cross Hospital before the war. And, oh, so kind.' She smiled at me. I found it hard to remember my father now.

'What does he look like?' I asked, hoping to jog a forgotten memory.

'He had dark hair and dark eyes,' Mrs Posadzka

said. 'Not at all like you. And a lovely gentle smile. I met him at the hospital. My daughter was ill, we were so scared. We took her straight to the hospital. We were in a terrible state, what with Joanna making all sorts of strange breathing sounds. She had gone quite blue in the face. Your father was working that day. He was wonderful. He didn't panic, he asked a nurse to see to us and then took poor Joanna away. A collapsed lung, he said later. Any longer and she would have died. He saved her life and I swore to him that day that if there was anything, *anything*, I could ever do to help him in return then he just had to say. Such a gentleman, he was, unlike those . . .' Mrs Posadzka looked at me and paused. 'Anyway, that's why you're here now, you, your aunt and Zazula. They'll have to get past me before they lay a finger on you.'

I had wanted to ask Mrs Posadzka whether she knew where my father was now but she said that she had stayed long enough and had work to do.

I liked being in Mrs Posadzka's house. Our hiding place was a small room on the first floor. The room was square with bare boards and no rugs to keep in the warmth or sounds so Aunt Adela told us to walk without shoes so that no one would hear us.

'Especially if you have to cross the landing to go to the toilet,' she said.

To the right of the door was a chaise longue and above it a window that faced out on to a small concrete backyard and over the wall into the street beyond. Zazula and I longed to look out of the window but Aunt Adela and Mrs Posadzka refused to let us go anywhere near it. Opposite the door, filling the whole of one wall, stood a large wooden wardrobe with two heavily carved doors. It was kept locked, the massive, swirly key sat in the door, but it was too difficult for me and even Zazula to turn even though we tried many times. Zazula and I often wondered what was kept hidden inside and we made up stories about that secret world behind the wardrobe doors.

The only other furniture in the room was a large, round, heavy oak table complete with three wooden chairs. It was covered with a plush, colourful Turkish carpet-like tablecloth that fell down in thick folds to the floor so that the chairs were never pushed completely under the table. It was the only splash of colour in a drab room into which the sun never shone.

Being isolated from the outside world, Zazula and I were bored and desperate for information, anything to suppress our fathomless pits of hunger and give us some idea of what was going on in the world beyond our window; to give some meaning to this life we were living. Mrs Posadzka came to our rescue.

'Let me tell you a story,' she said one day. 'How about one about this street?' she began. She told us what was going on outside, first describing in detail the houses, what they looked like and who lived there. Then she told us how people were dying from diseases and how they had to eat rats because there was so little food. She described the killings in broad daylight and of those who were taken away by train to camps far away. She told us about the Nazis but also about the brave people who were trying to stop the Nazis. She didn't tell us about all the 'nasty things' the Nazis did. She didn't have to. The gunshots and bombs that I could hear from our room together with Zazula's vivid explanations were enough for me.

Sometimes Aunt Adela and Mrs Posadzka would sit together in the corner of the room and talk in hushed voices. Zazula and I couldn't avoid overhearing snippets of conversation.

'. . . they were so thin, and so ill, that the soles of their feet fell off . . .'

'. . . the rats are everywhere, feeding off the dead bodies, living in the dirt and squalor . . .'

'. . . they smashed her poor baby's head against a wall before shooting her . . .'

'. . . the gas chambers are portable . . . going through all the remote villages . . . quicker than taking everyone away.'

'. . . what about Erwin's parents and sister? . . . Said they would be safe living so far away from . . . but Erwin tried to make Tosia and Renata go to stay with them when he . . . safer than staying in Przemyśl, he said.'

We heard the rumours about the people left in the ghetto—how they were made to gather together outside before the shootings started, before the burning of the bodies.

'So that's what the black smoke was,' Aunt Adela whispered, 'and the smell. They say death smells sweet and now I know why. I can still smell it even though the flames were put out days ago . . .'

We understood now why we had to keep quiet and stay inside and it wasn't just for our benefit, but also for the people with whom we were staying. They would be killed as well. The horror began to sink in more fully as Zazula found it more and more difficult to explain to me what it was that we were hearing. But we had worked out what would

78

happen if the soldiers found us, and we were scared.

* * *

Inside the house Zazula and I understood that this was no longer a game. We tried very hard to be obedient, not to complain about our confinement to a tiny room, and only talk in whispers. In the comparative safety of our room it all seemed a little unreal, distanced from us, normal, yet at the same time terrifying, if we paused for long enough to think about it. Sometimes we became so involved in our games, and our quarrels, that we forgot the seriousness of the situation. We were always listening for any change in the noises from the street below, for the wail of sirens or the staccato sounds of the gunshots in the distance.

'Let's have a story,' Aunt Adela would announce when we were especially worried or bad-tempered, and she would take us back to the land of fairy tales and instead of pictures in a book I had to concentrate on the pictures in my head.

'"... what big eyes you have ..."' and my aunt would open her eyes wide.

'"... what big teeth you have ..."' and I could see the open mouth of the wolf coming towards me, yellow teeth, saliva dripping—each time more vivid.

I would wake in the night petrified of opening my eyes or moving in case the wolf was at my bedside. The nightmares continued, combining the stories with memories of my parents. I'd find myself endlessly searching for my mother and father through woods full of gigantic beanstalks where trees pulled at my hair; witches fed me with sweets

79

and cakes that I should not have eaten but couldn't resist; wolves prowled and nowhere were princes to be seen.

I couldn't tell Zazula about these awful dreams; she would have laughed and called me silly and a baby. I wanted to be ten and grown-up and able to listen to the stories without getting frightened, just like her. So I said nothing, keeping the horrors to myself.

Even though we were together all the time, Zazula and I never tired of playing together. Our games were limited by the continual need to be quiet, but we spent many happy hours cutting scraps of paper into shapes with a pair of blunt scissors, and drawing—with our stubby pencils—the princes, princesses and monsters from the stories. Zazula was good at drawing, but I just scribbled, frustrated that what I saw clearly in my head wasn't what my hand was drawing on the paper. I preferred to act out the stories that either Aunt Adela had told us or Zazula and I had invented for ourselves. Our stories were always the same, about two happy sisters living in a beautiful, clean house with their loving parents and, of course, lots of good things to eat.

I loved my older cousin with all my heart. She was wise and knew everything. I wanted to do all that she did. Zazula didn't always like this and so sometimes we would squabble.

One dull autumn afternoon we were sitting in our room. Aunt Adela was seated as close to the window as possible with a sock wrapped around the darning mushroom in her hands. She was trying hard to cobble together a very large hole, which had been mended again and again and was now getting to a stage where there was more darning than sock. The light was fading and she wanted to finish before it became too dark to see. Zazula and I were playing at the table with small pieces of paper and pencils, bored and wanting more than anything to go and run outside.

'Be careful with the paper,' Zazula said. 'You know we don't have much of it. Why don't you let me do that for you?'

I didn't want Zazula to do it for me. I wanted to show her how clever I was and that I could do it on my own. I knelt up on the chair and stuck my tongue out of the corner of my mouth and concentrated really hard. Finally I finished and triumphantly I held up my piece of paper and waved it in my cousin's face.

'Look, Zazula. I can do real writing just like you.'

I had written some of the letters I knew from having seen them on the pages of the books that Aunt Adela had read us.

'That's not writing,' Zazula said, looking up from the drawing of a house she was making.

'Anyway you're too little to write.'

'It is writing. It's *real* writing just like yours.' She was being unfair. I thrust the piece of paper in front of Zazula.

'What does it say then, Miss Clever Clogs?' Zazula asked, concentrating once again on her picture.

'I'm not telling you,' I shouted, angry that Zazula wasn't as pleased as I was.

'You're just a baby. All you do is scribble. You're only six.'

'I'm not a baby.' I looked across the room to Aunt Adela for support. 'Aunty, tell her I'm not a

81

baby.'

'Be quiet, girls. Stop quarrelling,' Aunt Adela said with a sigh.

'Mummy, she is only a baby. Tell her. She can't write like me because I'm ten and have been to school.'

'Zazula, please don't be difficult, don't quarrel with your little cousin. I can't cope when you two are being so naughty.' Aunt Adela's voice broke and then she was crying—tears streaming down her face.

Zazula looked shocked.

'Mummy, please don't cry,' she said. Then she turned to me and said, 'I'm sorry. Renata, you're not a baby. I was only joking.'

So I had won. I beamed at her. I couldn't contain my pleasure.

'I'm growing up ever so fast and I'll be ten soon too. I'll get to ten and then I'll get older than you. You just wait and see.'

Zazula looked at me crossly but, seeing her mother's unhappy tear-stained face, she bit her lip and climbed down from her chair and went to give her mother a hug. After a while, she looked into her mother's face and said, 'Mummy, shall we go out for a walk? It's so boring being in this room all the time.'

'You know we can't, my darling. I only wish we could,' Aunt Adela said sadly, stroking Zazula's hair.

I thought that this was a great idea and decided that I would help change my aunt's mind.

'We could be back very soon,' I tried. 'Just a little walk. Please let us go.'

'How many more times do I have to explain to

you both?' Aunt Adela said wearily. 'We can't go out because it is too dangerous. We have to stay hidden and be grateful that we are alive.'

'When will we be able to go out?' Zazula insisted. 'Tell us, when?'

It was at that moment the door burst open and a white-faced Mrs Posadzka stood in the doorway looking as if she hadn't had time to comb her hair. Aunt Adela leapt to her feet and the darning fell to the floor.

'What's happened?' she cried.

'Soldiers!' gasped Mrs Posadzka with her hand on her chest. 'They are doing a house-to-house search up the street and they have dogs with them. They'll be here any minute.'

'We must get out of here. We have to hide. We must leave your house. We can't put you in danger.' Aunt Adela looked around the room, desperate.

Just then German voices, barks and loud banging were heard from downstairs.

'It's too late, they're here. We're lost.' Mrs Posadzka was shaking, unable to move.

Adela looked frantically round the room again, grabbed Zazula by the arm and pulled her towards the wardrobe.

'Quick, in here. Don't move. Don't make a sound, whatever you hear. Don't be afraid. Everything's going to be all right.'

She unlocked the door, pushed Zazula inside, turned the heavy key and slipped it into the pocket of her skirt. Then she looked round for a hiding place for me, still sitting at the table, terrified and unable to move.

'I'll go with Zazula. I can play hide and seek with Zazula,' I said.

Aunt Adela grabbed me by the arm, pulled me off the chair, lifted the heavy cloth and pushed me under the table.

'You're to stay there till I fetch you. Don't move, don't breathe, don't cry or we are all lost.' She let the heavy cover fall back in its place and I was alone sitting on the dusty wooden floor in the pitch black.

It wasn't the first time that I had been bundled into a hiding place without any explanation. I knew that I wasn't alone in the room; my aunt and cousin were somewhere there too. I also knew that I couldn't cry out or seek the comfort of my aunt's arms. I must keep still and quiet because the safety of the three of us, and that of Mrs Posadzka, depended on me. I cowered under the table, hugging myself for comfort, feeling the hammering of my heart in my chest and blood thundering through my ears. I was convinced someone would hear it. I buried my face in my lap and folded my arms over my head trying to block out the world around me.

From underneath the table I could hear everything but see nothing. Mrs Posadzka and Aunt Adela were frantically whispering in hurried voices but I couldn't hear what they were saying. Then I heard the sound of heavy boots coming up the uncarpeted stairs. Deep, muffled voices. A sharp command. The door bursting open. The scrabbling claws on the bare floorboards and the eager whining of a dog just the other side of the tablecloth. Thick male voices and that word: *Gestapo*.

Then a woman crying—my aunt. A slap. A scream. A brief silence. The silence was quickly broken by a harsh staccato command and then the excited single bark of a dog, too close. I heard every sound and felt the tablecloth move as the dog brushed past. I heard its panting and suddenly the volley of barks and scraping of wood as the dog leapt about. Then I heard Aunt Adela shriek as the sound of splintering wood was followed by the haunting screams of Zazula calling frantically for her mother.

'Mummy! Mummy!'

Aunt Adela howled, 'Leave her alone. Please leave her alone. She's done nothing wrong.'

I heard her cry over and over again. My heart was about to explode; I couldn't take much more. I wanted to run to Aunt Adela and hide myself in her warm bosom and let her arms hold me tight and tell me everything was going to be all right as she always did. But I couldn't. My arms and legs were frozen to the floor; I hugged myself closer to stop myself shaking.

Then the screaming began to fade. I could hear men's angry voices accompanied by the sounds of something heavy being dragged downstairs. Then silence. The sound of emptiness more terrifying than all the screams and shouts. But I remained rooted to my spot under the table, shaking, paralysed with terror and foreboding.

I sat there in that pitch-black silence.

Then from below there came a single bang. Seconds later another. Then total silence. Silence for hours and hours.

*   *   *

Eventually, many hours later, I heard other

footsteps hurrying up the stairs, this time softer and gentler, and then someone came into the room and tiptoed across the wooden floor.

'Renata,' a voice called into the deathly stillness. 'Renata, my darling, are you here?'

It was Marynia. I emerged from my hiding place under the table into the blinding light of the late afternoon and into the arms of Marynia, breathing in her familiar smell and drowning in the folds of her clothes. In the relief of having survived and the joy at being with Marynia, I didn't give my cousin and aunt another thought, at least not then. Having saved me twice, Marynia was my fairy godmother and I clung to her; I was never going to let her go.

CHAPTER SIX

November 1943

Marynia took me home. I couldn't remember ever having visited her house before the war and had only stayed there for a short time after she rescued me from the ghetto, but it didn't matter. It felt like home. Yet even here I still had to hide every time there was a knock at the door. Marynia would call out, 'I'm coming, one moment,' whilst waving quickly for me to go into the bedroom, with a finger over her lips so I knew to keep quiet. Then she would shuffle over to the door, wiping her hands on her apron, and start talking in a bright, cheerful voice. Quite often these visitors were Nazi soldiers coming to put in an order.

Renata's nanny, Marynia and Jusiek, Marynia's husband

'Why hello, Marynia,' they would greet her. 'Your husband is out, I see. Working hard. That's good. Now we have a little list here of things we would like your husband to get, if you would be so kind . . .'

Marynia would chatter away, teasing some, speaking kindly to others and, all the while, making her notes on small pieces of paper that she kept in her apron pocket with her short stubby pencil. She promised to pass the messages on to Jusiek and the visitors would leave.

When Jusiek came home she gave the list to him in silence, barely looking up from the task in hand. He shoved it in his jacket pocket with a sideways glance at me. We all knew that these lists were important and that both Jusiek and Marynia had to keep the soldiers on their side so they wouldn't ask any awkward questions.

With Jusiek at home, the mood in the house changed. He was kind enough but he wasn't friendly and he never really spoke if I was around. He waited until Marynia had put me into bed, tucked me up, given me a big kiss and closed the door behind her. Then almost immediately, in his deep urgent voice, he talked to Marynia in the room next door, on and on, until it lulled me to sleep.

In the beginning Marynia had been very forceful and spoken in a raised voice.

'She's here because she's like my own,' I heard her say repeatedly. 'What if it had been . . .'

'. . . of course she's staying . . .'

'. . . I owe it to her parents . . .'

I felt safe hiding behind Marynia's words. But as the days went by she said less and less until she stopped pleading altogether. I now tried even harder to please her so that she was happy to have me around. I tried to help her whenever I could but she would often smile at me in her gentle way and tell me to go and play. Sometimes she let me help her with the chores. I loved standing next to her peeling potatoes; I loved it when we stood side by side with our hands in soapy water doing the laundry, or when Marynia washed the dishes and I dried them, or simply when we swept the floor with our scratchy brooms. All I had to do was to point the broomstick skywards and jump on, and together we would fly into the endless blue and continue the search for my mother and father.

I loved the thought of being able to do *something*. Sometimes I imagined I was Cinderella but in my story she was living with her fairy godmother and not the wicked stepmother. At other times I pretended I was the Sorcerer's Apprentice fetching pail after pail of water.

I felt safe and loved. Marynia told stories to keep me entertained: fairy tales, stories about my family, and stories about the life we had led in Jagiellońska Street. She would make me laugh by telling me things about when I was little, like how I would stand up in my cot and with both hands push the knob on the wall that was between my cot and the door to my parents' room. She told me that I was very clever because I quickly worked out that whenever I pushed the bell it would ring at the front door. Once I knew this, I became mischievous, hiding in my cot, listening to my grandmother scurrying along the hallway in her slippers, murmuring under her breath, to open the door, only to find no one there. She would call out in surprise. I sent her again and again on this fruitless mission and most of the time she did it just to hear me crow with delight.

Marynia also told me stories about my father and his parents. I learned that my grandfather, the chief postmaster in the village of Żurawice, just outside Przemyśl, loved reading. He loved books as much as I did. He read everything he could lay his hands on and decided that, because books made him so happy, his children should go to school so they could read books too. My father also liked books and he ended up reading so many that he knew enough to go to university to train to be a doctor. His sister, Aunt Lusia, also read a lot of books and she became a teacher.

'Where is Aunt Lusia now?' I asked.

'I don't know,' Marynia replied. 'We never saw much of her after she married. Your father was so upset. He adored his older sister and would have done anything for her. But she wouldn't let him. Her husband even made her give up teaching.'

'Did they have any children?'

'No. It was a great pity, your father said, because she loved children so.'

'Your father made your grandfather very proud,' Marynia said. 'Your mother used to say that the other children at school were unkind to your father because he was Jewish and even later the students at the university weren't nice to him. Your grandfather was quite poor and it cost a lot of money to send your father to university, so to save money your father only ate black bread, day after day. Fancy that.'

I thought back to the ghetto and how a piece of black bread every day would have seemed like luxury, but said nothing.

'So, your father trained to be a doctor and when he'd finished his training he worked in a hospital before coming to Przemyśl where he met your mother and lived happily ever after.'

Although Marynia always spoke as if everyone were still alive, I had begun to realise that, along with my mother and my grandmother, I probably wouldn't see my Aunt Adela or Zazula again. With each day that passed, with little to think about, I began to miss them more and more and to dread the thought of being left an orphan. Above all else I did not want to be an orphan. Being an orphan, I knew from the stories, was by far the most awful thing that could happen to a child.

At night, I would lie awake and stare into

the darkness, listening to the heated exchanges between my nanny and her husband, thinking about my family and trying to remember their faces. I could see my aunt and Zazula clearly but it was more difficult to see Babcia and Mamusia. I would concentrate my thoughts on the last time I saw them; how my mother had given me the chunk of sausage and how wonderful it had tasted. I would lie and imagine what it would be like if I was to go back to my home in Jagiellońska Street and walk up the road, climb the stone stairs, open the front door and call out to Mamusia to tell her I was home.

In my thoughts, I could see her running into the hall and gathering me up in her arms, burying my head in her shoulder and covering me with kisses. I could see Babcia following closely behind, in her slippers, arms outstretched and the wrinkles smooth on her face. Big fat tears would roll down her cheeks, as she too would hug me over and over again. Then the memories would fade, leaving me alone in the darkness.

I think Marynia could see into my mind because no matter how busy she was, she could always spare a few minutes to tell me about my mother and father. One time she said, laughing, 'Oh, your mother is one in a million. Kind as the day is long. And she is funny, she would have us in stitches for hours. Full of life, she is, always the life and soul of any party.' She stopped and her voice sounded more serious. 'My word though, she can be stubborn when she wants to be. Sometimes I think your father finds her a little difficult to live with but he knew what he was taking on when he married her. Your Babcia told me that your mother had many admirers. Lots of young men all wanting

91

to marry her and everyone was so surprised when *she* decided—I told you, she's stubborn!—that she was going to marry a serious young doctor from the country. Well, everyone said that it would never last. He was nice enough, they said, but in time she would find him too boring and get tired of him. This was before I knew them of course, so I can only tell you what your grandmother told me. But they were all wrong. Your parents adored each other and because they were so different it made them love each other all the more.'

'What did my mother do?' I asked, eager to know more. 'I can't remember her being with me all the time.'

'No, that's right. She worked,' Marynia replied. 'She was a teacher at the university. She taught Polish literature. That's why they asked me to come and look after you when you were just this small.' She held up her hands to show me how small I had been, the size of Baby Doll. 'After you came along your mother had to go back to work and so she asked me to come and give you my mother's milk and take care of you. Oh, your parents adored you with your little pink feet, your golden curls and your baby-blue eyes. They didn't understand how you could look like that when they both had dark hair and dark eyes, and your grandparents too. They used to laugh about it and say that they had the most perfect angel child.'

At other times she used to tell me about Babcia and how fond she was of her, how gracious she was—a real lady.

'She was always helping others. Never a sour word crossed her lips, at least not when I was around. Her life hadn't been easy. Your mother's father—your other grandfather—won a lot of money on the lottery before the Great War in 1914. Can you imagine? They were immensely wealthy but then he went and lost all that money. I don't know what he did with it.'

How careless, I thought. 'Was Babcia very angry?' I said.

'Not for long. He went and died. Of pneumonia, I think she said. He was only thirty-five. Then she had a problem, what with no money, no husband and two young children, your mother and your Uncle Cesio, to bring up on her own.' Marynia paused for a moment. 'So, she ran a place where people could come and stay, a boarding house. She bought it eventually. But she also loved books and so when your mother and Uncle Cesio were old enough, with all her saved pennies she sent them to university. Just like your father's father sent his children. So it's no real surprise that you love stories. I just wish we had some books about this house.'

Although Marynia's house was empty of books, she had somehow managed to find another doll for me. It was a pathetic little doll with stringy hair and a raggedy dress, but I loved her and talked to her for hours every day, repeating the stories that Marynia had told me and making up more of my own.

*   *   *

One afternoon Marynia came into the room with a sombre expression on her face. She sat in her usual seat by the window and took me on to her lap. We sat quietly together for some time, my head leaning

93

against her chest. I watched the dust dance in the sunlight, soothed by the rise and fall of her soft, comfortable bosom as she breathed. The constant rhythmic sound of her beating heart had always comforted me whenever I felt sad and unhappy, or when she gently rocked me if I couldn't sleep. My head was beginning to clear and I felt peaceful again. I wished that we could stay like this for ever. Living here with Marynia, who knew me so well, I felt safe.

I felt Marynia take a deep breath and I knew she wanted to say something.

'What is it, Marynia?' I asked, not raising my head, still watching the dust making circles before me.

Whatever she said, I'd do. I had promised myself this so that I would never have to leave, and there would be no reason for her to leave me. I would never put her in any danger. With bad things lurking round every corner, I felt at last that I understood what was expected of me; I wasn't going to make any mistakes again. Then Marynia began to speak. At first I couldn't take in what she was saying. The soothing beat of her heart was drowned out by the thudding in my ears. Bright lights flashed in front of my eyes.

'What did you say?' I asked, hoping that I had misheard her.

'I said, my darling, that you can't stay here.'

'But why not?' I asked, panic setting in and closing its cold fingers tightly round my heart.

'I don't have anywhere safe to hide you,' Marynia replied. 'Jusiek and I don't know who is watching the house and if the Gestapo come here and look around there is nowhere to hide you.'

94

Panic fixed its grip and began its familiar squeeze on my chest as my head began to spin.

'But why can't I just stop hiding? I don't understand. What have I done? I have tried my best to be good and I know I argued with Zazula and that I didn't always do as I was told when I lived at home but I have tried to be good, I really have. And I have promised that I will always do what you tell me and never disobey you. Please, Marynia, you can't send me away. You *can't*!'

I was sobbing now. I felt the tears in my eyes running down my cheeks, wetting Marynia's blouse where moments earlier I had happily laid my head.

'Darling, it's not because you've been naughty. You are such a good girl.' Marynia took my face in her hands. 'It's just a wicked, wicked world and it's because you are Jewish.'

'Because I'm Jewish?' I was so surprised that I stopped crying. 'What do you mean because I'm Jewish?' Zazula had said something about this too but I wasn't sure what she meant and it seemed so long ago now. 'Is being Jewish wicked? Is that why Mamusia and Babcia were taken away—because they were wicked?'

'No, there is nothing wrong with being Jewish. You must never, ever think that,' Marynia said sternly. 'There is *nothing* wrong with being Jewish,' she repeated. 'It's just that . . . just that . . . well, the Nazi soldiers don't like people who are Jewish and they want to get rid of them.'

This made no sense to me at all. What was she talking about? I was a good girl but the soldiers wanted to get rid of me. Nothing made sense and I felt that I was sinking deeper and deeper into a black hole and I couldn't find a way out. I couldn't stop myself falling. I couldn't save myself. My mind was working fast. No Mamusia. No Babcia. No Aunt Adela. No Cousin Zazula and now no Marynia. This couldn't be happening again.

I thought for a moment and then blurted out, 'I can stop being Jewish if you like. If I stop being Jewish can I stay with you?'

'It's not that simple,' said Marynia, hugging me closer as she went on speaking. 'To be honest, Renata, I really don't understand it either. They don't like Jews because they have dark hair and eyes and they say they have big noses.'

This is what Zazula had said too. I felt as though a lifeline had been thrown into my dark pit—I could begin my escape. I was delighted and exclaimed, 'But then I don't need to hide because my eyes are blue and my hair is yellow and my nose isn't big at all. So the Germans can't know that I am Jewish. And anyway, how do *you* know that I am, Marynia?'

'I know because your mummy has beautiful dark hair and very soft brown eyes.' I tried to picture my mother's face but it was fuzzy and kept floating away. I was beginning to forget what she looked like.

'I can't remember. *Does* she have a big nose?'

'Well, maybe a little bigger than mine, but I wouldn't have said it was big,' replied Marynia.

'And do *you* hate her?'

'No, my love, I adore your mother. She is the most wonderful person. And you're going to grow up just like her.'

'I wish I could see her,' I said, desperately trying to remember what she looked like. 'When I'm grown-up, I'm going to be a teacher like her.' I felt pleased that I had remembered *something* about her.

'Now that's a good idea,' said Marynia. 'She would like that, but you're going to have to go to school and work very hard. She was very clever, you know.'

'I'm going to be clever too. When can I go to school?'

'Not just yet,' said Marynia. 'But soon, I promise. You're not quite old enough and besides there are no schools open these days.' She paused. 'Now, Renata, I want you to be a good girl and I will tell you about the nice people you're going to live with from . . . tonight.'

'Tonight? But who are they?' I asked. 'What are their names?'

I suddenly felt extremely tired. The thought of going to live somewhere else and this time with strangers was too much to bear. I started thinking about Mamusia again.

'Renata, you're not listening,' I heard Marynia say.

'No. I was thinking about Mamusia and Babcia.'

'Well, listen carefully. The people you are going to are called Maciej and Hanka. They are very nice and they have a room where they can look after you. You are not going to be alone because there will also be a little boy about the same age as you, called Jan. It will be nice for you to have a playmate again. I have told them that you are very, very good and will do everything they say.'

As much as I hated the idea of leaving Marynia, I did like the thought of having someone to play with again.

'Who is Jan? Is he Jewish like me?'

97

'Yes. He's a nice boy. His mother has to work so she is paying Maciej to look after him.'

'Do you have to pay for me?' I asked.

'Renata, you ask too many questions. Yes, we do have to pay for you. No one does anything for nothing in this world any more. But we are happy to pay for you. Jusiek is earning well and we can afford to look after you. Now let's pack your things, we must go this evening.'

CHAPTER SEVEN

November 1943

It was nearly dusk when we set off. As we came out of the house, Marynia drew her shawl up over her head and held my hand tightly. She said nothing as she pulled me along the deserted streets until we reached a dark alleyway. With a quick glance over her shoulder, she turned into the narrow alley, dragging me behind her. After a few minutes she stopped outside a wooden front door. She knocked quickly and waited, gripping my hand even more tightly. Eventually the door opened to reveal a tall, thin man with a mop of blond hair who was dressed in brown trousers and a thick sweater of the same colour.

'Hello, Maciej. I've brought Renata,' Marynia said, gently pushing me forward, her hands planted firmly on my shoulders.

'Hello,' I said politely.

The man looked down at me and smiled. I looked into his unshaven face. His eyes seemed kind—I thought I would like him—and I smiled back. He turned and beckoned us in. We followed him along the hall and up several flights of stairs. When we reached the landing the man pushed a partly open door and stood back to let us enter. The room was large and crowded with furniture. An old sofa covered in blankets stood in the middle of the room and to the side of it a rectangular wooden table with four chairs neatly tucked underneath, two on each side. Two mattresses lay on the floor against one wall and another two against the opposite wall. All were covered with grey blankets. Through another door in the third wall I spied a small lavatory. There was no kitchen, but a sink and a small stove stood in the corner nearest the window. The window was covered in black material. The room smelt of stale cigarettes.

A slim young woman got up off the sofa and came to greet us. She was not much taller than Marynia, but moved gracefully as she walked towards us. Her sharp eyes and pretty face were surrounded by neat brown hair that fell to her shoulders. She was dressed in a plain dark skirt and blouse and flat brown shoes.

'This is Hanka,' Maciej said. 'She lives here too.'

'Hello,' said Hanka, smiling at me. 'That's your bed.' She pointed to one of the mattresses and then turned to face the only chest of drawers. 'You can put your things in here,' she said, pulling at one of the handles. 'But make sure you keep them very tidy. We haven't much room.'

I handed my small bag to Marynia who was about to put my few things in the open drawer when Hanka put a hand on her arm to stop her.

'No, let her do it herself,' she said. 'We're not

here to wait on her hand and foot. She must learn to look after herself. It's enough that we have to share the room with her and the boy. I don't intend to be her slave as well.'

She was going to say more but Maciej put a restraining hand on her shoulder.

'She's only little, Hanka,' Marynia said. 'She will get used to doing things for herself soon enough.'

'You bet she will,' Hanka muttered under her breath.

Marynia then turned to me and smiling a sad smile said, 'Renata, I will help you this time,' and she emptied the contents of my bag, placed them carefully into the drawer, and handed me my doll. Just then we heard a faint knock on the door below. The man went out and quickly returned with two more people: a thin, frightened-looking woman whose huge dark brown eyes looked enormous in her hollow white face, and a small timid boy who clung fiercely to his mother's hand. He too was dark, with a sharply pointed, pinched face. He was wearing black cut-down trousers which hung off him in folds and a shabby navy-blue overcoat.

'Say hello to Jan, Renata,' Maciej said. 'He's going to live here too and you are going to be good friends and play together.'

'Hello, Jan,' I said obediently.

Jan didn't reply but hung his head and retreated behind his mother.

'I can see life is going to be a big bundle of fun,' Hanka remarked.

'Shut up,' Maciej hissed at her.

'Please excuse her,' he said to the other two women. 'Hanka isn't feeling well, which is why she is so crotchety today. Don't worry, everything will be all right. I have a lovely treat for you children,' he added, turning to Jan and me. 'For supper tonight you are going to have some meat, a delicious stew. Hanka's cooked it specially for you. Now go to that corner and get to know each other while we grown-ups have a little talk.'

Poor little Jan remained rooted to the spot, unwilling to leave his mother's side. I felt sorry for him and so held out my hand and then led him to the corner of the room that Maciej had indicated. I couldn't think of anything to say so we stood there looking at each other and listening to the adults' conversation.

Maciej was talking.

'We expect payment every Monday. Half the money will go to us and half to my wife who comes to collect her share regularly. In addition we expect contributions of food if you want those children fed. I insist that while they are here they are totally under my control with no interference from either of you. We are endangering our lives to look after them, therefore we must have absolute control. Can I also make it quite clear that, if the money for their board isn't paid on time, they will be thrown out on to the street. We are not doing this for charity.'

'You will be paid.' Marynia's voice was firm but cold.

Jan's mother promised too before wiping her eyes on a grubby handkerchief she pulled from her pocket.

'I think you both ought to go now,' Maciej said. 'We don't want them upset more than is necessary—the sooner they settle in the better.'

Marynia hugged me close. Over my shoulder I could see Jan's mother doing the same to him, her

101

eyes closed and tears escaping from under her dark lashes.

'I don't want to stay here,' I whispered urgently into Marynia's ear as I clung to her. 'I thought he looked nice, but he's not and Hanka's even worse. Please don't leave me here.'

'You'll be fine and I'll be back next week,' Marynia promised as she pushed me gently away. I saw that she too was fighting to keep the tears that welled up in her eyes from falling.

Jan, who had been silent up to now, began to sob as his tearful mother hurriedly left the room. Maciej showed his guests down to the front door and we were left alone with Hanka who immediately turned her back on us and stood staring at the blacked-out window.

*   *   *

'Right,' said Maciej when he returned. 'That's enough of all this snivelling nonsense from the lot of you.' He turned to Hanka. 'You nearly blew it, you bitch.'

Hanka just sniffed in reply.

Maciej turned to Jan who couldn't stifle his sobs any longer and began to cry loudly.

'Stop that moaning at once!' he roared.

With two large strides Maciej lunged at Jan, picked him up like a sack of potatoes and hurled him across the room onto his mattress. He turned to me. 'We're going to get some things straight. Right now,' he snarled. 'You and Jan are going to live here in this room with us. If you behave yourselves and do as you're told, then you'll be fine. If you don't . . .' He left the sentence unfinished

102

but unclipped the belt from his trousers and waved it in front of us. 'I hit very hard,' he said. 'Do you understand?'

We both understood quite clearly.

He softened his voice and added, 'Now that we all know where we stand, let's enjoy ourselves and have the stew Hanka has made as a special welcome treat. Say thank you to her for taking the trouble.'

'Thank you,' we whispered.

'Sit down and don't forget your manners.'

We sat down at the table in the places he indicated. Hanka fetched a rusty pot from the stove as Maciej put four bowls on the table into which he ladled dollops of a watery brown liquid with fat floating on the surface and lumps of red gristly meat. Maciej handed us both a hunk of black bread with which to mop it up. When everyone was served, Maciej and Hanka tucked into their meal and ate quickly not saying a word to each other or to us. Jan and I simply sat and stared at the bowls in front of us. Maciej finally looked up from his meal, still chewing on his food.

'Eat!' he barked.

Maciej had finished his first bowl and was helping himself to seconds. He then pushed the pot across the table towards Hanka who was scraping her bowl.

'I'm not hungry,' I said, pushing my bowl away. 'I would like to go to bed, please.'

'You're not going anywhere till you have eaten up every scrap,' Maciej said. 'This is good food and you should be grateful for the opportunity to eat meat. It won't come very often. And the same goes for you.' He turned to Jan who was sitting there, spoon in hand, with silent tears rolling freely down his pale little face.

'I can't, I feel sick,' Jan sobbed.

'You'll feel even more sick when I've finished with you.' Maciej leapt to his feet and grabbed Jan by the back of his jumper. He lifted him into the air and stared wildly into his face before returning him abruptly to his seat.

'Eat it at once,' he snarled.

Jan lifted a spoonful to his lips and slowly forced it into his mouth. He swallowed without chewing and then took mouthful after mouthful until all the stew was gone. Then he clapped his hand over his mouth and gagged. Without waiting for permission he rushed from the table to the lavatory whereupon he was violently sick.

Maciej was about to go after him but Hanka stopped him. 'He did what you said. He ate it all. Leave him alone.'

Maciej glared, but sat down again. He turned his attention to me.

'Pick up your spoon and eat . . . *Now!*'

I picked up my spoon and managed to swallow a little bit of the gravy. I swallowed another spoonful. It was horrible.

'Eat a piece of meat.' Maciej leant across the table and took the spoon from my hand and shovelled the biggest piece of fatty meat onto it, then handed me the spoon. At this point I, too, was crying.

'*Eat!*'

I put the spoon to my mouth and tried to swallow the congealed greasy meat whole, in one gulp, but it was too big. I coughed, spluttered and gagged. I couldn't chew it because it was so tough. So I tried to spit it out.

'Don't you dare spit that out!' Maciej said. 'If you do . . .'

In that moment I felt anger rising inside me, but didn't dare disobey him. I could see Jan out of the corner of my eye and was terrified of what might happen if I angered Maciej still further. So I sat there, tears pouring down my face, my mouth full of the disgusting meat. I sat there for what seemed an eternity watching the film of grease gradually cover the surface of my bowl with a yellow crust that I would have to break through to get at the next piece of meat. My throat closed up. It felt as if that huge lump of flesh was stuck, refusing to go any further. I felt sick and terrified. My tormentor sat opposite me and watched my every move without saying a word. He never once took his eyes off me.

'For God's sake, leave the child alone,' Hanka sighed, fed up with waiting. 'If she wants to go to bed hungry, let her. She'll only be sick if you make her eat it and I can do without the stink and mess, thank you.'

'She's an ungrateful brat,' Maciej growled, glaring at me. 'It's the last time we waste horse meat on her. She can go hungry. Get to bed and don't you dare move a muscle, you spoiled pampered child. Move fast before I decide to whip you.'

I moved—very fast—towards my mattress, silently thanking Hanka for saving me from Maciej and for being more understanding. I undressed and slid under the blankets as fast as I could. Before I covered my head I glanced over to Jan who was invisible under his coverings on the mattress next to mine. Although I couldn't see, I knew he was crying

105

because of the telltale quivering of the blankets over his tiny back. I felt very sorry for him. I knew only too well what it was like to feel abandoned and all alone, not understanding what was going on. He was so small and unhappy. I decided then that I would try to be the best possible friend to him. Perhaps we could help each other. Perhaps he knew why Maciej and Hanka were being so horrid when they didn't even know us. I would ask Marynia next time I saw her and, at the same time, try and persuade her to find Jan and me another place to stay. I knew that I had to look after him for as long as his mother wasn't there for him.

I lay there staring into darkness feeling the itchy blanket against my arms, legs and face, my ears alert to every sound. As I lay there I wondered why Jan was so frightened of everything. Why was he here when he obviously had a mother to look after him? But if she was Jewish, why was she allowed outside? My thoughts turned once again to my Mamusia and I wished she was with me under the blanket. Where was she now? Did she think about me or had she forgotten me? The Germans took her because she was Jewish, at least I knew that. But where had they taken her? What was that name old Piotr had told me—Szeb, Szebn-something, Szebnie. Again I tried to picture her face in my mind but it was blurred. I suddenly felt very alone.

After a while I heard the click of the switch, plunging the room into darkness that seeped through my covers. Cautiously I pushed the scratchy blanket off my face. I felt safer now, hidden in the dark; at least Maciej couldn't see me.

I heard Maciej and Hanka getting ready for bed and in the dim light I saw them getting into bed. If they were using only one mattress, then the other one must be for someone else. Perhaps it was for his wife—he had mentioned his wife to Marynia. Perhaps his wife would be nicer than him.

Soon I heard a murmur from across the room, then a giggle.

'Shhhh, don't wake them!' I heard Hanka whisper.

I strained my ears as Maciej replied, 'Oh don't worry, they're both sleeping like babies.'

Through the darkness came sounds of movement and occasional little groans and sighs that went on for ages. They seemed to be very restless sleepers. But at last when the noises were replaced by deep regular breathing and snores I was finally alone in the darkness. Yet it was still a long, long time before I, too, was able to escape into sleep.

*   *   *

After that long first night, one day dragged into another. Jan and I weren't allowed outside and, as always, had to keep quiet.

'You stay on your mattress until we say you can come off,' Hanka ordered us the next morning. 'We don't want any of the neighbours knowing you are here. You wait until they have all gone out. Then this afternoon when I say, you will get back on your mattress and play quietly.'

No one visited. Maciej and Hanka stayed in the room with us; only occasionally during the day one or other would venture out and even then it wasn't ever for very long. They never left Jan and me alone and wouldn't tell us where they were going. Then Maciej started going out after dark.

107

'Meeting tonight,' he would say to Hanka over supper and Hanka would nod her head in reply.

What these meetings were about neither he nor Hanka would say and I was much too afraid to ask. Maciej would leave soon after supper and not come back for several hours. Hanka was always anxious when Maciej was away, pacing up and down, smoking strong, pungent cigarettes, one after another, until she heard his footsteps on the landing. Then she would quickly stub out what remained of the cigarette and open the door. Maciej would take off his coat and the hushed whispering would begin as he recalled the evening's events. Try as I might from my mattress on the floor I couldn't hear anything of what Maciej told Hanka other than a few snatched words that meant nothing to me.

During the day Maciej and Hanka kept reasonably quiet so that no one in the block had reason to visit and start asking difficult questions. Sometimes when they were bored or frustrated, they got cross with each other.

This would often lead to an argument but it was quickly over. Hanka would purse her lips and stare at the blacked-out window, just as she had done when Jan and I arrived on that first evening, and Maciej, seeing that she wasn't going to answer him, stopped arguing. It was during these moments that I would think how strange adults were. Why did they shout at each other so much? Why were they kind to us, or each other, one minute and shouting the next for no apparent reason, telling us not to be so naughty or selfish or rude? I came to the conclusion that it was always best to stay out of their way and keep my thoughts and feelings to myself.

Jan and I settled quickly into the new routine. Jan was small and very quiet but not unfriendly. All his clothes were too big for him and they made him look smaller than he really was. His smooth hair surrounded his pale face and his large dark eyes always looked worried. I was becoming quite good now at picking up a new life, more often than not with strangers, and adopting their habits. I was able to tell what mood Maciej and Hanka were in and I quickly learned what I should and should not say or do. This made life easier for Jan and me. We didn't have much to amuse us during the long days and so I decided I would concentrate more on listening to the adult conversations and try and understand the words they used. If I didn't recognise a word, I would repeat it over and over again so that I would remember it and then ask Marynia what it meant on her next visit. I knew that things wouldn't stay the same for ever, they never did. Change was just around the corner and I waited.

At first Marynia visited regularly, always handing over the money and spending a few special moments with me explaining what the words I had learned meant, and helping me to understand.

'I'll be back soon, Renata, I promise,' she would say, giving me a tight hug and a big kiss before she left. 'Just six more nights.'

But after the first few visits, Marynia didn't come again. When Jan and I weren't playing, I would sit and wait listening for the knock on the door downstairs and her footsteps as she slowly climbed the stairs. I knew that Jan did the same. Sometimes I could read his face and feel his pain, knowing that he felt the same as me although he would never let on. Each evening as I lay under the blanket I would convince myself that I would see Marynia tomorrow. *Just one more night, Renata*, I said to myself over and over again.

But the days passed and Marynia still didn't come. I couldn't understand what had gone wrong because the last time I saw her she had promised faithfully that she would be back soon and Marynia always kept her promises. I knew nothing could have happened to her because Maciej had said he'd throw me on to the streets if Marynia so much as missed one payment.

But it was good to have a playmate: Jan and I got on well and at the advanced age of six, I felt very motherly towards him. Although he was just eight, a full two years older than me, he was always frightened. I had to take the lead and ended up doing the talking for both of us. He followed me around the room, sat beside me all the time and played whatever games I suggested. He would never quarrel with me like Zazula had done even when the boredom and frustration became almost too much to bear. In fact he hardly ever spoke at all.

I secretly enjoyed bossing him around—I wasn't the baby any more. I think he had always been with his mother and hadn't lived this sort of life before, unlike me who had been doing it for ever, and I found it much easier to get used to living here. On the first day we were together I couldn't get Jan to say a word. Then remembering all the tales Aunt Adela had told me I said, 'Shall I tell you a story?' Jan nodded his head and so it began. From then on I would involve him in my fantasies, recalling every smallest detail and sometimes elaborating

110

them with my own. We spent long hours sitting cross-legged on our mattresses, Jan facing me, happily lost in the tale I was telling, but always saying nothing.

'And the shoemaker and his wife peeped out from their hiding place behind the curtain to see two little elves leap up on to the work bench,' I said, watching as Jan's eyes grew wider. 'They sat cross-legged, just like us, Jan, next to the pieces of soft leather and began to stitch ...' I imagined being a small elf and being able to escape through the crack under the door.

Some days if Hanka or Maciej were in a more tolerant mood, we would act them out. Jan, who knew no stories, listened eagerly. I would choose to be the wolf in *Little Red Riding Hood* or the little heroine herself. He would be the granny and the huntsman. I was Goldilocks, whilst he was given the role of all three bears. Usually he would object to being the rats in *The Pied Piper of Hamelin* but seemed happy enough to be the fat mayor or crippled child whilst I, of course, was the Piper. I particularly loved this tale, the Piper with his twinkling eyes and his half yellow, half red coat and the rats, *great rats, small rats* ... who drowned in the River Weser.

I thought of the view of the River San, the only big river I could remember, and imagined the rats running into its dark waters. I understood why the Piper was angry for not being paid as he had been promised. I was angry with the little yellow star for not keeping me and Mamusia and Babcia safe as it had promised. I felt for the little lame boy left behind as the door in the mountain closed before him leaving him all alone, helpless. I felt sorry for

111

myself for being left behind with no Mamusia or Babcia.

It was Maciej who had the book of translated English poems. He read us some poems by Robert Browning that were about love and murder— 'Porphyria's Lover' and 'My Last Duchess' by Christina Rossetti—as well as other more fanciful poems such as 'Goblin Market'. Because neither of us could read, I would often ask Maciej to read to us, especially 'Goblin Market'.

'Please, Maciej,' I would beg. 'Just one more time.'

For then we could be transported into a world full of summer fruits and warm air as Maciej's deep voice led us through the verses one by one.

> *'Damsons and bilberries,*
> *Taste them and try;*
> *Currants and gooseberries . . .*
> *Sweet to tongue and sound to eye,*
> *Come buy, come buy.'*

I would imagine I was Laura and wonder whether I would have eaten the goblins' fruit.

> *'"No," said Lizzie. "No, no, no;*
> *"Their offers should not charm us,*
> *"Their evil gifts would harm us."'*

But there were days when the thought of summer fruits was too much to bear.

> *'She never tasted such before . . .*
> *She sucked and sucked and sucked the*
> *more*

112

Fruits which that unknown orchard bore,
She sucked until her lips were sore;
Then flung the emptied rinds away . . .'

On those days I knew that I would have done the same without a moment's hesitation even though, unlike Laura, I was only too aware of the outcome of doing such a forbidden thing.

Jan enjoyed being the goblins and he would make me laugh by going around the flat chanting, 'Come buy, come buy,' even when we had long since finished our play. I liked to hear his voice. For someone so frightened and silent, on these rare occasions he sounded almost happy. Jan's lead role was in *'The Forsaken Merman'* by Matthew Arnold when he was the deserted merman, suffering and longing for his human wife to come back. As the days passed, I found myself liking Maciej more even though his moods were unpredictable. I could see that he too loved books and the stories and poems that lay between their covers. When we were quiet and obedient Maciej would become friendly, offering to read to us and sometimes even joining in our games. He didn't hit us and had even given up threatening us once he knew that we could be trusted to behave.

Hanka on the other hand was more difficult to understand. She ignored us most of the time and rarely spoke to us, except to utter a command. She set food down in front of us without even glancing in our direction and at the end of each meal she issued orders to us to clear the plates. She showed us how to wash up and was cross if we did not do it properly. Even though she was neither friendly nor kind, underneath she was fair and would

113

defend, and sometimes protect, us against Maciej's outbursts of temper.

Living in one room, it wasn't surprising that Maciej and Hanka turned to each other. When they were not screaming at each other and sometimes even throwing things, they were hugging each other and kissing. I would stare at them wondering whether they really did like each other or not. I couldn't decide. I would watch them from my mattress as that feeling of jealousy rose up in my stomach and crept over me. I longed to be hugged even by Maciej or Hanka. My attention would turn to Jan: at least I had him to look after. I could take care of someone even if I didn't have someone to take care of me. Jan obviously missed his mother's affection too and so loved to lean against me whilst I tickled his back or stroked his hair. Sometimes I tried to put my arms around him and kiss his little face just like Mamusia used to do to me, but he didn't like that at all and would push me away, each time his face turning a deep shade of pink.

But even though Maciej read to us, I finally decided that I liked Hanka more. Although she shouted at us, what made me more uncomfortable was the way in which Maciej was so unkind to her. Sometimes their quarrelling became vicious, ending with Hanka in tears. Maciej would then clout either her or Jan and frequently both for no reason that I could ever understand. Thankfully he didn't hit me. But I hated it as much as if he had hit me because I simply could not see any reason for it. Yet as time went by I began to realise that this happened when his temper flared either just before, or just after, a visit from his wife. This was the time to keep out of Maciej's way. We all knew when she was due because Maciej was tense and irritable, snapping at Hanka and at us.

Jadwiga was Maciej's wife. She was a large woman with blonde hair scraped back into a bun and a loud, unpleasant voice. Her mouth was twisted and cruel; her eyes cold and unkind. Jadwiga visited every week, but never spent the night. Thankfully she never stayed long but whenever she came Maciej, Jadwiga and Hanka sat at the table in the middle of the room, speaking in low voices so that Jan and I, who had retreated to our mattresses to keep out of their way, found it difficult to hear what they were saying. Jadwiga took no notice of us at all. Sometimes their voices would get louder but, while we heard the words, we didn't always understand what they meant.

Jadwiga always began by throwing out questions to Maciej and Hanka.

'So, how have they been?'

'How much have you got now?'

'What are you going to do with—'

Then she would tell them off, in the same way that Maciej and Hanka would scold us.

'Idiots, can't you see that—'

'All you have to do is sit here with them! I am the one running around—'

Although Hanka sat at the table with Jadwiga, she hardly said a word to her. Hanka spent most of the time studying her fingernails as if she were cross and sulky but I could tell she was more than a little scared of Jadwiga. When his wife was present Maciej also changed. When Jadwiga was in charge he seemed to grow smaller and quieter—he too must have been a little nervous. This surprised me—how could someone as fierce as Maciej be

115

frightened of *anything*?

Jadwiga's weekly visit always followed the same routine. After the questions Maciej would take half the money Marynia and Jan's mother had given him out from his trouser pocket and place it on the table in front of Jadwiga. She would count the złotys, twice, and then put them carefully into a little cloth bag with pull strings, which she would stow away in an inside pocket of her coat. Once the bag containing the money was out of sight, Maciej would click his fingers and Hanka would get to her feet and busy herself at the stove in the corner with her back to Jadwiga who would eye her suspiciously. It was obvious that Jadwiga didn't trust or like Hanka and she didn't see why she should pretend to like her. As Hanka made the tea, Maciej and his wife sat in silence. Hanka would then hand them both a steaming mug and escape back to the stove. Then Maciej and his wife talked together, softly, until Jadwiga abruptly ended their conversation and, with a short goodbye, left the room.

There was one visit from Jadwiga that didn't follow the usual routine. Maciej was angrier and more hostile than ever.

'I'm sorry, Jadwiga, there's no money.'

'What?' Jadwiga leant over the table towards him and grabbed his jacket. 'You stupid idiot. What do you mean there is no money? Didn't they come? Did you go and look for them? Or were you expecting *me* to do that as well?' She released her grip and leaned back in her chair.

Maciej said nothing but scowled at her across the table. Jadwiga returned his stare until at last he looked away and said, 'They didn't show up, all

116

right? What could I have done? They'll be back. We'll just up the price.'

Jadwiga stood up, her face like thunder.

'Just get the money,' she hissed and grabbing her coat marched out of the room without even bothering to mutter goodbye.

Jan and I looked at each other but knew better than to say anything and kept out of Maciej's way for the rest of the evening. That night I lay awake and, as usual, tried not to listen to the muffled noises that came through the darkness from the mattress on the opposite side of the room. Hanka was moaning more than usual and I began to wonder whether I should get up and see if she was all right—Maciej didn't seem to care. Perhaps he was asleep. But somehow in the aftermath of Jadwiga's visit I didn't dare in case Maciej was in fact awake and got angry with me for being out of bed. Instead I lay very still and tried to focus my thoughts on Marynia and her promised visit. Finally the noises stopped and I could hear their soft, regular breathing allowing me to fall asleep too.

*   *   *

Two days after that strange visit from Jadwiga, Maciej was in a particularly good mood. He kept hugging and kissing Hanka and even patted me on the head.

'You are a good girl,' he said, smiling at me.

I couldn't remember him ever having called me a good girl before and the pleasure from knowing that I had pleased him felt wonderful. He had been nice to Jan too, not forcing him to eat all his gloopy porridge. Jan always ate like a bird, pecking a little here and a little there, and was constantly in trouble for leaving food on his plate. Sometimes when Maciej and Hanka were both away from the table Jan would quickly slide his plate over to me and in return I would push my empty plate in front of him. I had a hearty appetite and had learned to eat everything. Everything, that was, except horse meat.

On the rare occasions that Hanka returned from one of her short outings clutching a package of horse meat, the two grown-ups didn't waste it on us children. Hanka would make horse stew for herself and Maciej and the two of them would sit at the table and wolf it down. Jan and I didn't mind one little bit—in fact it was a relief. Whether or not Maciej was aware of how often Jan and I swapped our plates I never really knew. He turned a blind eye. Once or twice, when Maciej was in a bad mood, he did catch us and there had been trouble.

'You are more than ungrateful,' he snarled. 'There are people out there eating rats off the street because they can't find food. You are lucky and don't even know it. What makes you so special, I would like to know?'

Maciej and Hanka continued to spend most of their time focussed on each other, either gazing into each other's eyes and smiling lovingly, or quarrelling and shouting. The rest of the time they would talk together in earnest whispers. I listened to their conversations; after all there wasn't much else to do and I was always hungry for information and desperate to learn why Marynia hadn't been to visit.

'Another bunker has been found, the one in . . .'

'The Underground is ready but what they are

118

waiting for is . . .'

'They had been hiding a family of Jews and were all killed before the Resistance could . . .'

'This war can't go on for ever, we have to make sure that . . .'

They never mentioned Marynia, or Jan's mother either, and these snippets meant nothing to me. But it was the way that Maciej and Hanka talked in their urgent whispers that made the life outside these four walls sound strange and mysterious even though the world seemed to have forgotten about me and Jan cooped up inside this room behind the blacked-out window.

They would talk about the war, Jews, killing, Polish people fighting back, a hidden war, but I couldn't imagine what was really happening other than to draw on my own experience. War to me meant watching the starry sky or veiled clouds on a sunny day through darkened windows and only being able to imagine the warmth of the sun on my back or the cold splash of raindrops on my face. It meant men fighting and killing and taking what wasn't theirs, including those I loved; it meant the hole in my stomach that groaned and growled; the need to keep quiet all the time; having to tiptoe around adults whose moods would change in an instant without warning; and the fear of being found. But above all, war was the monsters in grey-green uniforms and peaked hats and shiny boots who continued to visit me in the night after everyone was asleep, reaching out and grabbing me as I lay frozen with fear on the ground before them.

*   *   *

One morning Maciej had just finished saying that he was going to teach us a new game when Jadwiga's familiar knock, two quick taps followed by four long ones, resounded through the door. Maciej's head jerked up and he and Hanka looked at each other.

'What the hell does she want?' Maciej snarled, trying to stay in charge. 'She isn't due for another five days. If she thinks she's going to get more money, she's got a surprise coming.' He got up off the floor and made his way to the door.

'Are you sure it's not a trap?' A look of terror crossed Hanka's face.

Maciej paused.

'I don't think so, but just in case . . .' Maciej returned to his mattress and after fumbling underneath it for a few moments pulled out a small revolver and approached the door holding the gun before him in his right hand. I looked at Jan who seemed as surprised as me that Maciej had a gun hidden under his mattress. The gun clicked as he held it. He unlocked the door and opened it a crack, then a bit further as far as the chain would allow. 'Who's there?' he whispered urgently.

'Who d'you think's here, you idiot?' came the unmistakably harsh voice of Jadwiga.

'What do you want? We weren't expecting you today.' Maciej stood firmly in front of the door, making no attempt to let his wife in.

'Open the door and let me in. Do you want the whole house to hear?' came the reply.

Maciej opened the door and in she came with a broad smile on her face. At first I didn't recognise her. I had never seen her smiling and I was surprised to find that she was in fact quite nice to look at. The smile extended to her eyes, which seemed to sparkle as she looked around the room in search of Jan and me. I found this new Jadwiga more disturbing than the usual one.

'Comes to something when my own husband locks me out of my own flat,' she remarked jovially, winking at me and turning her smile on Hanka.

'What d'you want? What are you up to?' said Maciej.

'What a suspicious mind you have, Maciej, dear,' she said. 'I'm not *up to* anything. I had a spare morning and I thought I would give you and Hanka the chance to go to the meeting together for once and I would look after these two. Get to know them better.' Still smiling, she looked over to where Jan and I sat.

'Well,' Maciej said. 'That is a turn-up for the books—my wife being kind and considerate, a rare event indeed. An opportunity too good to pass up. Thank you, my dear, we shall take up your offer most gratefully. In fact, Hanka needs to be at this one and so I was going to stay behind. I really do appreciate this, Jadwiga, especially as things are finally coming to a head.'

'So I gathered. That means you won't be able to stay here much longer. What d'you plan to do with *them*?' She raised her eyebrows and nodded towards Jan and me.

'Things will resolve themselves,' he replied. 'The mother is still behind with the money. I've warned her. She knows the odds.'

'No heart, have you, husband of *mine*. But that's when I like you best—when you show some guts.'

As she stressed the *mine*, she glanced across the room at Hanka. Hanka turned away and I saw her spit into the corner of the room. Why was Hanka

121

being so rude when Jadwiga was being so friendly for once?

'Right,' Maciej said. 'If you really mean it, we'll be off.'

'I really mean it. I know this is an important meeting. Don't hurry back. I have no pressing engagements today.'

Hanka and Maciej reached for their coats and then left before Jadwiga could change her mind, not together, but Hanka first and Maciej a few minutes later.

*   *   *

'So, here we are, just the three of us. Isn't that nice,' Jadwiga said, bending down to sit on the sofa, her smile making her look very different from the Jadwiga we knew. 'We have a whole morning to get to know each other properly. Come and sit here beside me and let's have a look at what I have in my bag.' She pulled her big cloth shopping bag onto her lap and started to undo the zip.

Jan looked at me and we shyly approached the sofa where she was taking up most of the available space and so we sat on the floor at her feet. Jadwiga rummaged in her bag and pulled out a small package which she carefully unwrapped and proudly displayed on her lap—two small sponge cakes.

'A little treat for two good children,' she said, holding them out temptingly. Jan and I looked at them in amazement. We hadn't seen a cake for months, years even. I couldn't tear my eyes away in case they vanished.

'Can we really eat them? A whole one each?' I

couldn't believe our luck.

'Yes, a whole one each. Eat them now before the others come back and make you share them,' Jadwiga added.

'Thank you!' Jan and I gasped in unison.

We ate our treats greedily, not savouring every mouthful as we should have done. But neither of us could remember having eaten anything so delicious for ages and ages. For the first time I noticed that Jan had no problem at all with eating. He finished his first and licked his lips over and over again so as not to miss one single crumb. Jadwiga watched us with a smile, not saying a word until every scrap was gone and our attention was focussed on her once more.

'I'm glad you enjoyed that,' she said. 'Now come and tell me all about yourselves. I want to know how you spend your time. Tell me all about what you do all day in just one room and how you amuse yourselves. Then later we'll have some of the nice lunch I've brought especially for you. It'll be our little secret. I may even have some sausage and more cake, who knows.' Jadwiga patted her bag and placed it on the floor beside her.

She turned to Jan and said in a soft voice, 'Tell me, little one, are you happy here?'

'I miss my mother,' he said.

'Of course you do,' said Jadwiga kindly. 'But Maciej and Hanka are good to you, aren't they? You do like them?'

Jan gazed at the floor. It surprised me how unfriendly he was being to this lovely lady who had brought us treats and seemed so concerned about whether we were happy or not.

'Everything's fine,' Jan said. 'When will I see my

mother again?'

'Soon. Sooner than you think,' Jadwiga replied. 'And what about you?' she asked, turning towards me and putting her arm round my shoulder. 'You never look very happy, my poppet. Tell Aunty Jadwiga what the matter is and why I never see a smile on your pretty little face.'

For the first time in ages I felt I had a new friend—one who would give me the hugs and the attention I longed for.

'I'm waiting for my father to come and get me. He's away with the Army, you see. Mamusia and Babcia can't come and get me, they will never come back. But sometimes I hope they will.'

'But who told you they won't come back?' Jadwiga asked, her arm still wrapped protectively around my shoulder.

'Marynia did. She told me the Nazi soldiers took them away and you don't come back if the Nazis get you. Do you know Marynia?' I asked. Perhaps she could explain the reason why Marynia no longer came to the flat.

'Yes, I know Marynia. I know her well,' Jadwiga replied.

'She hasn't been to see me and she said she would.'

'She's busy, and it isn't safe for her to come here,' said Jadwiga. 'It's safer for her *not* to come here—safer for you too. In fact I saw her only the other day, she sends you her love.'

Jadwiga dived once again into her bag and produced a book.'Would you like me to read you a story?' she asked.

We climbed on to the sofa and sat one each side of her and listened as she read us the tale of the

124

ugly duckling that turned into a beautiful swan. I wondered whether she had any children of her own. When she finished she laid the book to one side and delved into her bag and produced a wonderful lunch of soft bread, small slices of sausage and the tiniest sliver of rather dry and tasteless cheese. But, having survived on porridge, watery soup and sour bread, I found everything tasted so wonderful; my mouth came alive and my tongue was tingling. I enjoyed every mouthful.

When we had finished, Jadwiga looked worried. 'Now, my darlings,' she said. 'Do you usually have a little nap after lunch?'

'No,' I replied. 'Maciej says if we did we wouldn't go to sleep at night because we don't get enough exercise or any fresh air.'

'How sensible of him,' said Jadwiga. 'So, tell me, where do you two sleep?'

'Over here.' I pointed to the two mattresses against the wall. 'We have a mattress each. This one's mine and there's my doll,' I said, showing her my blanket. Then pointing to the second blanket, 'And that one is Jan's.'

'They look very comfy. But are you warm enough—do you have enough covers?' she asked.

'Oh yes, we are quite warm enough and the mattresses are comfy,' I replied. Jan nodded his head in agreement. I wasn't going to upset my new friend by complaining, even if the blankets were prickly and the mattress lumpy and hard.

'So, if you two have these mattresses, Maciej and Hanka must sleep on the other two then,' Jadwiga said. 'Now tell me which one is Maciej's and which is Hanka's.'

I was only too eager to explain our domestic

125

arrangements.

'Oh, Maciej and Hanka use the same mattress, that one over there.' I pointed in the direction of the one furthest from us.

'Do they always share one mattress?' asked Jadwiga.

'Oh yes, always. They put their clothes on the other one. It saves the bedclothes, you see, if they use only one.'

'How interesting,' Jadwiga said. 'Tell me, are you ever awake when they go to bed?'

'I'm always awake only because I don't sleep very well. But they don't know that. I keep ever so still but Jan is always asleep as soon as he gets into bed. He's lucky.'

'Do they talk a lot in bed?' Jadwiga's voice was soft and gentle and she stroked my hair. I nestled against her, eager to please and tell her whatever she wanted to know.

'Sometimes they talk and sometimes they giggle and most often they make funny noises.'

'Funny noises, what sort of funny noises?'

'Well, sometimes I think Hanka is crying. I think something must be hurting her. And sometimes they both breathe ever so hard. But they always go to sleep before me.'

'I see.'

Jadwiga suddenly pushed me away sharply and got to her feet. She seemed to have changed. Her face was no longer pretty. She looked angry, her smile had vanished and her beautiful mouth was twisted and ugly once again. I was frightened and stared at her. How had this happened? What had I said? What did I do to make this lovely lady so angry? I looked at Jan, hoping to find an answer,

126

but he seemed just as surprised as me. Jadwiga had been so kind and had given us such lovely treats and now she was angry with me. The wonderful day was suddenly spoilt; I felt so guilty and desperately tried to find the kind Jadwiga again.

'Are you cross with me?' I asked timidly as she moved away from the sofa.

No reply.

'Have I done something wrong?'

Jadwiga said nothing. Instead she kept walking quickly up and down the room, just like Hanka.

After a time she lowered herself on to one of the chairs and leaned her elbows on the table and just sat there staring into space, her face still twisted and ugly. She was ignoring us. I felt very afraid.

'She looks like a wicked witch,' I whispered to Jan after a while.

'I think she's horrible,' he whispered back. 'She really scares me.'

'Be quiet, the pair of you,' Jadwiga snarled. 'I've got a splitting headache and I don't want to hear a squeak from either of you.'

Confused and frightened, we cowered in the corner holding each other's hand for comfort.

*   *   *

After what seemed a very long time we heard the knocks that signalled the return of Maciej and Hanka. Jadwiga rose from the chair and opened the door.

'Thank you, Jadwiga ...' Maciej began, but she cut him short.

'I want these children out of the room while I have a conversation with you two.' Maciej and

127

Hanka exchanged glances.

'But the only place they can go is the lavatory,' Hanka said.

'Well, get them in there and lock the door,' Jadwiga ordered.

'But it's small and very cold,' Maciej said.

'Since when have you been so considerate? Do as you're told.'

Silently Maciej took our hands and led us towards the lavatory.

'Go on, in there,' he said quietly as he pushed us forward into the tiny space. Jan and I turned round to find the door closing and then the key turning in the lock. We stood there side by side totally unable to work out what was happening. Clinging to each other for warmth and comfort we listened to the adults in the room next door. We heard Jadwiga's cutting words, as sharp as a knife.

'On the same mattress, she says . . .'

'. . . grunts and groans . . .'

She was telling Maciej everything I had told her. Then we heard the deeper tones of Maciej's angry responses.

'It's not like that . . .'

'The brat doesn't know what she's talking about . . .'

And then crying, probably Hanka. Silence. Then Jadwiga's voice started again followed by the sound of the front door banging loudly. After a short time the lavatory door was unlocked and Maciej stood in the doorway towering above us. His face was stiff and white like a mask. Without saying a word he reached out a hand and grabbed me by the hair and with the other he grabbed Jan by his sweater and yanked us into the room and dragged us across to the sofa.

'Pull down your pants and bend over,' he shouted. 'Both of you.'

He slowly unhooked his belt from his trousers and raised it high into the air above his head. Terrified, I turned my head to see the thick leather about to descend on my bare behind. Maybe it was the way I looked at him, rigid with fright, small and helpless, that made him pause and as the belt came down his hand swerved to one side and hit the sofa beside me. Once again he raised the belt and once again he missed deliberately, and then again and again. The belt never touched me but I felt the pain of every blow and whimpered every time it struck the arm of the couch only inches away from my face. Suddenly he stopped, pulled me up and pushed me on to my mattress then turned to Jan who was cowering on the sofa. As Maciej raised the belt, Jan screamed loudly and Maciej brought it down so heavily on his buttocks that blood spurted from the long thin weal left by the leather. Maciej didn't hit him again but picked Jan up and threw him on to his mattress, his head hitting the wall with a dull thud as he fell. Neither Jan nor I dared to move and Maciej turned his back and left us lying there for some time, oblivious to Jan's moans of pain.

Eventually he turned round to face us. 'Get up, both of you, and go to bed. Stay out of my way or I may kill you.' His voice was soft but more frightening than if he had shouted at us. He walked over to where Hanka was standing and put his arms round her seeking comfort, but she pushed him away.

Maciej and Hanka began to argue.

129

'You're an animal, Maciej,' Hanka spat. 'A sadist. How can you treat a small child like that? You're not human. You are as bad as *them*. We are trying to rid the country of people who behave like you have just done . . .'

'But . . .' Maciej interrupted, 'Jadwiga . . .'

'Don't blame her,' Hanka shouted. 'I hate the woman but she didn't hit them. If you ever, *ever* do anything like that again I will go and I mean it. No second chances, Maciej—'

They didn't seem to care what noise they were making or who heard them. Maciej fell silent. Jan was lying face down on his mattress sobbing loudly into his pillow. I tried to offer some comfort to him by reaching out a hand. My greatest fear was that the things Hanka was saying would make Maciej even more furious.

Instead, as Hanka grew more angry and daring with what she said, Maciej seemed to get smaller. He didn't shout back, or hit Hanka, and he didn't turn on Jan who by now couldn't stop crying. Maciej just stood there and listened to all the angry things she was shouting at him and then to my amazement he went to Hanka and took her in his arms. Immediately she stopped yelling and leaned against him, then put her arms round his neck. They stood there in silence, eyes closed, all their noisy anger gone.

Then finally Maciej picked Hanka up and carried her over to their mattress.

'Maciej, the children . . .' I heard her whisper as he dropped to his knees.

'Bugger the children,' he replied. Jan turned his head away from me, calmer now that the arguing was over but still in pain. Blood from his buttocks

130

were beginning to seep through the blanket forming a red-black patch that slowly grew. Neither Hanka nor Maciej came to help him. Once again I simply couldn't understand adults. After a while I crawled out from under my blankets and went over to Jan. His pillow was wet through, but he didn't move. I put out my hand to touch him.

'Get back into your bed. *Now!*' Maciej's voice burst through the silence making me jump out of my skin with fright.

'But, Jan must be very sore,' I dared to say, safe in the knowledge of what I had just witnessed. 'He's not moving. You hit him very hard and that wasn't fair because you didn't hit me.'

'So you want a thrashing too, do you?' He was sitting up now.

'No, Maciej!' Hanka sat up too, hanging on to his arm. 'Please don't touch her. She's only little. She doesn't even know what they've done.'

Maciej was back in charge.

'How very touching that you are now defending those brats when you've done nothing but moan about them ever since they got here. Well, let me tell you that if the boy's mother doesn't turn up with the money soon, he will be out of here,' he added.

Hanka pushed past him and got up, straightening her clothes. Maciej didn't move as she walked across the room and, leaning over Jan, pulled back his blanket. She gave a little gasp as she saw the white weal and red, congealing blood.

'You brute,' she said, turning to Maciej. 'Get up and bring me a clean cloth and some water.'

To my amazement, Maciej, seeing what he had done, did as he was told. Hanka gently washed off the blood with warm water and then applied Vaseline ointment to the weal. Jan lay there silent and still.

'That will soon go down,' she said gently. 'Just lie very still. Would you like a drink of water?'

'Yes please,' he whispered, turning his frightened eyes towards her and trying to smile.

Hanka turned towards Maciej who was standing watching. She didn't speak, just clicked her fingers and pointed to the sink. Immediately he turned and fetched a cup of water.

What had happened that afternoon was never mentioned again and although things seemed normal from then on, life was far from what it had been before. Hanka now made the decisions, especially where Jan and I were concerned, focussing her attention on us and generally in charge of the day-to-day responsibilities. Meanwhile Maciej was much quieter, doing what Hanka asked and ignoring us. He didn't read to us any more. He didn't even really speak to us. After a few days I realised that I, too, was no longer frightened of Maciej.

One night, a few days after that terrible afternoon, I lay in bed listening once again to the two of them arguing in whispers. But this time I heard Hanka sobbing, and Maciej get out of bed. I heard the soft rustle of clothes being put on and then booted feet quietly crossing the floor. The door of the flat opened and the shadow of Maciej slipped out as he pulled the door shut behind him. I lay awake for what seemed a very long time, trying to work out whether Hanka was still crying, but didn't hear a single sound.

132

It was daylight when I woke up. The flat was very quiet. I sat up to see if Jan was awake, I wanted to know how he was feeling. His bed was empty. I looked around the room. Hanka was sitting at the table, her head in her hands. There was no sign of Maciej. He was most probably out at one of his meetings. But where was Jan? He must be in the lavatory, I thought. I climbed off my mattress and sat down with Hanka at the table.

'So, you're awake at last,' Hanka said, lifting her head to look at me. 'Do you want some porridge?'

'Yes please,' I replied, wondering whether she knew that I heard the happenings in the night.

'It's in the pan on the stove. You can finish off what's left.'

'What about Jan?' I asked.

'Oh, he won't be needing any.' Hanka looked away.

'Has he already had his? He doesn't usually wake up before me. Where is he? He's been in the lavatory a long time.'

'He isn't here, he's gone,' Hanka muttered.

'Gone? Gone where? Did Maciej take him to the meeting with him? Is it safe?'

'He's gone with Maciej who's returning him to his mother. He won't be coming back.'

I couldn't understand what Hanka was saying. Jan's gone? Without saying goodbye? Not coming back? What was she trying to tell me?

'But why? He didn't tell me he was going. He didn't even say goodbye.' I began to cry. 'I would have said goodbye if it was me who was leaving.'

'Stop that at once,' Hanka snapped. 'He didn't

know he was going. Eat your porridge and stop pestering me.'

I spooned the mess into my mouth in silence, tears splashing off the end of my nose and on to my plate.

A while later the coded knock broke the silence of the room and Maciej came into the flat, alone.

'Does she know?' he asked Hanka, who had stepped forward to meet him, nodding his head towards me.

'Yes, she knows. What did his mother say?'

'She wasn't there. It appears she left a couple of weeks ago. They don't know where she went.'

'So what did you do with the boy?'

'I left him.'

'*Left him?* Where?'

'I left him on the street near where his mother used to live and told him to find her.'

'Maciej, he's eight years old and you left him alone on the street! He will either starve or, more likely, the Gestapo will find him and shoot him. How could you?'

'I warned his bloody mother we weren't running a charity,' he said. 'I told her what would happen if she didn't pay. I gave her two weeks to pay what she owed. Well she didn't, so too bad.'

Hanka looked first at Maciej then turned away and picked up her coat that was lying on a chair.

'Get your coat,' she said to me. 'We're leaving— you and me. I'm taking you to Marynia.'

'Good thinking,' Maciej said. 'You're a really great girl. It's not safe to keep her here. Not safe for us to stay either. I've had a tip-off. People are getting suspicious so the sooner we get out the better. We'll go somewhere else where people don't know us.'

'You are not included in my plans,' Hanka said in a voice sounding like broken glass. 'You can do what you like. I warned you. As far as I'm concerned you don't exist. I never want to see you again and, if you try to stop me now or contact me in the future, I shall inform on you. Do you understand?'

'You bitch!' Maciej swung round towards the door and left, slamming it behind him.

Completely at a loss as to what was happening, I looked at Hanka expecting her to be crying as she always did after a row, but this Hanka was dry-eyed and calm. She was shoving my few possessions into a bag.

'Here's your doll,' she said, handing her to me. 'You mustn't forget her, must you?'

'Where are we going?' I asked. 'Are we going to find Jan? He might be very cold waiting for his mummy to come back. Perhaps we ought to take an extra jumper for him?'

'No, we're not going to find Jan. Someone will look after him, I expect. We're going to find Marynia. I do know where to find her. She will look after you and make arrangements.'

'That will be lovely. I want to see her so much. Will you stay with her too?'

'No. I have a job to do.'

'With Maciej?'

'You ask too many questions, Renata. No, not with Maciej, never again with him. The organisation I work for will find me someone else to work with.'

'Oh, what work do you do?'

'I told you, you ask too many questions. You're too bright for your own good. We must go. When

135

we're in the street, hold my hand tight and don't speak for any reason. If we are stopped by soldiers, or anyone in fact, don't speak even if they ask you a question. Do you understand?'

'Yes.'

I felt quite safe with this new Hanka. She opened the door of the flat, stepped out, looked around and then beckoned.

'Now remember, not a word, my brave little friend.'

CHAPTER EIGHT

November 1943. Skierniewice, about 220 miles north-west of Przemyśl

'But I don't understand,' Marynia was saying. 'What can you possibly have against Jadwiga? She's been so kind to you. It was she, after all, who made the arrangements for you to stay with Maciej and Hanka. Now that it's unsafe for you to be with them, she has offered to have you in her own house in the country. It will be so much safer there.'

It was the first time I could ever remember not wanting to do what Marynia said. Hadn't I promised always to do everything she told me? But I simply couldn't go and live with Jadwiga after what had happened. I had to protest even though in my heart of hearts I knew that it wouldn't do any good.

'I don't want to stay with Jadwiga. I'm not going.' I stamped my foot. 'She's horrid. *Please* let me stay with you.'

136

'You're not staying here, get that in your head once and for all,' Jusiek, sitting in the chair by stove, growled. 'We do enough for you as it is . . .'

'Be quiet, Jusiek. You just stay out of this,' Marynia said quickly.

'Fine, I'll stay out of this as long as she stays out of our place. Why you go on looking after her beats me. What d'you get out of it except a lot of sleepless nights? You're putting us both in danger we can well do without. I'm fed up to the back teeth with it.'

Marynia ignored him and bent down so that her eyes were on a level with mine. The effort of doing this was considerable, causing her to become short of breath, but she spoke in a wheezy voice. 'Listen to me, sweetheart,' she said softly, holding me by the shoulders and looking directly into my eyes. 'There is no choice. You have to go to Jadwiga. It's very dangerous for you to stay in Przemyśl. The Nazis will get to know about you and if they find you, they will kill you.'

'Why?'

Marynia sighed.

'Because you're Jewish and the Nazis hate Jews.'

'But why do they hate me? I haven't done anything bad to them, have I?' I began to cry. 'Please don't send me to Jadwiga.' I clung to Marynia's skirt. 'I'll go anywhere else. I'm frightened of her.'

Marynia looked worried. 'Has she ever hit you or punished you in any way?'

'No,' I muttered, looking at my feet.

'So, what has she done to make you so afraid?'

I was far too embarrassed to explain what had happened and how Maciej had behaved after

Jadwiga's last visit. How could I? It was my fault. I had made Jadwiga angry and then she had been angry with Maciej and Hanka. I still didn't understand what I had said or why Maciej had been so angry. But it was all my fault and there was nothing I could do about it. I was so ashamed I couldn't tell anyone, not even Marynia, about the way he had beaten Jan and made me lie across the sofa forcing me to listen to the thud of his belt. And then Jan had disappeared without a word. I must have done something terribly wrong. Even the thought of it made me feel sick and dizzy.

'I just don't like her,' I answered.

'Let me tell you something.' Marynia heaved herself up off her knees and took my hands. 'Do you remember your Cousin Fredzio's wife, Frederika?'

'The one with curly red hair?'

'Yes, that's the one.'

'I think so. Not very well. I remember she was nice.'

'Frederika came to see me a few days ago to ask if I knew where you were. I told her I did and she got very excited and said she wanted to see you.'

'Why hasn't she been to see me before?'

'Because she couldn't. She has been looking after her parents, her brother and her husband. You remember your Uncle Karol and Cousin Fredzio, don't you? They were all hidden like you from the Nazis but now her brother and Fredzio are both dead.'

'How did they die?'

'Well, Karol was in an organisation called the Resistance, that's a secret organisation fighting against the Nazis, and he was captured and shot.'

'Oh,' I exclaimed. 'Maciej and Hanka talked about something called the Resistance.'

Suddenly what I had so often heard in Maciej's apartment was beginning to make a little sense.

'I hope Hanka doesn't get shot. Did Cousin Fredzio get shot too?'

'You ask a lot of questions,' said Marynia. 'He was killed when the hospital where he was working was blown up.'

'Did a bomb fall on the hospital?'

'Yes.'

'When the bomb fell on us we weren't killed, so why was he?'

'You were lucky. It must have been a bigger bomb that hit the hospital. He wasn't actually *in* the hospital when the bomb fell, he was on his way to the hospital to help the injured people who were hurt by the bomb and he was shot outside his home. But let me finish my story,' Marynia said. 'Frederika has been looking after her parents and also your Great-aunt Zuzia and Great-uncle Julek. She heard about a small, golden-haired girl who was found hiding in the ghetto and for some reason wasn't taken away during the last clearances. People talked about it because no one could believe that a child had been able to remain there for so long without being found. Of course, she immediately thought that there was a possibility that the little girl might be you and, you know Frederika, she had to find out. Eventually, she made contact with me and I told her everything. She was beside herself with joy but devastated by what had happened to Adela and Zazula. She's said that she will look after you . . .'

I looked at Marynia, a smile spreading across my

139

face.

'But,' Marynia continued quickly, 'Renata, she can't look after you herself, not just yet.'

The smile stopped.

'That is why you have to go and stay with Jadwiga. Frederika has given Jadwiga a lot of money and you will be well looked after. Then you will go and live with Frederika. When she's ready.'

Marynia looked into my eyes to make sure I had understood. 'You are a very lucky girl to have so many people who love you and want to look after you. So, don't fuss about going to Jadwiga. I'm sure she'll be nice to you and you'll like her a lot once you get to know her properly. Anyway, it won't be for long. Frederika will come and get you as soon as she can arrange it.'

'Will you come and visit me?' I asked.

'No, my darling,' Marynia said, hugging me tight. 'She has a house out in the countryside a long way from here. It will be too far for me to come and that is why it's a good place for you to stay. But,' she added, 'she has a garden that you can play in.'

I could see that there was no use arguing further and maybe it wasn't so bad after all. It would only be for a short while and the thought of being able to go outside cheered me up, even if it was just a little.

Then I had a thought. 'Can Jan come too?'

'Jan is back with his mother. He'll want to stay with her.'

'No he isn't,' I insisted. 'I heard Maciej tell Hanka that his mother had gone away and he had left Jan in the street. He'll be so cold and unhappy. We must go and find him and then he can come with me to Jadwiga.'

Marynia seemed not to be listening. She was reaching for her coat that was hanging on its hook by the door.

'Where the hell do you think you're going?' Jusiek jumped up angrily from his seat and went to stand in front of the door.

'Get out of my way, Jusiek,' Marynia ordered him. 'Where do you think I'm going? I'm going to find that child.'

'Oh, no you're not.' Jusiek pushed her back into the room. 'You're not getting us involved with that as well. If he really left the boy in the street, do you think he's still there or even alive? Not a chance.'

'Don't talk like that in front of her,' Marynia hissed. 'She's only a child.'

'That's right,' Jusiek answered. 'She's only a child and she doesn't understand what we're talking about.'

But I understood, and only too well. Jan would be dead and Marynia wouldn't be able to find him. Marynia slowly removed her coat and returned to her seat. Nothing more was said.

*   *   *

Jadwiga took me to her home in the country herself. She lived just outside the small town of Skierniewice and to get there we had to go by train. Marynia and I went to the railway station early the following morning and amongst the crowds of people Marynia somehow managed to find Jadwiga. She handed over a bag with a few clothes and bent down to give me a quick peck on the cheek. Then she released my hand.

'Be a good girl now,' she said before pushing me

away gently and turning and walking back the way we had come. I didn't have time to say goodbye, give her a hug or to tell her how much I loved her. I felt tears welling up in my eyes as Jadwiga took my hand and pulled me towards the waiting train. I looked for Marynia amongst the crowds of people but my eyes wouldn't focus. I wanted to run after her and hug her. But she had disappeared. I felt terrible that I was going such a long way away. I didn't know if I would ever see her again.

*   *   *

'It's over 200 miles north-west of Przemyśl and we are about halfway,' Jadwiga replied when I asked how long we were going to be on the train. We had been travelling for some hours and I was tired of staring at the wooden floor, trying to peep out through the knot holes in the sides and avoiding looking at the other passengers like Jadwiga had told me.

I was fed up with standing in the corner of the wagon, my legs were stiff, and I wanted to run. There was no room and everyone was grumpy and tired. It was a relief when we finally arrived at Skierniewice station and I could finally stretch my legs. But the walk to Jadwiga's cottage tired me out and my legs began to ache long before we had reached the outskirts of the town. After we had left the last houses some way behind us Jadwiga announced that we had arrived.

Her cottage was small and set back from the lane. A narrow path led up the garden to the front door. All around were tall trees that made me feel small and safe. I decided that I would like living

142

here, for a little while. It was quiet and much nicer than living in one room.

I followed Jadwiga up the path and through the front door. Inside there were two bedrooms that joined the kitchen-living room. Jadwiga led me into the smaller bedroom where I was to sleep and put the bag Marynia had given her on the bed. It was dark as the window was covered by a black-out curtain. The bed stood against the wall, and there was a chair and a hook for hanging clothes. There were no ornaments or pictures of any sort. I knew then that Jadwiga had no children of her own.

It was the first time that I'd ever had a room to myself and I loved it because it was mine. But sometimes at night, when I lay in the dark unable to sleep, I felt very afraid and very alone. Then I would have terrible thoughts: Would Frederika be able to find me? What about Tatuś, would Frederika tell him where I was? What if she was to be taken by the soldiers, how would I ever find my father again? But when I heard Jadwiga's loud snores from her bedroom next door, just knowing that there was someone nearby comforted me.

Jadwiga's room was bigger. Her single bed was positioned just under the window and a large wooden chest containing her possessions—and firmly locked—was set against the opposite wall along with a wardrobe and dressing table. The dressing table was crowded with all kinds of interesting-looking jars and bottles of different shapes and sizes, which I was forbidden to touch. The kitchen-living room was much larger and was kept warm by the big iron stove in the corner. This stove was also used for cooking and three blackened saucepans hung from the ceiling rafters above. In the middle of the room stood a wooden table with two chairs and around the remaining three walls were bookcases crammed with books.

'Why do you have so many books?' I asked soon after my arrival.

'I was a teacher,' Jadwiga told me. 'Because of the war all the schools have closed down, including the ones in the town, and so now I have to earn a living in a different way.'

I knew that by this she meant looking after the likes of Jan and me. Even so, I wished she could have been a bit friendlier. After all, having been a teacher she must have been used to children, and I was trying very hard to please her, even if I didn't like her very much.

At the back of the cottage were thick woods that reminded me of the story of 'Hansel and Gretel' and how, like me, the children had been hungry and lost. Sticks and branches, blown down from the trees, lay strewn across Jadwiga's garden where no one had bothered to clear them away. I looked for a stick like the bone Hansel used to poke through the bars of his cage, a bone that resembled a long, thin finger. I spent a long time looking for the right-sized stick since it was my job to gather them up each morning so that Jadwiga could use them to feed the large iron stove inside the house. I dragged out the task for as long as possible. This was partly because I found it difficult to carry enough sticks and twigs in one go and I would have to make several trips before the basket by the fire was full enough to satisfy Jadwiga. But the reason was that I was able to be outside again. I had been kept indoors for so long that once let out I couldn't get enough of the feeling of space, the warmth of the weak sun on my skin, the early morning smell of the fresh air and the feeling of dew wetting my feet as I left footprints on the silvery cobwebs that magically appeared overnight to cover the grass. Every time I went outside I stretched my arms as wide as I could and lifted my face to the sky and felt free, for the first time in a very long time. Now I let myself begin to hope that perhaps the fairy tales were right after all; perhaps there was such a thing as happy-ever-after.

'Here is the vegetable patch.'

Jadwiga was showing me around. We were standing looking at a large patch of earth covered with greenery.

'These are potatoes.' She indicated a row of yellow-looking leaves coming out of the earth. 'Behind them are the carrots and the—'

'But, Jadwiga, where are they?' I interrupted. 'Where are the potatoes and carrots?'

Jadwiga looked at me as if I were one of those hated spiders that had crept into her house.

'Don't you know where *vegetables* come from?' she snorted. 'They are under the ground. You will have to dig them out, or pull them. Look.'

She grasped a bunch of green feathery leaves and pulled gently and firmly and out popped a handful of beautiful long pointed orange carrots with lumps of muddy earth clinging to them. 'See, they are hiding, away from all the little animals that want to eat them up. This can be your job, maybe you'll learn something.'

From that day on I was able to spend more time outdoors, either digging potatoes, pulling carrots or collecting the firewood. Jadwiga also had a small orchard of fruit trees that did not produce much fruit but there was enough for a dish of stewed apple from time to time.

'Here you are, some stewed apple,' Jadwiga said one day, putting a bowl of green gloop in front of me.

My mouth began to water; I could still remember how much I loved the stewed apple that Babcia used to make, eaten with cream or as a filling in pastries. I took a mouthful. To my horror the sour cooking apples hadn't been sweetened and I could feel my taste buds shrivel. Still I ate it, and as time went on I grew accustomed to the sharpness and began to enjoy the tang on my tongue.

Jadwiga hardly ever left the cottage and no one ever came to visit. Sometimes the old postman dropped a letter in to the box outside the gate and, if Jadwiga happened to be in the garden, she would chat to him for a short time. Once when he called whilst we were both outside she introduced me to him, calling me her niece from the city. Jadwiga wasn't unkind, yet nor was she caring. Most of the time she took no notice of me unless she wanted a job done. She taught me how to sweep the floor with her hazelwood besom and fill basins of water for the washing up. The water came from the well outside the back door. I longed to peer down inside the well but the large wooden lid was too heavy to move. I imagined the still, clear pool deep in its mysterious cave underground and thought of the princess, banished from her father's castle for saying she loved him like salt, tending to the old woman's geese and washing herself in water from the well by moonlight. I remembered how the ending had been so happy. The king and queen had found their daughter and it made me long for my

146

parents to find me and to take me home.

To one side of the well there was a handle which I would pump up and down until my arms ached and the lovely crystal water spurted out. It was hard work but I loved getting the water to shoot out in long silvery ribbons.

Once a week Jadwiga washed our clothes. This meant pumping and carrying bowlfuls of water and emptying them into a large bucket that she would boil on the stove. That was my job.

'It'll put some muscle back on you,' was Jadwiga's answer when I complained how heavy I found the pump arm. 'Don't be such a baby. You're perfectly capable of carrying water.'

Once the water was boiling she poured it into a tin bath that stood on the floor. The clothes were thrown into the tub followed by the rubbing board. The rubbing board was made of metal, with one side that had ridges, and set into a wooden frame. Jadwiga would pick out one garment at a time from the water where it was soaking; she would soap it with a large cake of horrible-smelling yellow soap and then rub the garment quickly up and down the ridged metal, to remove all the dirt. It was not long before she had me rubbing too. I didn't mind because it made me feel grown-up, with something important to do, and I liked the feel of wet, slippery clothes between my fingers and enjoyed hiding my hands under the slightly greasy water feeling the warmth travel up my forearms. It reminded me of doing the chores with Marynia, although that seemed like such a long, long time ago now. I was fascinated by the way my hands changed, becoming red and wrinkled after being in the water.

When all the clothes had been washed, we wrung

them out, put them back into the bucket and took them into the garden where we hung them out on a long washing line—a rope that stretched between two trees. I loved watching the drips fall off the clothes making patches of wet grass beneath. When the clothes were dry, I would bury my nose in their sweet-smelling freshness. The washing water was never wasted. When the clothes had been removed and the water was still warm, Jadwiga would strip naked and climb into the tub and bathe right in front of the stove in full view. She didn't seem to care whether I was present and in turn I was amazed by Jadwiga's saggy belly and hanging breasts. It was so different from my own skinny body.

Jadwiga told me that one day my bust would grow big too. So I would carefully examine the two pink nipples on my chest that Jadwiga had said were my 'bust-to-be', to see if they had grown. But they remained flat. Sometimes I worried that they would never grow.

'If they don't grow, will I die?' I asked her once.

'Don't be so ridiculous,' she had laughed. 'They'll grow and with it will come more trouble than you care to know.'

When Jadwiga had finished her bath she would climb out of the tub and then it was my turn to stretch out, close my eyes and enjoy the comforting warmth as Jadwiga had done. But all too often the water was chilly and unpleasant because Jadwiga had soaked too long. Then I would have to wash as quickly as possible and get out, shivering, and rub myself warm with a towel. I wasn't very good at that and Jadwiga never offered to help. More often than not I would climb back into my clothes, teeth

148

chattering and half damp. Jadwiga would watch me struggling.

'Anyone would think you'd never had a bath before,' she said.

I didn't bother to tell her that I couldn't remember the last time I had had a bath as I had had to make do with a strip of cloth and a bowl of cold water.

Sometimes she hung the floor rugs on the washing line, which would sag with their weight, and it was my job to beat the dust out of them with a carpet beater made of sticks twisted into a pretty pattern at the end of a long handle. As I whacked at the rugs, dust flew in great clouds, making me sneeze over and over again. This task seemed to take for ever; Jadwiga always tested them herself to check that I had done them properly. She was very keen that everything was clean in her cottage but didn't worry that I was covered in dust after having beaten the rugs as hard as I could.

'You'll just have to put up with it till the next time you have a bath,' she told me when I complained. 'Perhaps that will teach you to be a bit more careful about keeping the house clean.'

*   *   *

One morning not long after I arrived, I was looking at the rows of books on her bookcases.

'Jadwiga,' I asked shyly, having spent the best part of the morning plucking up the courage. 'Could you read me a story from one of your books? This one with the pictures?'

I held open a book with little black-and-white sketches which broke up the solid wall of words on

149

each page. Jadwiga had read me one or two stories before but nothing from this book. She rarely read to me and only did so when she was in one of her good moods, which only seemed to appear when the postman had called to give her a letter.

'It's high time you learned to read,' she said. 'I have better things to do than spend my time reading to you all day. You can do it for yourself. You're not stupid.'

I was pleased to think that Jadwiga didn't find me stupid. After all, she often called me a dimwit and questioned whether I knew *anything at all*. Yet at the same time it seemed strange that Jadwiga said she had no time to read to me. As far as I could see, she spent most of the day doing very little and making me fetch and carry, dig and wash. Still, the idea of learning to read pleased me very much. I often picked up books from Jadwiga's shelves and wished I knew what they were about.

'I'd love to learn!' I said excitedly.

'Right,' said Jadwiga. 'We'll make a start and you will be reading fluently in two weeks.' She got up and took a book from one of the bookcases. 'By the end of today you will know the alphabet by heart. I will test you on it tomorrow, for every mistake you make you will get a smack . . .' She walked over to the broom cupboard and reached inside. 'With this,' she added, laying the carpet beater on the table.

'Now, there are thirty-two letters in the alphabet . . .'

I worked hard that day, only breaking off to do my chores as quickly as I could and then returning to my place at the table so that by the next day I had memorised every single letter and escaped the

150

beating. I was extremely quick at putting the letters together so that by the end of the third lesson I was able to stammer out a whole page of simple words such as *mysz* (mouse), *ryba* (fish), *dach* (roof). I felt so pleased with myself when Jadwiga praised me.

'Well, who would have thought it,' she said. 'For someone who didn't even know where potatoes came from, you are a quick learner, I have to say.'

Jadwiga had been right. I was reading within two weeks—not fluently but enough to be able to practise on my own, which I did every spare second I could find when I wasn't expected to do chores around the house. Jadwiga was a good teacher and, better still, if I had done well the day before, she rewarded me by allowing me to pick out any book from the shelves. Without any guidance I picked out the books with the attractive covers and the ones that had the odd picture inside to help me to work out the meaning of the words.

I wanted so badly to read and tried hard so that within a very short time I was able to read any, and every, book. It didn't worry me that a lot of the words made no sense. In the beginning I would ask Jadwiga to explain their meaning but after a while she became impatient.

'I've taught you the skills. Stop pestering me and work it out for yourself. I haven't the time to be answering your questions.'

Jadwiga had a lot of books by authors from around the world translated into Polish, including the works of Charles Dickens, who seemed to have written hundreds of books. I found a copy of *Grimm's Fairy Tales*; the familiar stories were not the joy I had expected but brought back fresh horrors and made me remember dark, forgotten

151

things that gave me the most awful nightmares. So I looked further until I found *Swallows and Amazons* by Arthur Ransome. I was hooked at once; it opened up a whole new world, of fun and laughter and excitement. I became the fifth member of the Swallows, living their life and sharing in the adventures of John, Susan, Titty and Roger and their sailing dinghy on holiday beside a big lake in a place called England.

Then Jadwiga suggested I read *David Copperfield*. As soon as I began to live through David's miserable childhood, I forgot my own. I learned from David's experiences to fear the idea of school. I read about the sea and sand, not knowing what they were or that they even existed until I was transported to Yarmouth. I cried at the brutal treatment of David and his mother by Mr Murdstone and in turn adored Miss Betsey Trotwood. Even when I wasn't reading I was thinking about the events in the book. Real life seemed less important than the trials faced by David Copperfield.

As time went by I began to read faster and faster. I didn't stumble over the words as often and I was able to make sense of their meaning. After I finished *David Copperfield* I turned to another novel about a small boy forced to go through the most terrible unfairness at the hands of his tormentors, the grown-ups. This was *Oliver Twist*, a story about a boy whose mother dies and he was left an orphan. I had got no further than his life in the workhouse when I had a thought. I looked at Jadwiga sitting at the kitchen table.

'Am I an orphan?' I asked.

'Looks like it,' Jadwiga answered.

She was reading one of the letters she had just received but this time was in a particularly bad mood.

'But an orphan has no mother or father and I do have a father. Does that make me half an orphan?'

'If you do have a father, he isn't making much effort to find you or support you,' Jadwiga spat.

'I think you're very unkind,' I protested. 'Marynia told me that my father is a doctor with the Army and that as soon as he can he will be back to look after me.'

'Well, he'd better hurry up,' Jadwiga replied. 'I've just had this letter from your cousin's wife.'

'From Frederika? Is she coming to get me? She will be so pleased that I can read!'

'No, she's not coming to get you. More's the pity,' she added. 'She's asked me to hang on to you for a few more weeks. And to add insult to injury, she hasn't sent the money she owes me for this month. I don't know how I'm expected to feed you.'

'Isn't she going to send any money at all?'

'She says she is. But I'll believe it when I see it. That's the trouble with you Jews. All big-mouth promises. No wonder everyone hates you. Well, I'm writing back to tell her that the money had better turn up in two weeks or that's it.'

She picked up her pen.

'What if it doesn't come in two weeks?' I was terrified, remembering how Jan had disappeared. I still hadn't heard whether he had found his mother but knew he must be dead—like Jusiek said he was.

Jadwiga didn't answer.

'You won't leave me in the street alone, like Maciej left Jan, will you, Jadwiga? Please say you won't. I wouldn't know what to do. *Please* say you

153

won't.' I went up to Jadwiga and put my arms around her, looking for comfort and reassurance.

She pushed me away.

'No, I won't leave you out in the street. I'm not a murderer like my beloved husband. But you won't be staying here, I can tell you.'

'What will you do with me?' I spluttered, tears welling up.

'I'm giving your cousin two weeks to do something about you, which is very generous of me—just you remember that. Now leave me alone before I get angry. Go and get some more firewood and then peel those potatoes I've put out.' She turned to the blank sheet of paper on the table in front of her and began to write.

CHAPTER NINE

December 1943

I was sitting at the kitchen table, engrossed in my book, when Jadwiga had a visitor, the first since I'd arrived at the cottage. He was obviously expected, for Jadwiga stood up as soon as the knock sounded, and went quickly to the door, quite unworried.

'Please, come in,' she said, then turning to me, 'Go and read in your room, Renata. I will call you when I need you.'

Obediently and happily I did as I was told, taking my doll and my book with me. Now that I had my new friends Titty, Roger, Susan and John, I wasn't alone. In *Swallowdale*, their second adventure, I found Titty in a beautiful hidden valley up on

154

the moors above the lake. Of course, I could only imagine what their boat, or the lake, or the secret valley looked like but at that moment when the visitor arrived I couldn't wait to find out what the strange *pemmican* was that Titty was busy cutting into thick slices. It sounded so special and marvellous and it was making my mouth water. Life on the boat in the company of children was far more exciting than any visitor Jadwiga might have so I took little notice of the man in the doorway, blocking out the winter sunlight, looking at me intently.

It occurred to me that John, Susan, Titty and Roger really had very little to worry about. There were no Nazis in their lives. They didn't have to hide. They never went hungry and were never punished for no reason. They were happy children and I wanted to be one of them. I longed for someone of my own age to play with and missed Jan dreadfully, and Zazula even more. I knew Zazula was dead. I had asked Marynia to tell me what happened to her, over and over again, until finally she gave in. Her words haunted me still.

'Your aunt didn't find anywhere to hide,' Marynia told me. 'The dog found Zazula hiding in the wardrobe and then the soldiers took your aunt and Zazula down the stairs and out into the street. The officer in charge told Zazula to run on ahead and she did so, of course, she was such a good girl.' Marynia paused then she looked me straight in the eyes and said, 'I am only going to tell you this because you want to know. I am going to tell you the truth—they are your family after all.' She paused again and took a deep breath. 'The soldier shot her, just like that, through the back of the

155

head as she was running down the street. She didn't see anything, she didn't know what was going to happen. She felt no pain.'

I stared back at Marynia, unable to say a word.

'But your aunt . . . your poor, poor aunt saw everything. She tried to reach Zazula but the soldier turned and shot her too, just like that, at point-blank range, without a thought as to what it was that he was doing.'

'And Mrs Posadzka?' I asked, feeling light-headed and sick. 'Did she get away?'

'I don't know what happened to her,' Marynia replied softly. 'I only know what the neighbour told me. Her body was found lying at the foot of the stairs. He saw what happened in the street. He was fond of Mrs Posadzka but didn't know about you all hiding in her back room of course. Renata, I am telling you all this so you can remember, because no one else will tell you. This is your family and one day when the war is over and things are back to normal most people will want to forget but there may be a few who want to know what really happened, and if you remember you can tell them. Not all of us Poles hate the Jews and there are many people, many ordinary everyday people in Poland, helping to save you and the gypsies and other people the Nazis hate. Remember this, Renata, so you can tell your children and your grandchildren what it was really like. If you forget, everyone forgets.'

I had clung to Marynia, shocked into silence. At the time I couldn't think of anything to say but now I wanted to see her and ask how she knew about Aunt Adela and Zazula and how she knew to come and find me under the table. I wondered if I would ever know.

Although there was now no doubt about Zazula, I still held onto the slight hope that both Jusiek and old Piotr were wrong and that Jan would come back, that all the people I loved would come back. Maybe, a miracle would happen and a fairy godmother would appear, wave a magic wand and all would be well. I would be with my Mamusia, my Tatuś, Babcia and Marynia. Things would be as they were long ago. We would be living happily together in our beautiful apartment. Babcia's room with her secret stash of sweets and chocolates that she always kept there, just for me. Our lovely ceiling-high stove would be glowing with warmth and we would sit on the sofa, Mamusia, Rabbit and I, and whilst Babcia busied herself in the kitchen, Mamusia would reach for her big fairy tale book. But then I would take the book from her and *I* would read the stories to Mamusia and she would be so happy, so proud of me, and she would hug me and hug me . . .

Lost in Titty's adventures, I didn't hear Jadwiga calling until she appeared in the bedroom doorway.

'How many times do I have to call? Come into the living room at once.'

'Sorry, Jadwiga,' I said. 'I didn't hear you. I was reading.'

'I'm perfectly aware you were reading, but that's no excuse for not coming when I call you.'

Jadwiga pushed me into the kitchen ahead of her.

'Now say good afternoon to Mr Policky.' I looked at the man now seated at the table.

'Good afternoon,' I repeated.

He didn't smile. He just sat there staring at

157

me hard through a pair of round, wire-framed spectacles.

'A pretty, blonde child,' he said, looking at Jadwiga. 'When will you bring her?'

I felt a cold shiver run up my spine. I was afraid of this man but didn't know why.

'As soon as it is convenient for you, Mr Policky.'

'Very well. Let's say a week from today at two o'clock. By then all arrangements can be made.' He got up and for the first time spoke to me.

'I am sure you will settle quickly with us. You may bring one toy and one book with you, no more. Do you understand?'

I didn't understand at all.

'Please, where am I going?'

'You are going to the State Orphanage.'

'An *orphanage*?'

Immediately I thought of Oliver Twist. He had been an orphan and he had had a terrible life in the orphanage.

'Yes, an orphanage.'

'But I'm not an orphan, am I, Jadwiga? I have a father who is away with the Army and my cousin Frederika is coming to fetch me to live with her very soon. I would far rather stay here with Jadwiga.' I turned to her. 'Jadwiga, please, let me stay. I know my cousin is paying you to have me here.' I felt my heart beating very fast.

'Your cousin wrote to me last week to say that she can't pay me at the moment and can't offer you a home just yet. I am not a charity. I can't afford to keep you and feed you. Mr Policky is the Warden of the orphanage and has, as a special favour, kindly agreed to take over the burden of keeping you until such time, if it ever comes, that that cousin of yours

158

turns up to shoulder her responsibilities.'

Jadwiga's voice was cold and hard. But as she spoke she didn't look at me but over the top of my head, at something on the far wall.

'*Please*, Jadwiga, I'll do all the work if you'll let me stay. I'll be ever so good, I promise.'

'There is nothing to discuss. All arrangements have been made for you to go to the orphanage.'

'Is it far away?' I asked. 'Will I still be able to read your books?'

'It isn't far away. In fact, it is just on the other side of the town,' Jadwiga replied. 'But you will not be able to take my books. You heard what Mr Policky said, one book and one toy. Besides, as soon as I have got rid of you I shall be leaving too.'

'Where are you going?'

'That's none of your business. After next week you will never see me again. I've done my bit for you.'

'That child talks and argues too much,' Mr Policky said quietly. 'We shall soon put a stop to that sort of behaviour. Until next week then, Jadwiga.'

'Thank you, Stefan. I am very grateful,' Jadwiga said, showing Mr Policky to the door. 'You really have taken a great weight off my mind.'

She shut the door behind him and turned to me. I wasn't crying but, standing in the middle of the room, I was unable to move. I felt more alone than I'd ever felt before. Since Jadwiga had introduced me to the world of books, I thought we shared something special and we were becoming friends, and now I was being pushed out and worst of all I wouldn't have any books to read. I wanted to curl up and die.

'If you're trying to make me feel guilty or change my mind, forget it,' Jadwiga said. 'You won't. I didn't take you in for love. I took you in at great personal inconvenience and danger as a source of income that seems to have dried up. That's all there is to it. So don't you dare beg and try to make me change my mind.'

*   *   *

The orphanage looked similar to the one I had imagined Oliver Twist lived in. It was a grey-stone building with two rows of small, caged windows and a thick wooden front door with metal studs all over. It was surrounded by flat, bleak farmland. There were no other buildings except for one old tumbledown barn off in the distance. As I stood on the steps that led to the front door, I could hear the wind howling and moaning around the cold grey walls and over the fields full of blackened tops of beets and turnips, frozen into the ground. I could see the dark clouds that rushed across the sky above my head reflected in a plaque nailed to the front door. It read: *State Orphanage*.

'You are very lucky, very privileged in fact, to have a place at the orphanage,' Jadwiga had told me earlier as she closed her garden gate. 'What did I tell you this last week? You could have ended up like Jan, abandoned on the street, when his mother failed to pay for his keep. I am not a charity and I can't afford to become fond of you.' She paused. 'We all have to survive as best we can. It's the safest place for you, *if* you keep quiet about being Jewish, of course.'

I had tightened my grip on my doll and tried to

160

keep up with Jadwiga as she hurried along the lane.

'Just remember you must tell *no one* that you are Jewish. Because if you do, they will throw you out and you will die of cold and hunger.'

'Why does everyone hate the Jews?' I had asked, still looking for an answer I could really understand.

Jadwiga seemed to know. 'Because anyone with any sense hates Jews.'

'Do you hate me?'

'What I feel about you is my business, not yours. All I know is that I have been far kinder to you than you deserve.'

'Have I done anything to make you cross with me? I have tried ever so hard to be good and helpful. Please tell me what I have done wrong. Please let me stay with you. Please—'

'Stop it, Renata.' Jadwiga was getting angry but I didn't care, anything would be better than going to an orphanage. 'You are going to the orphanage and that's it, so stop arguing because it will get you nowhere except to make me more angry than I already am. You're lucky I made arrangements for you rather than throw you out on the street.'

'But, Jadwiga,' I had begged her, 'I will die without books. I'd rather be dead than go without books to read.'

She had suddenly stopped, grabbed my shoulders and whirled me round to face her.

'If you don't stop arguing and moaning I shall get *very* angry,' she shouted. 'Books are not essential— they are a luxury. You just be grateful that you have survived this far. That's all there is to it. Now I don't want to hear another word.'

I didn't care. This was my last chance. I tried

again.

'I have been really, really happy with you since you taught me to read.'

Silence.

'You know Frederika won't ever leave me. She loves me, she always told me she did and she *promised* to send you the money.'

Silence.

'What if she doesn't find me in the orphanage? Will I have to stay there for ever?'

But still Jadwiga refused to answer and had marched on in silence whilst I trotted along behind desperately trying to keep up with her stride, tears rolling down my face. Dressed only in the thin coat with my teeth rattling from the numbing cold and from being so nervous, I felt more miserable than ever. Jadwiga held my hand so tightly that it hurt and she dragged me along behind her. She didn't speak to me again and ignored my whimpering.

Then, as we approached the looming building, she had suddenly stopped for a second time.

'Pull yourself together,' she said and glared at me. 'It's not my fault that I can't afford to keep you any longer. If your relations fail to keep their side of the bargain and don't bother to pay for your keep, then *I* certainly have no obligation to look after you. Just count yourself lucky that Mr Policky agreed to take you as a special favour to me. So you'd better behave yourself. You're a miserable little brat and I shall be glad to be rid of you.'

As we stood on the steps of the orphanage, Jadwiga raised the iron knocker and let it fall back loudly. We waited but no one came. She tugged a rusty bell pull and I heard the dull clanging from inside the building. It seemed a very long time before there was a sound of bolts being drawn back and the door opened a crack. A bent man all shrunken and old, with shabby clothes hanging off him, peered out at me. His face was purple, with blotches of darker red on his cheeks and nose. He stared angrily.

'What do you want?' His voice was thin and reedy.

'Mr Policky is expecting me,' Jadwiga said. 'Take me to him, please. I'm in a hurry.'

The man stared at me before opening the door wider to beckon us in. He didn't say another word but set off down the corridor at a brisk trot. Jadwiga followed while I had to run to keep up with them.

The narrow corridor went on and on. The floor was made of hard, square stones and the walls were flaky and green. The halls were cold and dim with just a few bulbs hanging from the peeling ceiling. It felt like the dungeons where princesses were imprisoned by wicked witches or where brave knights were kept with chains around their ankles. I had read about these dungeons and now I was in one. Sadly, I wasn't a princess and there was no brave knight waiting to rescue me.

Three little girls came down the passage towards us. I hadn't seen any children for such a long time and I gave them a little smile but they flattened themselves against the wall to let us pass and just stared at me. All three wore stained white aprons over black dresses and I thought they looked very thin and very unhappy.

At the end of the long corridor we stopped outside a big door. Our guide knocked and after a pause we heard a voice call out, 'Enter.'

The old man pushed the door and stepped away.

163

Jadwiga marched in, dragging me behind her. Sitting on the far side of a huge messy desk was a large man with a bushy black beard. He didn't look up and we had to stand there waiting. When eventually he did look up, he had the cruellest eyes I had ever seen and his mouth was a thin tight line.

'I have come to see Mr Policky,' Jadwiga said. 'Where is he?'

The man got to his feet. His stomach was huge and bulged over the top of his trousers like an over-inflated balloon. He almost knocked me over as he brushed past, hand extended towards Jadwiga.

'Jadwiga, may I call you that? Mr Policky sends his apologies; he was called away very suddenly. I am his deputy, Mr Mackiewicz. How are you?'

'The better for being here,' Jadwiga responded with a curt nod towards me. 'She's bright enough, but spoilt. Needs a firm hand.'

'We shan't have any problems with her,' Mr Mackiewicz said. 'She will find it pays to behave. We haven't time for rebels. They all learn soon enough that life isn't fun and games. We feed them, we house them, but we don't have the time or the resources for anything else. They all have to work for their keep, whatever their age.'

All this time he hadn't as much as glanced in my direction, but I'd had plenty of time to examine him—to notice how red his face was and how his thin, greasy hair lay plastered to the top of his shiny head. With his thick, bushy beard, he looked as if he had put his head on upside down. His eyes were so small that they almost disappeared into the puffiness of his cheeks and his lips, only just peeping through his beard, were wormy pink lines.

164

I thought about the ugly troll in 'Three Billy Goats Gruff'.

The adults exchanged a few more words and then Jadwiga turned to me.

'I'm going now,' she said. 'Be sure you behave yourself and everything will be all right.'

'I shall miss you, Jadwiga,' I said, trying not to cry. 'Please come and see me, and thank you for teaching me to read.'

Jadwiga paused. For a moment I thought her face looked kinder, just a little, and then it was gone. She quickly bent down to give me a small peck on the cheek, then stood up and walked out of the room without another word or backward glance. I stared after her willing her to change her mind. Then I was alone with Mr Mackiewicz.

'Go and stand by the window,' he commanded. He returned to his chair, sat down and stared at me. 'Turn round very slowly.'

I did as I was told.

'You're very blonde and quite pretty,' he said. 'Obviously pure Aryan stock.'

This was another strange word that I would try and remember.

'Where's your mother?'

'I don't know.'

'Sir. You say "sir" whenever you speak to me. Do you understand?'

'Yes.'

He leapt from his chair, grabbed my hair and jerked my head up so that I was forced to look at him.

'What did I tell you?'

I nodded. Tears began rolling down my face.

'I'm waiting!'

165

'Yes. Sir.'

'That's better.' He released me. 'Don't you ever again dare to forget. I won't have disobedience or insolence from anyone. How old are you?'

'Six. Sir.'

'Quite old enough to know how to behave and certainly old enough to do a full day's work.'

He pushed a bell set in the wall above his desk and said nothing more until, moments later, there was a timid knock on the door. I stood where he had left me, not daring to move. I felt a surge of anger towards Jadwiga for having left me here.

'Enter,' Mr Mackiewicz ordered and the door opened and in came two girls about the same age as me.

They stood just inside the doorway and curtsied. One of them was twisting the edge of her apron round and round her finger.

Mr Mackiewicz opened a drawer in his desk and pulled out a black book. He looked at one of the girls, picked up a pen, dipped it in ink and wrote something in the book.

'Do you know what I've just written in the crime book, Basia Lipska?' he asked, fixing his mean stare on the smaller of the two girls who was now twisting the end of her apron even more nervously.

'No, sir.' Her eyes were wide with terror and she could hardly get the words out.

'You don't? Well, I will tell you. I have written a black mark against your name for ruining your clothes, so who knows what will happen to you at the end of the week.'

Basia immediately dropped her apron and I could see that she was shaking all over. I wanted to go and comfort her, but didn't dare move.

166

'In the meantime,' Mr Mackiewicz went on, 'you two girls are to take this new one and show her where she will sleep. Then introduce her to Matron who will allocate her duties. This is Basia Lipska and this is her sister Cesia.'

Cesia was a little taller than her sister and very thin. She too looked frightened.

'Take her away now,' Mr Mackiewicz said, waving his hand towards the door and turning back to the papers on his desk as if he had already forgotten us three children.

I followed the two girls out of Mr Mackiewicz's room and into the hallway.

'What's your name?' Cesia asked in a whisper as we went back down the long corridor.

'Renata. Why are you whispering?' I asked, not thinking to lower my voice.

'Shhh. We're not allowed to talk in the corridor. We get a black mark if we're caught. Come in here. This is where we sleep.'

The girls went into a long room with iron bunk beds down both sides. The floor was bare and beside each bunk stood two chairs, one at each end. All the beds were covered with grey blankets. I counted ten bunks down each side of the room. At the end of the room the girls showed me a small door that led into a washroom with six washbasins and a lavatory.

'Your bed will be under mine at this end of the room,' Basia said. 'We're lucky because we're near the lavatory. Cesia is at the other end because she's older.'

'What is a black mark?' I asked. 'What happens if you get one?' I was worried by what I had seen in Mr Mackiewicz's room.

Cesia looked at me. 'You get it read out on Punishment Day and if you have more than one you get punished.'

'Have you ever been punished?'

'Yes. I was locked in the coal cellar for a whole afternoon, in the dark. It was horrible.'

'Why did you get a black mark?'

'I forgot to make my bed and fold my clothes.'

I decided there and then that I would never forget to be tidy. I was frightened of the dark and felt quite sure that if I was ever locked in a dark cellar I would certainly die.

'We'd better go to Matron now,' said Cesia, 'or we'll be in trouble for wasting time. We're all orphans here so we have to be grateful and obedient,' she added. 'Are you an orphan?'

'I hope not,' I said. 'I have a father who is away with the Army and my cousin Frederika is coming to take me to live with her as soon as she can fix it. So I don't suppose I'll be here long.'

'You're so lucky,' Basia said, looking sad. 'Our mother died because a bomb hit the house. She only went out of the cellar to get some food and at that very moment the bomb landed and killed her.'

'Oh no,' I said. 'That's awful. I was in a house when a bomb fell, too, but we were all in the cellar and didn't get killed. Are there lots of orphans here?'

'Loads. Probably about a hundred but I think you must be the only one with a father.'

'Who brought you here?' Cesia asked.

'Jadwiga. She looked after me and taught me to read. Do we have books and lessons here?'

'No.'

'So what do we do all day? Isn't it boring?'

'We have to work, sweep and scrub floors, wash dishes, things like that.'

I didn't like the sound of this at all, but at least it was nice to have people of my own age to talk to again and I liked these two sisters.

'We *must* go and find Matron or we'll be in trouble.' Cesia looked around nervously.

We set off once more along the long corridor, down a flight of stone stairs to an icy-cold, dark passageway and finally to Matron's room. Cesia knocked and led the way into a room steamy with drying clothes—grey-white aprons, shapeless black dresses and endless grey knickers—hanging in long rows in lines attached to a pulley on the ceiling.

Matron looked bad-tempered with hair scraped back from her face into a bun. Strands of her hair were trying to escape and had got as far as her neck.

'This is Renata, miss,' Basia said. 'She's just arrived and Mr Mackiewicz told us to bring her to you.'

'More trouble,' the woman said, staring at my hair.

'We're going to have to cut that blonde mop off before the lice eat it.'

She grabbed my arm, spun me round and poked around in my hair.

'No lice at the moment, but we'll take precautionary action.'

She picked up a pair of large scissors and began to snip vigorously. As I stood, head on one side, I saw my long golden curls tumbling to the ground around my feet. I couldn't believe what was happening. Everyone used to tell me how beautiful my thick golden curls were and now this woman

169

was getting rid of them.

'What are you doing?' I cried, trying to pull my head away, but Matron held me even tighter, then after a minute or two said, 'That will do,' and put down her weapon.

I looked at my two new friends and saw that they were giggling, hands over their mouths.

'You look so funny,' Basia said. 'Naked.'

'We've no time for vain misses here,' Matron said strictly. 'And you two had better get back to work instead of standing around being silly. Go and get on with your jobs and come and collect this one in time for supper.'

The sisters, still giggling, went and I was left alone with Matron.

'Now I'm going to scrub your scalp with soap,' she said. 'In case you've brought any nits in with you. Bend over this basin.' She pushed my head down and with a small bucket poured a stream of icy water over my hair. It made me gasp and cry out.

'Don't be such a baby,' Matron said, rubbing a horrible-smelling liquid into my hair with such force that I felt as if my head would fall off. More icy water followed then she rubbed my hair with the roughest of towels leaving my ears and neck raw and smarting.

'Here's a comb and there's a mirror over there. Make yourself respectable and then we'll see about your clothes.'

Looking in the cracked mirror, I saw a pale-faced stranger staring back at me with spiky hair cut so short that, even wet, it wouldn't stay flat. I felt anger bubbling up inside me but this time I couldn't stop it coming out.

170

'I hate you, I hate you,' I screamed at the woman. 'Look what you've done. You've stolen my hair. It will never grow again, never. Wait till my cousin comes. She'll punish you for this. I am going to tell that man what you've done to me. You're cruel and wicked and I hate you!'

The next thing I knew, the woman was shaking me by the shoulders then pinning me against the wall. She raised one hand and brought it down hard upon my left cheek.

'You're going to learn some manners, my young miss,' she sneered, her face in mine. 'Just try complaining to Mr Mackiewicz and you'll see what you'll get. Why should you think yourself special just because you've got pretty hair? We've no time for prettiness around here, or vanity either. Don't you dare utter another word or it will be your last, I can tell you. Now are you going to behave yourself?' She waited until I nodded.

'Over there,' she ordered, 'are your clothes.'

'But I brought some with me.'

'*Brought some with you?* Well you won't be needing them. You wear the regulation stuff here. Everyone's the same.' She put out a bundle of grey, slightly damp garments and proceeded to go through them.

'One nightdress to be washed every two weeks; while it's drying, you sleep in your vest. One pair of knickers to last the week. One vest, two weeks, and one dress and apron, two weeks.'

She tossed the bundle into my arms.

'I haven't heard the words "thank you",' she said.

I stared at the floor.

'Thank you,' she thundered.

'Thank you,' I whispered to the floor.

171

'That's better,' she said. 'Now we'll go along to the dormitory and I will show you where to put your things and collect what you've brought with you.'

'But I *can* keep my dolly,' I said to Matron's back as she headed off to the dormitory. 'She was a present from my nanny and she goes everywhere with me.'

'No dolls allowed round here,' Matron said over her shoulder. 'Toys are not allowed. You're orphans and you have to work for your keep, not play and be little babies that need looking after.'

'Please.' I was clinging desperately to her arm, trying to get her to stop and listen to what I was saying. Fear had made me brave. 'Please let me keep my doll. She's all I have to love. I'll die if you take her away. I'll be ever so good and do anything you tell me and not mind about my hair, but please don't take my dolly.'

But I might as well have been talking to the peeling green walls or the hard stone floor.

CHAPTER TEN

January 1944. Skierniewice State Orphanage

There was a lot to learn at the orphanage. Rule number one was don't trust anyone. There were one or two children, such as Cesia and Basia, who I thought I might be able to trust but even with them I had to be careful. If you told on someone else's wrongdoings, you got a reward, like extra food. I soon realised that the children were always telling lies about each other just to get more food. If you cried or showed that you were unhappy, you were told off as it might make other children think they were unhappy too. If you were kind or tried to help another child, you were told off as well. I quickly realised that it was best not to say anything at all and to keep out of everyone's way. I decided to copy the other children and keep myself to myself and then days went by without me saying anything at all to anyone.

The other children also scared me. I was terrified by the way they behaved; some acted more like frightened animals than children, making strange sounds and trying to hide themselves even when there was nowhere to hide. Others just stared ahead as if they were asleep with their eyes open. But the worst of the lot were the children who kept hurting themselves over and over again. I couldn't understand why they kept on wanting to hurt themselves so badly and make themselves even more miserable.

I was scared and jumpy being surrounded by so many children who acted in such strange ways. I knew that I could not get away from them. But then I would remember Babcia and her stories and how we used to leave the living room at home and fly to the places inside my head. So I thought about those stories, and the ones Aunt Adela and Marynia had told to me, and those that I had read myself. And I found I could still 'fly' and so I left the horrible orphanage and the scary children to join my story-book friends in my head and share their lives instead. I told my friends my problems and they always tried to help even if they didn't know what to do. I tried to copy their behaviour when they had been in difficult situations like when

173

people were being cruel to them or when they were frightened. If I felt miserable scrubbing stone corridors with a scrubbing brush too big for my hands, or carrying buckets of water which were too heavy for me, I would imagine myself as Cinderella working in her stepmother's kitchen. At times when I felt a bit better, I imagined myself in a beautiful land full of fairy godmothers and happy children, loving parents, where knights in shining armour were waiting on big white horses to rescue beautiful damsels in distress. While struggling to swallow the orphanage food, I sometimes pretended that I was eating delicious fruits off golden plates, like those Laura ate at Goblin Market, and drinking nectar, the drink of the gods. My friends inside my head always told me that they loved me and I felt happy and I was able to get through to bedtime where I always dreamed of finding my Mamusia and Babcia and Tatuś.

All the time I thought about food because I was constantly hungry. I now understood why Oliver Twist dared to ask for more even though he didn't like the food, but I was never brave enough to do the same. Most of the time we were given a gloopy, tasteless porridge—but never enough. For a while it made me feel bloated and then suddenly I would be starving hungry again. It tasted better and went down more easily if it was warm, but usually it was cold and had hardened into a repulsive slime that was difficult to swallow. Sometimes we got thin, watery cabbage soup instead. We could tell when it was soup day because the whole orphanage stank of boiled cabbage. The smell got everywhere, into our unwashed clothes, our hair, our beds and our dreams at night. You couldn't escape it, even outside. The stench would get into the walls and it tasted even worse than it smelt. On soup days I imagined that the whole world had turned into an enormous cabbage. And then as we tried to eat it it would grow back and get bigger and bigger until finally the cabbage would unfurl and start to eat us.

We were also fed bread, which was given out in small quantities. It was black and sour, hard to chew and even harder to swallow. But at least it was filling—if we were given the chance to eat it. The youngest children, like me, were watched by the older, bigger boys who used to hide round corners and then suddenly appear, knocking us over and snatching the bread and gobbling it up greedily. When I first arrived I was quite glad to hand it over, but soon the hole in my tummy made me think again and I would hide my ration, usually in my knickers, until I could find a place where I could eat it without any of the big boys seeing. In the morning we were given a mug of warm, dark coffee made of ground acorns and for the rest of the day we had to make do with water.

If not trusting anyone was rule number one, then rule number two was stealing. The horror of living at the orphanage made me learn quickly and for the second rule Cesia was my teacher. My first lesson took place on the morning of my second Sunday at the orphanage when I was feeling utterly miserable. Those of us who had shoes were marched in a long crocodile to church. Those whose shoes were too small or had worn through had to stay behind. We liked the weekly visit to the church because it meant we could escape our prison.

On this Sunday Cesia introduced me to turnips. Cesia and I, wrapped in our thin coats and hugging

175

ourselves for warmth, joined the crocodile of children making its way towards the town. Basia was not with us that day because both her shoes had great big holes in them and there was snow on the ground. She had walked in them like that for a long time but now everyone could see the holes and her toes all red and swollen with chilblains.

It was bitterly cold. A howling wind drove the sharp, icy flakes of snow into our faces and it took for ever to walk the two miles to the church. Inside there was no escape from the cold, it was as freezing as outside and we sat there shivering in our pews, hands in laps and heads down. Apart from the children from the orphanage there weren't many others—a few old people all wrapped up in shawls and nodding asleep throughout the long service. I looked round in the hope that I would catch sight of Jadwiga but she had never gone to church when I stayed with her and so I really knew that she wouldn't be here now.

Today the sermon went on for ages and ages. The priest was talking about being grateful and I couldn't think of anything at all to be grateful for. Cesia, who was sitting next to me, noticed that I had begun to cry.

Under cover of the pew in front she took my hand in hers and squeezed it hard. Then I had something to be grateful for. I was grateful that she was being so kind when I really needed it. When at last the service was over we walked out into the churchyard where, although the snow had stopped falling, the cold was just as numbing. Cesia and I left the church together and joined the end of the crocodile as it snaked slowly back on to the muddy frozen road. I kept my head down, trying to shelter my face from the icy wind and keep up with Cesia beside me. After a while I realised that Cesia had begun to slow down and was now walking very, very slowly. I looked up and saw that we were now some distance behind the others.

'We'd better hurry and catch up with them,' I said, worried that Matron would notice, but Cesia grabbed my arm and pulled me back.

'No, wait. Let them get ahead. We'll soon catch up, don't worry.'

We were by now out of the town and in the open countryside. It was freezing and grey angry clouds were gathering above us stopping any sunlight coming through that might have helped to warm us. I saw Matron ahead leading the children back up the dirt track to the orphanage. She was cold herself and wanted to get back quickly and so was hurrying on, not bothering to check that we were all keeping up.

Suddenly I felt Cesia pulling me sideways off the road.

'Come on,' she hissed.

'What are you doing?'

Cesia took me completely by surprise by saying, 'I'm going to show you where to get food.'

She pulled me again and I fell off the side of the road and into the field. When I scrambled to my feet, my clothes were soaked and covered with freezing mud.

'Look what you've done!' I cried.

'Stop fussing. The mud will brush off when it's dry. Quick, grab a turnip, there are loads on the ground, and then hide it under your coat. Nobody will notice.'

'What am I going to do with a frozen turnip?' I

asked, still cross that my clothes were so dirty and afraid of Matron's anger, but Cesia wasn't listening.

'As soon as we get back, say you need the lavatory but instead go and hide it in your bed, under the pillow is best. Then you can eat it tonight. It will be warmer to bite by then and if you keep under the blanket no one will hear you crunching. There's one, take it. I must get one for Basia too.'

Confused, I did what my friend told me. I bent down to pick up a turnip half sticking out of the earth but I couldn't move it. I tried another and managed to free it from the frozen ground.

'But it's like a lump of ice, and ever so hard. How can we eat that?' I gasped. 'I can't carry that under my coat, I'll freeze to death.'

'Don't worry,' said Cesia, 'it will have thawed out by tonight,' and she stood up, clutching two turnips that she tried to hide under her coat. I copied her and with the icy turnip close to my body I felt colder than ever. Cesia scrambled back on to the road and ran to catch up with the others, telling me to hurry. I was still not convinced that these 'hidden treasures' would be worth the bother.

Once back inside the orphanage, still hugging ourselves and our turnips, we were sent straight to the kitchen to get on with our chores but, as Cesia had told me, I asked to go to the lavatory. Matron tutted and said, 'Hurry up, for goodness' sake. I shall be timing you.'

I rushed off to the dormitory and pushed the turnip under my pillow before returning to the kitchen as fast as I could.

That night long after everyone was asleep, I bit into my 'treasure'. Cesia was wrong, it was still very cold and it hurt my teeth. The skin was gritty and bitter and didn't taste at all nice but, once I managed to get into the turnip itself, I was surprised at how sweet it tasted. Best of all, it filled the hole in my stomach and made me feel calm inside, for a while at least. Over the following weeks I became a real expert in stealing turnips and began to look forward to my weekly crime. I never came to like the taste but a large turnip would last nearly all week so I saw stealing as an adventure that helped to make me less bored and give me something to tell the friends in my head. For the rest of that winter I came back after the service every Sunday with a cold, hard turnip and an urgent need to rush off to the lavatory. No one suspected a thing.

It was not just the food in the orphanage that I hated, but mealtimes themselves. Each day we would be hard at work and then a bell would clang through the building. We had to stop what we were doing, make our way to the dining hall and form a long line outside the door. Then, and only when ordered to do so, slowly, one by one, we filed in, holding our hands out in front of us ready for inspection. This was silly, I thought, as we almost never washed ourselves, or our hair, or our clothes. Anyone with very dirty hands was cuffed and sent out to wash them and then had to queue up all over again.

Most of the time there wasn't enough food to go round, so the children at the back quite often missed the meal. As we filed into the dining hall we had to pick up a bowl and spoon from a table near the door, then walk in line to queue for food at another table across the room. Three women stood behind the table poised over a ladle and a large, dirty-looking metal pan. As each child came forward with an outstretched arm one of the women would drop a dollop of porridge or soup into the bowl. No one said anything. Then we would file to the nearest empty space and sit in silence at the table watching our food grow cold, waiting for all the others to be served. Then, and only then, could we begin eating. We could not choose who we sat next to or where we sat, it simply depended upon where you happened to be in the long queue.

Sunday was a little different. Although we always had the same porridge, we were given a small blob of jam as a special treat so that at least it tasted of something. It was on Sundays that we girls wished that we were boys, because if there was any food left the boys were given seconds. We girls were never given any more.

One Sunday Basia, Cesia, I and some other girls managed to get into the dining hall together and were able to sit next to each other at the table nearest the serving women. As usual we sat in silence with our bowls untouched, watching the food grow cold. Usually I didn't mind waiting as the food was horrible, hot or cold, but today for some reason I was hungrier than ever. I was miserable too for it was a particularly cold day and on our return from church we found the turnips frozen into the ground. No matter how hard we tried we had been unable to yank them out of the soil—so today there was no Sunday treat to look forward to at bedtime.

At last all the children were served and seated and the signal given for us to begin. Everyone ate greedily and quickly. For some reason that day the jam had been sweeter and the porridge tastier

180

so when I finished, I longed for more. When the boys were called to come up for seconds, I longed to join them but instead had to watch as the ladles dipped in and out of the pot and more dollops were dumped into the boys' bowls. I thought that it was so unfair and I had to try very hard to stop myself crying. Jorik, the person I hated more than anyone in the world and someone who scared me to death every time I saw him, was the last in the queue. As he passed by my chair he gave me a kick which almost made me cry out. I quickly turned my cry into a splutter because if Jorik was caught and punished he would look for me everywhere and then take his beating out on me.

I watched as the server dipped her ladle into the pan and tipped a spoonful into his bowl. But it wasn't only porridge that landed in his bowl. I also saw a cooked mouse slide from the ladle and land on top of the porridge with its tail hanging neatly over the edge. I saw the look of surprise on Jorik's face before loud screams filled the hall and I was violently sick all over the table, my clothes and the floor.

Matron appeared at my side, slapped me hard across the face then pulled me to my feet and shook me until my teeth rattled. I could hear someone still screaming but now it was far away and, even though I saw Matron's hand rising and falling in front of my face, I could feel neither the slaps that came fast and furious, nor the shaking that left bruises on my arms. Matron then dragged me out of the dining hall and outside into the icy cold. Even this didn't stop the screaming. It was only when a doctor was called and he had given me an injection that I began to calm down a little.

181

'That child has suffered a terrible shock,' I heard him say. 'She must not be left alone in the night. She might die.'

* * *

Through Jorik I learned rule number three: how to hate. Before I had heard people saying that they 'hated' the Nazis and I knew that I should hate them too because I was Jewish; because they had taken my mother and grandmother, killed my aunt and Zazula, and made me come to this orphanage. I was scared of them finding me but I didn't really understand how I should be hating them as they were not real to me. They only appeared as monsters in my nightmares and even then I couldn't always see them. Now that I was older I knew that I was often unhappy and I knew I was terribly lonely and frightened and I knew how these feelings made me feel inside.

But when I met Jorik, I then knew what it felt like to hate someone. Jorik was a lot older than us. He was at least fifteen and had been in the orphanage longer than any of us. The first time I met him was soon after I had arrived when I saw him tumble out of the Warden's office holding his hands under his armpits. He was crashing down the corridor bouncing from one wall to the other as if he couldn't see and although I tried to get out of his way he bumped straight into me. As I started to cry, he stopped, let out a big roar and bent down over me, his teeth clenched in a horrible grimace and his fingers stretched out like claws. His face was round and red, his chin was very small and the breath that came out of his mouth and on to mine was smelly and full of spit. His staring eyes were popping out of his head. They were strange and wild and did not seem to see me although his face was nearly touching mine. He could tell I was more frightened of him than anything in my life and he roared at me again. I scrambled to my feet and ran off down the corridor. He followed me, caught me and held my shoulder in a tight hard grip, spun me round and began roaring and roaring in my face until Matron came running down the corridor and saved me.

'Jorik!' she screamed, grabbing him by the ear and leading him back towards the Warden's room.

That night he came to me in my dreams. He was now the faceless monster chasing me down the corridors. All the doors were locked and I knew I couldn't escape from him. He got closer and closer and closer until my nightmare woke up the whole dormitory and brought Matron rushing in. I dreamed it again, night after night. During the day I did everything I could to stay out of his way.

'Here comes Jorik,' Cesia began to whisper whenever he was near and I would try and find a place to hide from him until he passed.

Cesia and Basia had warned me about him soon after my first encounter with him.

'No one likes him. He's not normal. Make sure you keep out of his way.'

'Children like him don't live very long,' Basia had added.

But the more I tried to avoid him the more I seemed to bump into him. Often it was after he had been punished that he would come roaring down the corridor to terrify the life out of me. He never missed an opportunity to bellow at me. He enjoyed seeing my frightened face and would bare his teeth and roar like a wild beast. But he also enjoyed hurting me. Whenever he saw me he pinched or kicked me even when he hadn't been punished himself. He knew I would never tell on him because I was too afraid of what he would do later. Every time he hurt me I wished he was dead.

Like everyone else in the orphanage, I dreaded Punishment Day. At five o'clock every Monday afternoon we were summoned by the clanging bell to line up outside the dining hall. We were all so scared that no one ever uttered a word. No one was ever sure if their name was on the list of those to be punished or not. So far I had managed to escape everyone's notice and had not been punished but each week I shook with fright in case I would have to walk forward for a public punishment.

When we were all assembled and standing in straight rows facing the raised podium at the far end of the room, the doors behind us were locked. Then after a long silence a short procession entered through the doors at the back of the dining room, climbed the three steps up on to the podium and took their places. The Warden, Mr Policky, always entered first, holding a little bell, followed by his deputy, Mr Mackiewicz. Matron would remain on ground level with us but she too was one of the judges. The Warden then stepped forward and gazed long and hard at us. Sometimes some of the younger children cried with fright and the Warden then looked at Matron who went and grabbed the child, dragged them to the front and made them kneel down on the floor in front of everyone until Punishment Day was all over.

The Warden then rang his little bell and two of the older boys came in carrying canes and straps

184

that were laid out on the table in front of him. The two boys stepped back, one on each side of the table, and the Warden slowly picked up each cane and strap and swished them one at a time in the air. We all had to watch and listen. After he rang his bell for a second time a third boy came in with the black crime book. The boy opened it and handed the book to the Warden. The Warden looked through it for a few minutes and then began to read out the names of all of the criminals for that week: the children who had been late for work; the children who had been disobedient or rude; the children who had stolen, and the children who had not worked as hard as they should. Every time a name was called, the child made their way to the front and climbed up the steps on to the podium. The Warden read out their crime, and then their punishment was shouted out so everyone could hear. If it was your first time you might be let off with a warning not to do it again. But if you had been called before then you were punished. We had to watch as some children were caned on their palms, others were bent over a chair and held down by the two big boys while the Warden beat them with a cane or a strap. If they screamed, they were given extra thrashes. I couldn't bear to watch the punishments and sometimes I dared to shut my eyes and try to block the screams from my ears. It was so horrific it felt as if it was me that was being hit, and afterwards I couldn't get the screams out of my head and the visions away from my eyes.

But it was Jorik who suffered most and there was never a week when he wasn't thrashed over and over again. He would be dragged howling and fighting to the front.

'Jorik. Crime? Bed wetting,' the Warden would bellow every week. 'This antisocial behaviour *will* stop. You will be beaten every time you wet the bed. We will beat this antisocial behaviour out of you and we will go on beating you until it stops. Bend over!'

Every week Jorik was thrown across the table, held down by the two boys and caned again and again across his bare buttocks, all the time begging for it to stop. As he raised the cane above his head, I noticed that the Warden always had a small smile on his face as if he was enjoying himself.

I knew that I had to keep out of Jorik's way on Monday evenings because he would want to get revenge for his beating. When he was being beaten, I felt a tiny bit sorry for him but later when he was roaring in my face, pinning me to the wall or hurting me I only felt sorry for myself and I hated him with all my heart.

*   *   *

'Unser Führer! Sieg Heil!'

Sometimes inspectors came to visit the orphanage. We knew when these inspections were going to happen because it was the only time we saw the Director, Dr Kempf. He stood on the podium in the dining hall and raised his right arm and saluted the *Führer*. Then, letting his arm fall, he looked across at us all, standing as still as statues and quiet as mice.

'The time has come for another inspection from the authorities. They will be here to ensure you are learning how to be useful citizens. Some of you will contribute to the advancement of science.

186

Others will go on to become citizens of the new Fatherland, the new Germany. Citizens with true blood, of pure stock, embarking on a journey to rid the world of cowards and parasites, racial poisoning and contamination.'

I was surprised and very frightened when Dr Kempf sent for me. I had never seen him except on the podium and didn't realise that he knew I was even at the orphanage. It was Matron who told me.

'Renata, come here, please,' she said, as I was making my way back to my chores after we had been dismissed from the dining hall. 'I was just coming to look for you.'

I followed her into her room, fearful and worried that I had done something wrong. She closed the door behind us.

'Dr Kempf wants to see you this afternoon,' Matron informed me. 'You have to be presentable. Let's have a look at you.' She spun me round. 'Your hair needs washing, and you need a clean dress.'

'Why does Dr Kempf want to see me, miss?' I asked.

'You are a very lucky girl. You are to go to his house this afternoon and I will take you.'

'Why? Have I done something wrong, miss?'

'No, just wait and see. But you must make sure you behave yourself when you get there. Now go and collect a clean dress from the laundry, and wash and comb your hair. Be back here at one o'clock sharp. Make sure you don't talk to anyone else about this. Do you understand what I'm saying?'

'Yes, miss,' I replied.

'You mean, "Yes, thank you, miss,"' she corrected me.

187

At one o'clock I knocked at Matron's door.

'There you are,' she said and led me to a sink in the corner where she washed my face and hands again and helped me into the clean dress and apron.

'Let me look at you,' she said. 'Yes, you'll do. Now, remember your manners, Renata, I won't be having you let the orphanage down. If they ask any questions and you are unsure of the answer just tell them you don't know. I don't want you saying things that will get you or anybody else into trouble, including the orphanage. Do you hear?'

She handed me my coat and then led me out of the office, through the building and out the front door. We went along the lane that I had only walked that morning to church but this time we went past the church before turning off along a pretty street with large houses on either side. She stopped outside one of the houses and knocked on the door.

It was answered by a man in a grey-green uniform and Matron gently pushed me forward. 'This is Renata. Dr Kempf is expecting her.' She then turned away and started walking back down the street. The man shut the door behind me and took my coat before leading me into a room with soft rugs, beautiful furniture and colourful paintings on the wall. Three men sat facing the door in large armchairs. Two were soldiers wearing Nazi uniforms. Seeing them so close to me, I shivered and my heart began to beat very fast inside my chest. The third man was old and kind-looking with white hair and a friendly smile—this was Dr Kempf. I looked at him as he got up from his chair and patted me on the head.

'This is Renata,' he said to the other two men. 'An orphan from the Skierniewice area. No parents around. I think you would agree that she has all the necessary qualities.'

At first the soldiers didn't say anything but remained seated, still staring hard at me. Then Dr Kempf made me walk around the room and the soldiers fired questions at me.

'Where is your father?' the first one asked.

'He is in the Army, sir,' I told him.

'Your mother?' asked the second.

'I don't know. Sir. I think she's dead. Sir.'

'Do you go to church?'

'Yes, every week. Sir.'

'Do you know what Germans think of Jews?'

'They hate them. Sir.'

'Do you hate the Jews?'

'I don't know. Sir.'

'Do you like the orphanage?'

'No. Sir.'

'Why not?'

'There aren't any books to read. Sir.'

'Can you read?'

'Yes. Sir.'

'Who taught you?'

'Jadwiga taught me. Sir.'

'Would you like to leave the orphanage and go to a home where there were lots of books—a nice German home?'

'Oh yes, I would like that very much. Sir.'

The soldiers looked at each other, smiled without smiling and came over to pat me on the head.

'Charming,' said one.

'Good. Good,' said the second and gave me a slice of cake.

When I had finished eating, Dr Kempf led me out into the passage and helped me on with my coat and as he did so he dropped to one knee, so that his face was on the same level as mine. He looked into my eyes.

'You did very well, Renata, very well,' Dr Kempf said. 'But tell me one thing, when did you last see your mother?' His voice was gentle and his watery grey eyes looked worried.

'Just before she was taken away by soldiers, Sir,' I replied, repeating what I must have said a hundred times before, not thinking about its meaning.

'Do you know where she is now?' Dr Kempf asked.

'No, Sir,' I said. 'She was taken away in a lorry to a camp, with my granny, Sir.'

Dr Kempf paused and was just about to ask me another question when the man in uniform came back. Dr Kempf stood up, patted me on the head and asked the man to take me quickly and safely back to the orphanage.

CHAPTER ELEVEN

March 1944. Skierniewice to Warsaw

Matron was back to being her horrible self again and everything was the same as before. I hoped what happened to Oliver Twist was going to happen to me. I would leave the orphanage and go and live with a lovely, kind lady and gentleman who would give me nice food to eat, a warm comfy bed to sleep in and lots of books to read. Then I would discover that they were my Mamusia and Tatuś, the same way that Oliver Twist had found his grandfather. But I didn't hear anything else about me leaving Skierniewice and going to live in the house in Germany with the nice family. Perhaps I had dreamed the whole thing. Perhaps there had been no meeting, no cake, no kind Dr Kempf who had asked me about my mother. I had started to believe that I would have to stay at the orphanage for ever when Matron called for me once more.

'Renata,' she said. 'You will be leaving us to start a new life. Tomorrow morning after breakfast I want you to put on these clothes and return your uniform to the laundry. Then you must wait in your dormitory. Someone will be along to fetch you.'

She held out a bundle of familiar clothes—the clothes I had been wearing when I first arrived.

The next morning I followed Matron's instructions. I left the dining hall and returned to the dormitory where I quickly changed into my old clothes, which were much shorter than I remembered. But before I sat on the end of my bed to wait, I took the turnip, the one I had stolen only yesterday, and quickly placed it beneath Basia's pillow. I returned to the end of my bed hugging myself at the thought of Basia's delight when she found it this evening. It was my way of saying goodbye.

I sat there for what seemed like hours and still no one came. After a while I began to panic. Perhaps I had misheard. Perhaps I had dreamed up the meeting with Matron, but I had the clothes. I was beginning to doubt myself and thought perhaps I was finally going mad like the other children in the orphanage. Then Matron entered the room.

'Renata, there has been a change of plan. Here is your uniform. Put it back on and go and join the others scrubbing the long corridor.'

I knew better than to ask what had happened. I did as I'd been told then went to join Cesia and Basia at their work, angry that I had lost my precious turnip for nothing. Swallowing my disappointment, I decided then that I would forget about my meeting with Dr Kempf and the promise of my new life with lots of books. He had seemed kind enough but after all, promises were never kept by anyone, were they?

But a little later that morning, I was called for again. This time I didn't have to change clothes, just make my way to Mr Mackiewicz's office. There was someone who wanted to see me. I expected to find Dr Kempf or one of the Nazi soldiers who had shown so much interest in me a few weeks before, but to my surprise I found a lady with her back to me. I recognised the hair. That beautiful dark red hair. I would know it anywhere. My head went dizzy and my heart was beating so hard I thought it would burst. I wanted to rush into her arms and shout her name but Mr Mackiewicz's eyes made me stay where I was, studying the floor.

'Renata,' Mr Mackiewicz said at last. 'This is your cousin Frederika. She informs us that you are not an orphan after all. Now she has found you, she will be taking you to Kraków where she can look after you.'

I looked up and saw Frederika turn towards me, a secretive smile on her lips.

'Mr Mackiewicz, I would like a few moments with Renata, if that is all right with you,' Frederika said and to my surprise Mr Mackiewicz agreed.

Frederika

'Renata, go to your dormitory and you may have a few moments there. Matron will be along to show your cousin the way out.'

Frederika took my hand in hers and together we left the room. I couldn't believe it. Frederika had found me at last. I said nothing. I just led her down the maze of corridors to my dormitory where we closed the door and finally Frederika swept me up into her arms and hugged me tight, kissing me and hugging me again. I felt my heart would break.

'How did you find me, Frederika?' I asked finally. 'How did you know I was here?'

'Jadwiga told me,' she answered. 'Jadwiga wrote and told me that she couldn't wait any longer for the money. But it was so silly because I had already sent the money I owed and enough to cover the next two months. It must have arrived soon after she took you to the orphanage. In her letter she said that she had waited long enough already and that she had no alternative but to take you to the orphanage. But she said you would be properly looked after and given enough food to eat and a warm place to sleep. I was so relieved as it meant that you would be safe because being in a Catholic orphanage no one would ever suspect anything. It also gave me a little more time to get everything sorted out before I came to get you. Oh Renata, I am so sorry. If only I had known, I would have come sooner. I thought you were happy and well looked after. I never dreamed that you would be in a place such as this.'

But I no longer cared. I no longer felt cold or hungry or alone. I no longer felt angry at giving my turnip away. Someone *had* been thinking of me and now I had been found—that was all that mattered.

Matron appeared before we could say any more and Frederika regained her composure and, in a loud, calm voice, said, 'I shall visit Renata again tomorrow, every day in fact until I have made arrangements for us to return to Kraków. It won't be long, a few days at most.'

I watched Matron's face as Frederika spoke but Matron just nodded and stood back from the door allowing my cousin to pass.

The next day I was allowed to return to the dormitory after breakfast to see Frederika again. We sat in each other's arms on the end of my bed for a few precious minutes and I asked Frederika whether she had heard from my father.

'No, my darling,' she said, 'I haven't, but things are so difficult at the moment. I expect he is somewhere safe waiting for you.'

Then there was silence; neither of us knew what to say, where to start.

'Tell me a story,' I said finally, breaking the silence. I just wanted to hear her kind, soft voice; it didn't matter what she said.

Frederika thought for a moment and then she began.

'Once upon a time, not so very long ago, there was a beautiful little girl. She had golden hair, big blue eyes and a pretty little nose and lived with her mother and father and her grandmother in an old town nestled at the foothills of the mountains and on the banks of a large river . . .'

Over the next few days she told me stories about my family and our life before the war. As she described what Mamusia looked like and how she acted, the memory of my mother began to stir inside my head.

'Oh, your mother was such fun,' Frederika said, 'everyone loved her. And she loved music and dancing. She could dance so well. When she went to parties, and there were so many to go to before the war, she would wear her little dancing slippers . . .'

At night, long after Frederika had gone, I lay in bed staring into the darkness as, gradually, I joined together, little by little, all the pieces of information that Frederika had given me. The image of Mamusia became less fuzzy until I could see her at last, right there before my eyes—my Mamusia clear for the first time. Her gorgeous wavy hair that she would flatten in curls around her ears, her dark eyes and the tiniest of gaps between her front two teeth. That night I slept more deeply than I had slept for a very long time.

'I'm going to be a teacher like Mamusia,' I told my cousin the following day after listening quietly to Frederika's stories about my family.

'That would be nice,' she replied. 'Your mother would be very pleased to know that.'

'Will you help me to go to school and university like my parents did?'

'Of course. But I expect your father will be back by then.'

'I don't ever want you to leave me.'

'I don't want to leave you, my darling.' Frederika gathered me up in her arms and gave me a huge hug. 'But you never know, your father might marry again and then you will have a new mother to take care of you.'

'If he comes back, if he is alive, I shall tell him that he must marry you because I want you to be my mother,' I declared, returning the hug.

Frederika laughed.

'Do you like Tatuś?'

'Of course I do. We used to spend a lot of time together. We were a very close family.'

'Tell me again, what is he like?'

'He is tall and dark and has the kindest eyes and the gentlest smile. He was very quiet, not lively like your mother, but wise and very clever. She adored him. Everyone did, especially all his patients . . .'

'What about my grandparents, his parents?'

'I only met them a couple of times. They lived in the country. His father was in charge of a post office and his mother was called Johanna.'

'Where are they now?'

'We don't know what happened to them. They

196

disappeared at the start of the war. They have probably died . . .'

'Like Mamusia?'

'Yes, but darling, it's not safe to talk about these things.'

*   *   *

The big day finally arrived. Frederika had received all the signed papers from Dr Kempf that meant I could leave the orphanage. I wasn't allowed to tell anyone that I was leaving and I couldn't say goodbye. I would have liked so much to have given Basia and Cesia a hug and told them that there *was* such a thing as a happy-ever-after, you just had to keep hoping. But I never got the chance.

We left the orphanage and made our way to the station, Frederika with her small suitcase and I with nothing other than the clothes I was wearing. It was early in the morning and I was surprised that we did not take the train heading south to Kraków as Frederika had told Mr Mackiewicz. We took one heading in the opposite direction, towards Warsaw. Only when we were on the train did I ask why.

'I wasn't going to tell them where we were going,' said Frederika. 'I bought two sets of tickets and only showed them the ones for Kraków. We don't want them following us, now do we?'

I laughed with her and clasped her hand.

The journey was slow and I grew tired of standing and squatting, and once again I longed to be outside, where I could see the sun was shining through the slats in the wagon sides. Frederika realised I was getting restless and so she pulled me on to the suitcase next to her and whispered in my

197

ear, 'Shall I tell you another story?'

'Oh yes,' I said. 'Tell me *your* story, Frederika.'

And so to pass the time, in her soft voice interrupted only by the clanking of the wagon, Frederika told me the story of her life since I last saw her and how she had finally managed to rescue me from the orphanage.

'I have been looking after my parents and Fredzio's parents, your Great-aunt Zuzia and your Great-uncle Julek; you remember them, don't you?'

I nodded at the memory of my butterfly aunt who had changed into a moth and grumpy Uncle Julek.

'Are they still alive?' I whispered.

'Oh yes,' Frederika replied. 'Your aunt and uncle managed to survive what happened in Przemyśl. They had connections and used them. They had to disappear of course but now they have different names and live in a small flat but are safe and well.'

'And your parents?'

'My parents went to live in the country. They had a friend, an artist, who owned a remote house outside Warsaw and they were able to go there. No one bothered them.'

'Fredzio was killed, wasn't he?' I asked. 'Marynia told me he was on his way to help people who had been hurt by a bomb.'

'Yes,' Frederika replied. 'Fredzio is dead. He wanted to help everyone. It didn't matter who they were or what they did. He only went because the hospital took a direct hit and he knew he was needed. I told him it was too dangerous, that he mustn't go until his usual time at night but he wouldn't take any notice. He was a doctor, you see. He said he would be all right but he never got further than the doorway of the house in which we were hiding, when he was shot by some Nazis who happened to be passing. They never stopped, just drove on. He never got there to help. Such a waste.'

Frederika tried to laugh but the laugh got caught in her throat and she had to cough.

I gave her hand a squeeze and tried to change the subject. 'What did you do, then?'

'It's been tough,' she said, 'not as tough as it has been for you, of course,' and she tousled my hair and put her arm round my shoulder. 'But when the war started, I realised that I really couldn't *do* anything. I had been to school, of course, and then on to study art in Vienna. But I hadn't trained to do anything sensible. Not like your mother. She went to university and then went back to teach Polish literature there. But my summers were one long round of parties and fun, and in the winter I spent most of the time skiing in the Carpathian Mountains, or the Austrian Alps, depending on who was where. It all seemed so important then.' This time Frederika did laugh. 'That's where I met Fredzio, you know, on the ski slopes. I didn't have to worry about things like working,' she said. 'My father was a very wealthy man. He was a dentist in Lwów. After I was married we came to live in Przemyśl and we visited you often, although you were probably too small to remember.'

'Did you have any children?' I asked.

'No, we didn't, but we were young, we wanted to have fun and we had all the time in the world, so we didn't think about it really. Of course we would have children in time, or so we thought. But then we just wanted to enjoy each other.

'But without Fredzio and without my father, all

199

the money disappeared like everything else. I had to start earning myself to look after you all so I made leather gloves and artificial flowers and sold them, to the Germans mainly. They could afford pretty, frivolous things. But then I managed to get a better paid job in Kraków. In fact that was where I was going when I decided to come and see you because Jadwiga had told me you were in the State Orphanage at Skierniewice so I knew you were safe and sent money for any needs you had. I was on my way to Kraków when the train just stopped in the middle of nowhere, or so I thought. There were problems on the line on the other side of the station and they said there would be a considerable delay. No one could tell me for how long. After a couple of hours I became angry and frustrated. The job was important to me and so I asked an official how long we'd have to wait and how far we had come. He told me he couldn't say how long the delay would be and that we were just outside a station called Skierniewice. I asked him to repeat the name to make sure I had heard him correctly—after all, there could only be one Skierniewice. So I decided that I would break my journey and come and visit you. I knew I had missed my appointment anyway and so another day wouldn't make any difference.

'I went to the station and asked how far it was to the State Orphanage and a very pleasant station master told me that it was in walking distance and offered to look after my case for me. I didn't want to lug it down the streets and so I let him put it in his office. I was stopped twice on the way by German soldiers wanting to see my papers. I let them see my papers and was very nice to them, so of course they let me pass.

200

'When I reached the orphanage,' Frederika continued, 'it was getting late and that ugly man who opens the door said that the Warden, what's his name, could not be disturbed. Well I wasn't going to let a man like him tell me what I could and couldn't do, not without a fight anyway. So I told him I would stay until he did have time to see me because it was a matter of the utmost urgency. And it was, wasn't it?' She smiled.

I smiled back, nodding in agreement.

'Well, he slammed the door in my face and left me there in the fading light and I didn't know what to do, I didn't know whether he was going to come back, or whether I would have to sleep right there on the steps. But he did come back, eventually, and told me that a Mr Mackiewicz would see me and led me to his office.

'Isn't he a horrid little man?' Frederika exclaimed. 'He was sitting behind his desk and didn't even bother to look up when I came in. So I didn't wait for him. "Mr Mackiewicz?" I said, "I have come for Renata." He looked up then all right with his little piggy eyes and that slimy smile.'

I giggled at Frederika's description of the man who had scared us witless with his black book and array of canes and straps laid out on Punishment Day.

'Of course, he said that it was impossible. "I don't think so," I said, "I am her cousin. I wish to take her away with me now that I have found her." "You're her cousin?" he said. "We were told she was an orphan. Do you have the papers?" "Not with me," I said, "but I can arrange for them to be sent." I didn't have any papers for you but I wasn't going to tell him that, now was I? "Mr Mackiewicz,"

I said, "I have travelled a long way to see Renata and I would like to see her." I wasn't rude, only firm and polite. Then he said, "I am very sorry, but I am afraid that it is impossible." "Impossible?" I said, "but why?" "Well, my dear," he said, his eyes looking me up and down making my skin crawl and my toes curl, "little Renata is leaving us, tomorrow morning." That shook me,' Frederika said. 'I didn't know what to say or do. I thought you might be dead or dying or terribly ill, but I tried not to let that toad see that I was concerned, so I asked him why. He said that this was your last night and you were already in bed and that tomorrow you would be leaving for Germany to start a new life with a new family where you would be looked after and loved. Well, I have heard about these new lives in Germany—' Frederika began but at that moment the train jolted and I was thrown headlong onto the floor of the carriage. Frederika pulled me back towards her.

'Go on, Frederika,' I said. 'What happened next, what did he say?'

'Well, Mr Mackiewicz said that you were one of the "lucky ones". You had been selected by the Director, Dr Kempf himself, for the very great privilege of becoming one of "our beloved *Führer's* founder members of the Great Master Race of truly pure Aryans. You have all the required attributes ... "to perfection".' Frederika stopped and looked at me.

'What does *that* mean?' I asked.

'It means that you have golden hair and blue eyes, and look like a little angel, just like your mother and father used to say you were, do you remember? Well what could I say? I had to think fast so I said what a wonderful honour and how delighted I was and that of course I wouldn't stand in your way but I would like to see you before you go. Perhaps I could come back tomorrow. The toad was unsure. He would have to consult his superiors, he said. So I said that I was sure a man in such an influential position as his could find a way for me to say goodbye. Even if it was only to tell me which train you would be travelling on, so I could wave you off from the platform. He obviously liked to think he was that important and was more obliging after that and said that he would see what he could do. I gave him one of my biggest smiles and left the room.'

'Oh Frederika, you are brave,' I whispered and Frederika laughed. 'But that wasn't the end of the story?'

'Oh no,' Frederika said. 'Mr Mackiewicz didn't have any control, of course, he couldn't help me, he is just a puppet. Only the Warden's deputy. I had to go and see the Director himself.'

'The Director? But how did you find him?' I asked. 'I've been to his house and it was a long way from the orphanage.'

'It was a long way, you're right,' Frederika confirmed, 'but Skierniewice is only a small place and I thought everyone was sure to know where the Director of the orphanage was living. So I returned to the town and asked the first person I saw. He was obviously unsure as to why anyone would be asking for the Director of the orphanage at that time of night, but thankfully he pointed me in the right direction and I found the house quite easily and rang the bell. Almost immediately a man answered the door and when I asked to see the Director of the State Orphanage he told me that Dr Kempf was unavailable and that I must make an appointment the next day. I told him that I must see the Director as it was a matter of urgency. The man hesitated but then agreed to go and speak to Dr Kempf. But he left the front door open and so I walked in. It was a beautiful house, so very different from the place you were in, wasn't it?'

I nodded.

'Well, I could hear voices behind one of the closed doors and so I knocked twice and walked straight in.'

I could see her, head up, sweeping into Dr Kempf's room, the one where I had been only a few weeks before.

'There he was, Dr Kempf, sitting in the armchair with a newspaper on his lap. I apologised and excused my entrance but said I needed to speak with him as a matter of urgency. He looked at me for a moment and then waved his hand to dismiss his butler and we were left alone. I then began to explain as briefly as I could that there had been a terrible misunderstanding, that you weren't an orphan at all, that you had a loving family waiting for you to be returned to them and I had been sent to collect you. He seemed convinced. I told him that I hadn't got your papers as they were being prepared and that I had been sent to make sure that you were still in the State Orphanage and to check that you were well and happy. Still he sat there, his chin resting on his fingers, and then he said to me, "Is Renata of pure blood?" '

'What does that mean?' I asked, thinking my blood was red, the same as everyone else's.

'He wanted to know whether you had any *other*
204

blood. I was so surprised I didn't know what to say because you don't look Jewish or like a gypsy and no one would know you were not a Catholic Pole unless they knew your family. Did you say anything to him, Renata? Did you say anything about your mother or your father?'

'No, I don't think so,' I replied. 'The soldiers asked me where my father was and I said he was away with the Army. Then they asked where Mamusia was.'

'And what did you say?' Frederika asked.

'I said she was dead. I don't think I said anything else. No, wait. When I put my coat on Dr Kempf asked if I knew where my mother was and I said she had been taken away by the soldiers with Babcia. Was that the wrong thing to say?'

'Well, if he thought you did have some *other* blood then maybe he was worried. After all, he had let you into the orphanage which was supposed to be for Roman Catholics only. If someone had said anything about him having a non-Catholic with dubious parentage in the orphanage then I can't imagine he would have been in his position for long. Perhaps that was why he didn't put up too much of a fuss when I asked if I could take you away with me.'

'But what did you tell him, Frederika? Did you tell him I was a Jew?'

'Of course not, my sweetheart. I didn't need to tell him anything.'

'But, Frederika,' I said in a low voice, making sure no one was listening to our conversation. 'You're a Jew, aren't you? Why don't you have to hide?'

Frederika leant closer and whispered in my ear,

'You just have to have courage and confidence.'

I beamed at her.

'So what did you do next?' I asked.

'There's not much else to tell. I asked for your release papers and said that I would come and visit you every day whilst I waited for them. I couldn't take you without them, it would have aroused suspicion, and I had to make sure that they didn't send you away without telling me. I then said that we would be going to Kraków and of course he wanted to see the tickets. I suppose the sooner he got rid of us the better for him in the end.'

'If we are not going to Kraków, then *where* are we going?'

'Because I missed the appointment, I couldn't take up the job in Kraków. I will have to find other work so I have decided that we will go back to Warsaw and stay with my parents, Hania and Leon. But you can call them "Grandma" Hania and "Grandpa" Leon if you like. They are so looking forward to seeing you.'

'Frederika?'

'Yes, my love.'

'Promise me that *you* will never leave me.'

'I promise my darling, I *promise*.'

*　　　*　　　*

We arrived in Warsaw around midday and made our way to the small apartment where Frederika's parents were now staying in Saska Ke̜pa. It was on the third floor of a house in what had once obviously been a very smart part of the city. Frederika's mother, Hania, met us at the door of the apartment and swept me up into her arms. After

206

a flurry of hugs and kisses she held me at arm's length and looked me up and down. She was small with a velvety pink complexion, soft wavy white hair and the sweetest of expressions. Her appearance matched her character; she was one of the loveliest people I had ever met. After feasting her eyes on me, 'Grandma' Hania spoke for the first time.

'A little thin and a bit peaky,' she said, 'but nothing good food and sleep won't cure. You're still our beautiful Renata,' and she led me to the table in the centre of the room, which was decked with plates of the most delicious cakes and pastries that she had somehow managed to obtain for the welcoming party.

Frederika's father, Leon, was a large cuddly bear of a man, fond of sausage and plum brandy and miraculously never seemed to be short of either. He was obviously spoiled and had been waited on hand and foot all his life and still expected the same treatment in spite of all that was happening around him. 'Grandma' Hania spent her time making sure that he was happy and well looked after.

The flat was small, consisting of one room, but it was unlike any room I had ever seen before—a wonder of glorious rugs that muffled any noise and created a feeling of peace and calm. Every inch of wall was hung with beautifully patterned rugs in lovely warm colours. One covered the table, several were laid on the divan bed that stood against the opposite wall. They were mysterious with an exotic, dusty smell.

'Oh how beautiful,' I exclaimed. 'It's just like Aladdin's cave.'

This pleased the old man mightily and he began to tell me that they were the remainder of a magnificent collection of Persian carpets that he had possessed before the Nazis took them all. My interest in his carpets made us friends at once and from that day I would sit on his knee for hours and listen to the stories he told me about life before the war. He was, of course, always the central figure, the hero of the tale, his life full of parties, outings and wonderful meals served by servants. He told me all about the apple of his eye, his beautiful Frederika, and what she was like when she was my age. How all her clothes were sent from the best stores in Vienna and of the wondrous holidays she and her brother, Karol, took every year: skiing in the mountains in winter, escaping the heat of summer by retreating to the mountains above Zakopane and bathing in the cool lake waters of Morskie Oko. Frederika had had a French governess to teach her at home and had not been sent to school until she was ten. Karol, being a boy, had of course gone to the best school in town. 'Grandpa' Leon talked about his collection of antique cameras, fob watches and jewellery. Most of which had either vanished in the war or been sold. He even told me about the many women he had loved and who had loved him back, ignoring his wife's disapproving tut-tuts, oblivious to the idea that his ever-faithful partner might be upset by the tales of his beautiful women friends and roving eye or that I, a child of six and a half, was his only audience.

Each morning I woke not believing my luck that my family had found me. No longer anxious and alone, I taught myself not to be afraid of the strange sounds I heard at night. I began to sleep well. I no longer had to race ahead, trying to understand the world. I could relax and begin to enjoy my life once again. I was so caught up with tales from 'Grandpa' Leon and the attentions of 'Grandma' Hania that I was unaware of Frederika's daily activities away from the apartment; she was always very quiet when she returned home in the evenings.

One evening after supper she called me to her and took my hands in hers.

'Renata,' she said, 'I want to talk to you. I am going to have to break the promise I made to you.'

My heart sank like a stone.

'I thought I could find a job and somewhere to live where I could keep you with me, but it's turning out to be impossible. You see, I have been offered a job that will involve me in a lot of travel and very long hours, so I won't be here a lot of the time to look after you. But this job is important because it will help both of us.'

I felt my new-found world, once again, come tumbling down around me. The room began to spin and I could barely keep upright. I grabbed the chair in front of me.

'You aren't going to send me back to the orphanage?' I stammered, wide-eyed with fear. 'Jorik will kill me. *Please* don't send me back.'

'I would never do that,' Frederika assured me. 'Never.'

I was so relieved. 'I have an idea,' I said, thinking hard of a solution before Frederika changed her mind about the orphanage. 'I could always stay here with your parents. I should like that very much.'

'They would like it very much too,' said Frederika, 'but it's not possible for you all to live in this one small room. No, I have made far better arrangements for you where I know you will be very happy with someone you know well and love. Try and guess who I mean,' she teased.

'I can't think of anyone. I know Hanka and Jadwiga well but they don't love me and don't want me. It can't be Marynia because Jusiek didn't want me either. I don't know.'

'No, none of them. Let me tell you. I have decided to send you to live with your Great-aunt Zuzia and Great-uncle Julek. Do you remember them? Aunt Zuzia used to come and see you every day before the war. She is your Babcia's sister.'

'I do remember her a bit,' I said. 'Babcia used to call her a butterfly. But I don't really remember Uncle Julek except that he was always grumpy. Where do they live now?'

'They still live in Przemyśl where you were born. They have an apartment with several rooms and enough space for you. I had a letter from them today and they are longing to have you live with them. You will be very happy there.'

'But will I ever see you again? Will you come and get me to live with you?'

'Yes, my love, I told you I would and I will keep that part of my promise. I think the war will be over soon and then we will be together for ever.'

I so wanted to believe her but I had heard these sorts of promises before, too many times.

* * *

'But are you sure you're doing the right thing?' Hania was asking her daughter. 'That child is so insecure. She has been pushed from one person to the next and now it's going to happen all over again. Can't you see it from her point of view? Don't you think it would be better to leave her here with us? She's settled in so nicely and she's so happy. She's quite a different child.'

'Oh Mother, I sincerely wish I could, but it just won't work. You have so little space and enough problems without the added responsibility of Renata.'

'Renata is not a problem. She's a really good child and we have grown to love her.'

'She is a growing girl. She is going to need more space than this and anyway it's too dangerous here in Warsaw. She will be safer with Zuzia and Julek, and now Julek has been allowed to work again they are in a better position to provide for her.'

'But, darling, you know what a difficult man Julek is. He's going to hate having a child there all the time. You could hardly call him tolerant. As for poor Zuzia, she is broken after the death of both her boys. It would only serve as a reminder . . .'

'Yes, I know all that,' Frederika whispered impatiently, 'but what am I supposed to do? I am at my wits' end. I'm filled with guilt about Renata, worried about you and Father and all I want is that we all survive this ghastly war. You know,' Frederika continued, 'I think Renata may turn out to be Zuzia's salvation. Renata will give her less time to think about her two boys and she will be someone Zuzia can devote herself to and pour her love on. I think it may turn out better than you imagine.'

'Well I hope you're right,' her mother responded.

'Believe me, Renata will be loved and happy.'

'How do you intend to get her to Przemyśl, and when?' asked 'Grandma' Hania.

'She will go by train the day after tomorrow,'

Frederika replied.

'Does Zuzia know she is coming?'

'Mother! What do you take me for? Of course she knows. Remember they will be good for each other, and it may even make Julek a little less self-absorbed—though that would be a miracle.'

'One other thing,' Frederika said. 'I'm counting on your support. You must make Renata believe that you are fully behind the idea of her going. It's not going to help her if she knows you are upset.'

'She won't know, I promise,' her mother replied.

But of course I knew. Lying on my bed of cushions on the floor, I had been wide awake and heard every word of their whispered conversation.

CHAPTER TWELVE

April 1944. Warsaw to Przemyśl

Bożena Lipowska was waiting when Frederika and I arrived. The station hall was heaving with German soldiers checking people's documents. It was clever of Bożena to spot us but she was tall and could see above people's heads. She waved and Frederika waved back as Bożena fought her way through the crowds to get to us.

'Renata, this is Bożena,' said Frederika. 'She is a very good friend of mine and she is going with you to Aunt Zuzia's. She will deliver you there and then she'll let me know that you have arrived safely. Tonight you will be staying with some friends of hers in the country and this time tomorrow you will be back in Przemyśl. Won't that be nice? You have absolutely nothing at all to worry about, my darling.'

'Why can't you take me yourself?' I asked, clinging on to Frederika's arm. I hated all the loud noise, the fact that the monster soldiers of my nightmares were so close, and the crowds of people were bumping and jostling us.

I was stalling for time, knowing that Frederika would soon be gone. I felt very unsure and unhappy. I did not like this at all. I was going to be left alone with a stranger, *again*, and I'd had enough of being passed around, hidden by strangers, told to be quiet, having to stay indoors, being frightened and confused. Why could I not stay here where I knew people loved me and wanted to care for me? I tried again, knowing it was my last chance.

'Please, Frederika, please can I stay with "Grandma" Hania and "Grandpa" Leon?'

'Sweetheart, we've been through all this.' She sighed. 'And I've explained the situation to you. You're a big girl now. I promise it won't be long before I come to see you and I'll write often and you must write to me. Now say hello to Božena.'

The strange woman bent down so her face was level with mine and smiled at me. She had very short brown hair and a plain, open face, but she was smiling and looked friendly enough.

'Hello, Renata,' she said in a kindly voice, taking my hand.

'Hello,' I said.

Božena kissed me and then stood up and turned to Frederika.

'I'll contact you as soon as I'm back. Don't worry about a thing. We'll be fine.'

'I know you will. Thank you, Božena,' Frederika

said and then turning to me for the last time she said, 'Right, my darling, I will fight my way out of here and leave you to get on the train. It should be here at any moment.'

Before I had a chance to cry or say another word, she turned away and was instantly swallowed up by the crowd.

'Now it's just you and me,' Božena said, giving my hand a gentle squeeze. 'We're going to have a fine time. Listen, when the train comes, remember to hang on to me so we don't lose each other. If by any chance we do get separated, don't panic. Just go and stand by that tall, stone building over there till I come and find you. But if you hang on tight, there should be no problem.'

We pushed our way to the platform, which was full of people. Some were carrying suitcases, others had heavy baskets filled with different sorts of vegetables, or live animals—squawking chickens and fluffy rabbits. Everyone appeared to have a purpose. Soldiers in uniforms and shiny boots were everywhere, their guns raised. I tried to hide behind Božena so that they wouldn't notice me. People were shouting at the tops of their voices and it seemed to me that the whole world had decided to board our train. With difficulty Božena steered me to the front of the platform where people were either sitting on the ground, squatting or standing. Everyone was waiting like us for the train to arrive.

Eventually, after what seemed like an eternity, a cloud of smoke appeared in the distance and with a hissing, hooting and puffing, a train slowly pulled into the station. Instantly the whole platform began to move. People began shoving and pushing, battling their way on to the train before it had even come to a standstill. Some were forcing and squeezing their belongings in through the door while others were even hanging on to the side of the train and climbing on to the roof. I could see that there was not enough room for everyone—Božena told me that this was the only train of the day, so everyone would try and get a ride somehow.

Božena was an expert at getting through a crowd, which was lucky for me. She was a big woman and she didn't think twice about shoving people aside with her elbows and her large bottom. When we finally reached the door to the carriage, she picked me up and struggled on board as someone handed her my bag from below. She raised her hand in thanks and then forced me further into the overflowing carriage. She spied a small space against one wall and firmly wedged me between the side of the wagon on one side and her body on the other. Although we had to stand, I could at least lean against her.

A loud whistle sounded and the train jerked forward, sending people lurching against each other. We were off. The train slowly picked up speed and steamed away from the station. I felt cold and sick. I was on the move again to another location with people I didn't know. Božena rearranged herself with difficulty, pulling me sideways and lodging me between her big knees so that she wouldn't lose me. I couldn't see outside so I looked at the wicker basket held by the woman next to Božena. It was full of chickens and rabbits so tightly squashed in together that they too couldn't move. As the hens squawked their displeasure I forgot how uncomfortable I was as I felt so sorry for these poor creatures.

215

After a while I felt the nagging urge to go to the toilet, so I pulled at Božena's skirt.

'What is it?' Božena shouted, peering down at me and swaying from side to side.

'I need the lavatory, please,' I said quietly, not wishing to draw attention to myself.

'You must shout louder. I can't hear you,' she bellowed back.

'I need the toilet,' I yelled, realising that no one would hear me above the noise of the train and the chickens.

'Can't do a thing about it. Sorry. You'll just have to wait.' Božena returned her gaze to the far side of the wagon.

I tried to ignore the feeling in my bladder, but after a while a little puddle formed around my shoes. I looked about the carriage and to my relief we were so tightly packed that no one had noticed. But I felt so ashamed. I remembered Jorik and was worried that Božena would punish me when she realised what had happened.

The train eventually came to a halt. The doors opened and people pushed their way outside to stretch their legs and breathe in the fresh air. To my surprise the train hadn't stopped at a station but somewhere out in the country and it was already getting dark. Božena helped me to the door and then jumped down onto the rough grass below. She held out her arms to help me do the same.

'Right,' she said. 'Now's your opportunity to do your business.' She pulled down my pants and didn't seem to notice that they were wet, or if she did, she made no comment.

'Squat here,' she said, 'and get on with it. It's going to be at least another couple of hours before we stop for the night.'

'I can't,' I said, my face all hot, 'not here.'

'What d'you mean you can't? You told me you needed to go, so here's your chance.'

'I can't, not with all these people around.'

'Miss Vanity Box, is it? Who do you think cares if a child of your age does a pee? Don't give me that nonsense. Get on with it before I get angry with you.'

As she spoke Božena pulled down her own pants and squatted. I watched, horrified, as a great golden frothy stream flowed out from under her skirts. I felt I would die from shame but no one seemed to even notice Božena. In fact I could see others doing exactly the same thing.

Suddenly the train whistle sounded and everyone began a mad scramble to clamber aboard again. Božena stood up, straightened her skirts and then helped me back into the wagon.

'All right?' Božena shouted as we found our places once more.

I shook my head to indicate that things were far from all right.

'You're spoiled,' Božena bellowed, not bothering to ask what the problem was. 'The train in which your mother travelled was a hundred times worse than this, believe me.'

I was flabbergasted. How could Mamusia and Babcia's journey have been any worse than *this*? Did their journey take this long? Where did they go? Now I couldn't stop thinking about them and the fact that they too had gone on a train.

Eventually after what seemed a lot longer than two hours, the train clanked its way into a small station where it would remain until the next morning. Most people were forced to sleep either in the wagons or on the platform and, when no further room was available, some bravely crept underneath the train to sleep as best as they might. But just as Frederika had told me, Božena had made other arrangements.

'Come on,' Božena said, pulling me towards the door. 'We're staying with some people I know who live in the village not far from here.'

We left the small station full of shadowy figures preparing themselves for the night, wrapping themselves in blankets and huddling against each other for warmth, all settling down across the platform and under the train, and made our way along a deserted lane, pitch black and full of holes. I could smell the sweet smell of farm animals and hear soft stirrings, rustling and snuffling noises out in the darkness. Božena held my hand tightly.

'Where are we going?' I asked Božena as I tried to keep up with her, my voice sounding loud in the dark silence.

'We are going to spend the night in a home belonging to an old farmer and his wife,' Božena told me.

'A peasant?' I asked nervously.

'Yes, if you want to put it that way.'

This was a terrible shock. I could remember my family talking long ago about peasants as if they were lower than servants. I felt peasants were strange people and different but had never met one. Marynia had been a servant, but she wasn't a peasant. Peasants lived in hovels in the country. They were dirty and they couldn't read and write. I knew that I had been helped by all different kinds of people since I had been taken away but I

218

was worried about meeting a peasant. What would Mamusia, Babcia or Marynia say? Bożena must be making a mistake.

'I'm sorry, but I would prefer to sleep on the train if that's all right,' I said.

Bożena let go of my hand and stopped in her tracks. She then bent down so that our faces were on a level.

'And why might that be?' she asked in a cold voice.

I could see the whites of her eyes through the darkness.

'Because . . .' My voice was shaking but I had no choice but to explain. 'Frederika would be upset if she thought I was sleeping in a peasant's house. She would prefer me to stay on the train.'

'My God, you are a horrible, ungrateful little snob,' Bożena said. 'I can't believe what I'm hearing. After all you've been through, I would have thought you'd have felt honoured and thankful to be invited into the house of kind, generous people who don't even know you. And what's more they are putting themselves in danger for you, a little Jewish girl. They would be killed if anyone ever found out. How can you stand there and say what you just have? I don't want to hear another word from you, d'you hear?'

I nodded, unable to understand why Bożena was so angry. I hadn't said anything wrong—everyone knew that peasants were different.

We walked the rest of the way in silence. Somewhere in the distance a low hooting made me jump and hurry after Bożena in case the ghosts came out of the darkness to grab me. I didn't dare to share my worries with Bożena in case she

219

shouted at me again.

We stopped at last in front of a small dark hut. As we walked up to the door, I could smell strange scents coming from inside. Božena knocked three times very quickly and the door opened a crack to reveal a chink of candlelight that lit up the grass at our feet. I heard a few whispered words and only then was the door opened wide enough to let us in. Behind the door stood an elderly woman with a flowery apron tied around her middle. She hugged Božena tightly, kissed her on both cheeks and then bent down to enfold me in her arms. She smelt of garlic and carbolic soap. In the candlelight I could see that her face was like leather with lots of little lines and creases. When she smiled there were gaps between her yellow teeth.

'This is Renata,' Božena said to the woman, and then turning to me, 'This kind lady, who is risking her life to give us hospitality, is my Great-aunt. She brought me up because I am an orphan and I lived here all my childhood. So that makes me a peasant too but I'm proud of it.'

I simply stood there unable to think of anything to say, smiling shyly at the old peasant woman and feeling embarrassed by what Božena had said.

The hut was one large room and everything was made from wood—a wooden floor, a wooden ceiling and a rough wooden table with benches on either side. Garlands of onions, garlic and herbs hung high above my head under the reedy roof. A huge stove, rising up from the floor to reach the ceiling, stood in the middle of the room beside which a thin old man slept in a large wooden chair. Even in the dim candlelight I could tell he was very old and crooked from the way he rolled forward in his chair with his head lolling from side to side. He was covered in a thick dark blanket even though the room was very hot. At the furthest end of the hut I could make out the outline of an enormous wooden bed. The room was filled with a familiar smell— cooked cabbage.

'Come, come.' The old woman urged us forward towards the table. 'You must be so hungry after your long journey. Here I have your supper ready. Sit down.' And she gave me a toothy smile then placed huge bowls of cabbage soup and hunks of black bread on the table. I stared at the soup and bread and sat down reluctantly and raised a spoonful of the dreadful liquid to my lips and took a sip. But to my complete surprise it tasted wonderful. It wasn't thin and watery but thick and full of flavour and the bread was the most delicious I had ever tasted. I gave the old lady a big smile.

I was enjoying the food so much that I didn't concentrate on the conversation the two women were having. Once or twice I heard my name so I knew they were talking about me. When I did try to follow what they were saying, I found that I could understand very little of what the old lady was saying. A lot of the words sounded funny and mixed up and not quite right. I hoped that Božena wasn't repeating what I had said about staying with peasants. The women continued to talk well after I had finished my second helping of cabbage soup. Now I was too full and sleepy to try and take in what they were saying; I understood nothing except the words *money* and *Russians* that were repeated from time to time.

The old man suddenly woke up and his wife placed a bowl of soup on a small table in front of him. He took one spoonful but his hands were shaky and the soup slopped all down his front and over the blanket that lay across his knees. Božena got up from the table, took the spoon from him and fed him like a baby. Her aunt smiled gratefully and watched them happily. After a while she spoke to me slowly so that I could understand her.

'I think it's time for the little one to go to bed.'

'Yes,' Božena agreed. 'We have to be off very early. The train is supposed to leave at seven in the morning and,' she turned to look at me, 'it's a good half-hour's walk back to the station.'

'I'll have breakfast ready for you at six,' her aunt said.

The old lady beckoned me towards the big bed. 'You and Božena will sleep in here,' she said. 'I put clean sheets on for you this morning. You will be snug and comfortable. But first you had better use the bucket. It's just outside the door. I can't leave the door open because of the light, but you'll be fine. Just knock when you're ready to come back in.'

'I'll go out with her,' said Božena. 'She isn't used to being outside in the dark on her own.'

After relieving myself in the bucket and washing my hands and face in a metal bowl filled with warm water that was waiting for me on the table inside, I undressed and climbed into the big bed. Božena pulled the covers over me.

'Božena?' I whispered. 'I can't sleep on these sheets, they are so rough and hard.'

'You are the most ungrateful little brat,' Božena hissed back. 'These are my aunt's best handwoven linen sheets that she has washed and put on the bed specially for you.'

I was too tired to argue so just pulled the covers up to my chin and, breathing in the flowery smell of clean sheets, I fell into a deep sleep and never heard Božena climb in beside me.

*　　　*　　　*

Božena shook me awake just before six.

'Wake up, sleepy head. It's time to get back to the train. We don't want it to go without us, now do we?'

I was having a lovely dream that I didn't want to end. I had been lying, with my arms folded behind my head, in the bottom of a boat as it rocked gently on a lake. Overhead the sun shone from a clear blue sky and at the back of the boat sat a man with a gentle smile. Beside him was Mamusia. I knew that the strange man was my father and in my dream I knew that I was going to be happy for ever. It was hard to leave behind this wonderful feeling and wake up, but I got up obediently and let Božena rub a wet cloth over my sleepy face. The cold woke me with a shock and by the time I had crouched over the bucket outside in the freezing early morning air, I was fully awake ready for the day ahead. I drank a bowl of warm milk and ate another slice of the black bread, which I dipped, like Božena and her aunt, into my milk.

The old man was still nodding in his chair by the stove where he must have spent the whole night. Seeing a quilt on the floor near his chair I understood where the old lady must have slept. For the first time since arriving I realised what Božena had been trying to tell me. I felt totally ashamed of what I had said about staying here and about sleeping on the rough sheets. Now all I wanted was to say thank you and show the old lady that I wasn't ungrateful. But I felt embarrassed and suddenly very shy.

'It was very kind of you to let us have your bed,' I said.

The old woman smiled at me. Božena looked pleased.

'It was a pleasure, *kochanie*,' the old woman said and beamed at Božena who got up and kissed the top of her head.

'We must be off,' she said. 'The train won't wait for us.'

'When will we see you again?' the old lady asked.

'I'll try and stop off on the way back,' Božena replied. 'So in a couple of days hopefully. I have to get back to Warsaw as quickly as possible so I won't hang around in Przemyśl longer than necessary. As soon as I've delivered Renata to her relatives I'll make my way back. So I'll probably spend another night with you then. But please don't expect me. Things are coming to a head, thank God. Don't worry if I don't come. I'll be in touch one way or another.'

I listened carefully to Božena. Over the last week of listening to 'Grandpa' Leon and 'Grandma' Hania I was becoming more aware of what was going on outside the rooms I was being hidden in. I was beginning to understand that the war had changed the lives of so many people, not just my family and the people I had met.

I watched Božena as she went over to the stove and kissed her sleeping uncle.

'Casimir,' the old woman said loudly making me

224

jump. 'Our Božena is leaving, but she'll be back soon.' The old man didn't move.

'Don't wake him,' Božena said. 'He's a very sick man. He looks a lot worse than last time.'

'I think he's dying,' the old lady said. 'It will be better for him to go, but for me . . .' She stopped talking and Božena hugged her again.

'We really must be off. It's getting late.'

She didn't need to remind me to say thank you.

'Thank you so much for letting me stay with you.' And I meant it with all my heart. 'I would love to visit you again one day when my father's back, or perhaps you could visit us.'

'Perhaps, who knows. At any rate I'll never forget you,' the old woman said, hugging me again. 'You're a real little lady,' she added.

She remained in the doorway waving as we made our way back down the lane. I waved back until the bend in the road hid her from view.

'Božena, I really liked your aunt,' I said. 'I am sorry that I was so rude before.'

Božena looked at me and smiled, but said nothing.

When we arrived at the station the train was building up steam and most of the passengers were already aboard. We shuffled along searching for a space until one of the men hanging out of a wagon door pointed to a place beside him where we could stand. Helpful hands pulled us up and no one asked where we had spent the night. Now that the journey was in its last stage, people seemed to be more cheerful and talkative. A group further down the wagon had started singing and very soon the wave of cheerfulness spread along the wagons as more and more people joined in.

Just after seven, and on time, the train set off slowly building up steam until once again it was clanking along through the countryside. Through the slits just above Božena's head, light from the outside world filtered through. The rushing air chased out the smells inside. Božena tapped me on the shoulder and told me that we weren't going to stop for about five hours, until we reached the end of the journey.

Whenever the train went into a tunnel, the wagon filled with evil-smelling smoke from the engine which made us choke and cough and my eyes smart and water. I noticed the smuts of dirt on people's faces and rubbed my own face to see if mine was covered too.

'Have I got smuts of dirt like freckles on my face?' I shouted up to Božena.

'You had,' Božena replied. 'Only now that you've rubbed your face, it's covered with great big black smudges. You look more like a chimney sweep than a little girl.'

I could tell Božena was in a good mood today, she was much more friendly than yesterday. I remembered a story that I had read at Jadwiga's house about a little chimney-sweep who was sent up chimneys in big houses. One day he falls down a chimney into a little girl's bedroom and realises how grimy he is and runs away, falls into a river and is transformed into a water-baby.

'Have you read the story of the little chimney-sweep called Tom?' I asked.

'Never heard of it,' she shouted back. 'Can you read?' She frowned. 'You're very small to read.'

'Jadwiga taught me. That was before I went to the orphanage. I love reading.'

226

But the train was so noisy and the singing was now so loud, it was impossible to hear each other speak and we completed the journey in silence.

On the outskirts of Przemyśl, Božena pulled out a cloth. She made me spit on it and then wiped it over my face, rubbing vigorously to get rid of the black smudges.

'We don't want your aunt to take fright,' she shouted. At the mention of my aunt I began to feel butterflies starting to jump around inside my tummy. I was going to see my butterfly aunt again.

'Will she be there to meet us?'

'I hope so. That was the arrangement. Do you think you will recognise her?'

'I don't know . . . I was only little when I last saw her. What shall we do if there are lots of people on the station and we can't find her?'

'There will be a lot of people, but don't worry. I will recognise her. Look, I have a picture.'

Božena fumbled in her pocket and pulled out a tatty photograph which she handed to me.

'That's your Aunt Zuzia. It was taken before the war but I imagine she will still be recognisable after all this time.'

I looked with interest at the yellowing photo. It showed a lady with a longish face and dark, laughing brown eyes. She was wearing a suit with a fur collar and a hat with a feather that was pulled down over one eye. She looked very smart. She was holding a tiny girl by the hand. The girl was smiling, her chubby face surrounded by lots of light-coloured curls and a large bow was perched on the top of her head. She wore a pale dress, short white socks and little boots and in her hand she was clutching a toy rabbit.

'She looks nice. Who's that little girl with her?'

'You! Who else?' laughed Bożena.

I was amazed. Was this really me—this happy child in beautiful clothes?

'I don't look at all like that now, Bożena. I've changed a lot. Supposing Aunt Zuzia has changed too and we don't recognise her?'

'You mustn't worry, we will recognise her. After all, that's what *I'm* here for.'

* * *

The train's journey was meant to end at Przemyśl but when it pulled into the station, its brakes squealing and clouds of steam puffing into the air, people fought to get off as if it was due to pull out at any moment.

'We'll wait a few moments and let everybody get off,' Bożena said, holding me back. 'It wouldn't do to lose you now.'

'But supposing Aunt Zuzia won't wait? Supposing she thinks we're not on the train? Supposing she goes away?' I began to feel really worried.

'Calm down, child. None of these things will happen. Your aunt will wait. Anyway we've a greater chance of finding her if we wait for the crowds to lessen.'

Impatient as I was, I had little choice but to wait until Bożena decided that it was time for us to leave the train. When we climbed down from the wagon into the bright daylight the platform was teeming with passengers. Steam from the train was curling around everybody and everything making it difficult to see very far. But Bożena seemed to know exactly where to go and headed for a building on the far side of the platform.

At the booking office the crowds were thinner and everyone seemed to be in such a hurry. There were only two people standing still, one short man and next to him a lady, both old and wrapped in scarves and coats. They were scanning the faces of all the people that passed them. The man had white bushy eyebrows that peeped out from under his hat. He looked rather grumpy. The woman was taller and seemed very restless because she kept turning in every direction as if she was looking for someone. She was thin and looked worn-out with wisps of straggly grey hair coming out of the scarf she had wrapped around her head and fastened under her chin with a knot.

I had decided that this couldn't be Aunt Zuzia. She was far too old and didn't look anything at all like the fashionable lady in the photo, certainly nothing like the butterfly aunt I remembered. But Božena made her way towards her, held out the photograph she had shown me and muttered a few words. The woman looked at me, uttered a little cry and then held out her arms. Then there were tears pouring down her face as she hugged me so hard that I could hardly breathe.

'Zuzia, stop making such a hysterical scene,' the man at her side said in a gruff voice. 'You'll have us arrested or worse. Pull yourself together. You're being quite ridiculous. The child will think you're a complete idiot.'

But I didn't think anything of the sort—I was hugging my weeping aunt as hard as I could. It was wonderful to be recognised, to be wanted and welcomed.

Aunt Zuzia and Uncle Julek (*right*) with a friend,
1945–1946

I followed Božena, Aunt Zuzia and Uncle Julek
out of the station towards a waiting horse-drawn
carriage. I stood and stared at it—I had never
ridden in such luxury before.

'Don't get the wrong idea,' Uncle Julek growled.
'We can't afford luxuries like this. It's only because
your aunt was convinced you would be tired out
after the long journey. But you look perfectly all
right to me, so we've obviously wasted our money.'

As my uncle hadn't said one nice word to either
me or Božena since we had arrived, I decided he
wasn't at all pleased to see me. I remembered
Frederika's whispers to her mother that night

230

before I left so I sat quietly on a seat next to Aunt Zuzia, feeling the springs poke into me whenever the carriage bounced over a rut in the road.

The horses turned into Kolejowa Street. We came to a stop outside one of the tall stone houses and Uncle Julek helped us all down from the carriage, me last. As we waited for my uncle to pay the driver I looked around me at the wide road and the apartment blocks, and wondered which one was Aunt Zuzia's, and then I looked again at the house in front of which we were standing. The ground-floor window of Number 2 was filled with books.

'A bookshop,' I exclaimed happily. 'I've never seen one before. Does it cost a lot of money to buy books?'

'It's not a bookshop,' Aunt Zuzia said. 'It's a library.'

'A library, what's that?' I asked. I had never heard of a library before.

'You can't buy books there,' my aunt explained, 'but you can borrow the books, one at a time, and take them home to read. Then, when you have finished, you take it back and borrow another one.'

I stood there amazed. 'Will I be able to do that?'

'Yes, when you learn to read,' my aunt answered as she reached for my hand.

'But I *can* read. I've read ever so many books. I love reading more than anything else in the world. Can I borrow one *now*?'

'You can read?' My aunt seemed surprised, just like Bożena had been. 'They're closed today, it's Sunday. But tomorrow, if you like, we will make arrangements for you to join so you can borrow books.'

231

I felt as if I would burst with joy. Frederika was right. I was going to love it here.

CHAPTER THIRTEEN
April 1944. 2, Kolejowa Street, Przemyśl

Uncle Julek and Aunt Zuzia's apartment was on the third floor of Number 2, Kolejowa Street. They grumbled that the lift wasn't working and we had to climb hundreds of stone stairs to their apartment. We were all out of breath by the time we reached the third floor.

Aunt Zuzia unlocked the front door.

'Here we are,' she said. 'Come in, come in.'

We crowded into the small dark hallway and took off our coats. On the left of the front door was the kitchen, a warm room filled with the smell of cooking. Through the open door I could see that it was small but large enough to hold a stove, a small table with several chairs and a sink. I went inside and stood on tiptoe to peep out through the one small window. It looked out of the front of the building and down onto the street below. Next to the kitchen was another room filled with a number of stiff leather chairs. It smelt musty as if no one had been in there for a long time. In the middle of the room there was a high leather couch without a back or sides. Against the window was a large desk covered in untidy piles of paper.

And there were books here too! The shelves round the walls were all filled with books. I ran across and gently pulled some off the shelf to look at them but many were written in a language I couldn't read. I felt disappointed and returned those to their little holes.

'This is Julek's room,' Aunt Zuzia explained. 'He uses it to see his patients now that he doesn't have a surgery.'

'Is he still able to see patients?' Bożena asked.

'Officially no. It's a long story . . .'

At the word *story* my ears pricked up. I pretended to look through Uncle Julek's books that I could read but listened carefully to what Aunt Zuzia was saying.

'. . . but after the Nazis arrived and life became extremely difficult for the Jews, he and a couple of colleagues formed a committee to liaise with the Gestapo. I was worried because I thought that if he was to draw attention to himself he would be one of the first to be taken away. But there's no telling Julek, he will do what he wants.'

A loud harrumphing noise came from the doorway and we turned to see Uncle Julek standing there.

'I'm sure they don't want to be bored by all of that,' he said. 'Zuzia, I think our guests would like some tea.'

'Of course,' Aunt Zuzia said. 'Renata, why don't you come and help me.'

'But you are still able to practise?' Bożena asked again, once we were all seated round the kitchen table.

'We had to disappear,' Uncle Julek said. 'When things in the ghetto came to a head, we knew it was only a matter of time before we were taken too. We left everything behind and a close friend of ours moved into our apartment and lived there. He

233

looked after everything for us as best he could. Not much left by then of course.'

'Where did you go?' Božena asked.

'Into the country,' Uncle Julek replied, 'here and there, to and fro, until we were given new papers, a new identity and we returned. Not to our apartment of course but we found this one, much smaller and more discreet. I am not supposed to practise but I do.'

'He's too old,' Aunt Zuzia interrupted. 'He should be putting his feet up at his age but no, he's out there helping everyone just like he used to. Doesn't charge much, just enough to get by, but that way we're kept safe and our friends are kept healthy. He's worried about the orphans now. All those poor children who have lost their parents. Not much he can do though.'

Uncle Julek tutted.

'But don't they suspect anything?' Božena asked. 'People coming into your apartment all the time?'

'Oh, they don't all come here,' Aunt Zuzia replied. 'Mostly he visits. Occasionally someone might come here but not often enough to arouse suspicion.'

'It's all good exercise,' Uncle Julek added. 'Don't want to be sitting around all day with my feet up. Too much time to think then.'

Then it went silent. No one said a word until Aunt Zuzia put the teacups on the table with a loud clatter.

After the tea, Aunt Zuzia said, 'Renata, we haven't shown you your room, yet. Would you like to see it?'

'Yes please, Aunt Zuzia,' I said, jumping off my chair and taking her hand. She led me through

234

to another room. On the bed there was a bright blue bedspread. There was a narrow wardrobe for clothes, a chair, and a table positioned in such a way that the light from the window bounced off its shiny surface. I loved the room immediately and imagined myself lying on the bed reading books borrowed from the library downstairs.

'When you go to school,' Aunt Zuzia told me, 'you will soon make friends to play with and you can ask them to come and play here in your room.'

'As long as they don't make a noise and disturb me,' added Uncle Julek, who had just appeared in the doorway. 'I'm not going to have my home turned into a zoo by a lot of other people's noisy offspring. It's bad enough that we have been landed with one of our own.'

'Take no notice of your uncle, darling,' Aunt Zuzia said. 'He doesn't mean it. He's really happy that you're here. It's just a little joke. He's always joking.'

But I had already decided that it would be best to keep out of the way of my uncle and his little jokes. I had a funny feeling that he really didn't want me there at all.

'What a lovely room. You are a lucky girl. Wait till I tell Frederika,' Božena said.

'And that just leaves the bathroom and our room,' Aunt Zuzia said, leading us out of my room and opening the last two doors.

Their bedroom was small, a lot smaller than mine, and almost completely filled by a large bed but, unlike mine, there was no window.

'She insisted we gave up our room for the child,' Uncle Julek growled. 'Said she would need the space more than we do. Ridiculous.'

Aunt Zuzia and Bożena said nothing.

'Please, I don't mind having this room,' I said, trying to make my uncle like me a little, 'if you would like the other one back.'

'Don't tell us what to do,' the old man snapped. 'We decide which room you have. It's not up to you.' He turned on his heel and left.

'His bark's far worse than his bite,' Aunt Zuzia said to Bożena. 'He's taken the death of our boys very hard, even harder than I have. He feels guilty that he's alive and they are dead. It has made him very bitter. I try to be patient.'

She turned to me. 'Don't look so worried, my precious. Uncle Julek loves you very much and anyway it was his idea to give you the bigger room. So you see he doesn't mean what he says in his grumpy old way. He just enjoys a grumble.'

She led us back into the kitchen and invited Bożena to sit down again.

'We are very grateful to you for bringing Renata to us. Frederika wrote that you are a wonderfully kind person and would look after her well. What can we do to repay you?'

'Absolutely nothing. It is a pleasure to be able to help,' Bożena replied with a smile. 'Frederika is a dear friend who has helped me in the past more than once. I was glad of the opportunity to do something for her. Besides, she insisted on giving me money, which I really didn't want, but she wouldn't have it any other way. I have a letter for you from her.' She fumbled in her pocket. 'If you want me to take something back to her I would be delighted to do so. I shall be seeing her very shortly. We are working together at the moment.'

'Really, what are you doing?'

'I'm sorry,' Božena said, 'I'm sure that you will understand that I'm not in a position to say. It's safer for you that way. Please don't worry about Frederika. She's fine.'

'Our daughter-in-law's a saint,' Aunt Zuzia said. 'I don't know how we would have coped without her. Who would have thought that the young, pretty, fun-loving girl our eldest son married would have turned out the way she has. If only he were alive to see her now, he would be so proud.' Tears welled up in her eyes but Aunt Zuzia quickly pulled herself together.

'Take no notice of your silly old aunty, my darling,' she said, seeing that I was worried by the sudden change in the conversation. 'Everything will be happy now you are here. We're going to have a lot of fun and it won't be much longer, they say, until the war ends and things are back to normal.' She wiped her eyes on the sleeve of her cardigan and smiled at me. 'Now for some food.'

*   *   *

First we had a delicious potato soup followed by *paluszki*, little dumplings coated with fried onions. There was plenty to go round and Uncle Julek had two helpings of both. For a small man he ate a large amount. To finish there were more cups of sweet tea. I could remember these tastes from long ago but however hard I tried I couldn't remember where it was that I had eaten these things before.

'Now, Božena, it is far too late for you to start travelling back to Warsaw. You must stay the night with us. I can make a bed up for you in Julek's room.'

'That is very kind of you, but I really must leave this evening. The sooner I get going the better, but it is most kind of you to share your wonderful food with me.' Božena sounded as if she was ready to go and nothing would change her mind. 'My work awaits and there is a train in an hour which I plan to catch.'

'Then in that case I will take you back to the station,' Uncle Julek said.

'Absolutely not,' Božena insisted. 'You stay here. I will be fine. I am used to travelling alone.' Božena smiled at him. 'Well, Renata,' she said, pulling on her coat. 'I'm sure we shall meet again and I shall tell Frederika what a good little girl you've been and how happy you are here. She will be very pleased.' She bent down and gave me a big hug.

'Give Frederika my love,' I said, my face buried in Božena's middle, 'and her parents, and your aunt and uncle too.' I added, 'I hope your uncle doesn't die. Oh, and please tell Frederika about the library downstairs and all those books I shall be able to read and what a lovely room I have and what a good cook Aunt Zuzia is and . . . and . . . how kind Uncle Julek is because he insisted I should have the big bedroom.'

'Who told her that?' Uncle Julek growled.

But I was sure that I saw his face soften for a moment before he looked all grumpy again. I grabbed Božena's arm and stood on tiptoe.

'I'm sorry, Božena,' I said quietly. 'Really I am.'

Božena patted my head and smiled. 'I know you are,' she said. 'Don't worry about it any more but just remember, you are not alone.'

I wasn't sure whether she meant me, or my family, or all of us the Nazis hated.

Uncle Julek showed Božena to the door. 'That's an honest woman,' he said when he rejoined us in the kitchen. 'Now, Zuzia, for goodness' sake let the child breathe. You've done nothing but hug her and sob over her ever since she arrived. Give her a chance to settle in. You can ask all the questions you want later and then, and only then, will we think about what to do with her. But now she must be ready for her bed.'

He was right, I was very tired. Once again my life had been turned upside down, once again I was in another home with new people. But this time I wasn't with strangers, I was with my very own family and had my very own room. Božena was right. I wasn't alone. I belonged here with my aunt and uncle.

*   *   *

The minute the library opened the following morning Aunt Zuzia and I went there. I was so excited and hoped that I would see some of my old friends again. Aunt Zuzia enrolled me as a member and then I was free to look around. The books were mainly old and shabby without any pictures, but that didn't matter at all. In between two much larger, older books I read a familiar name on one of the spines—Charles Dickens. Eagerly I looked for other favourites but couldn't find any but I didn't mind, there were shelves and shelves of books, enough to keep me going for the rest of my life. This was the best library in the world. I took down book after book and looked through the pages. Each one was full of magical words that I hadn't come across before, and now that I had Aunt Zuzia I would be able to read them and remember them and begin to understand them *all*.

I read everything and anything, at breakneck speed, and it didn't matter that the stories were too grown-up for me, or that the facts were too complicated. There were hundreds and thousands of new words all waiting to be discovered.

'Not you again,' the librarian laughed on my third visit. 'I have never known anyone read as fast as you. Are you sure you are reading them? Three books in three days is rather a lot, even for an adult.'

'Oh yes,' I said. 'I have nothing to do except read. Aunt Zuzia helps. She tells me what all the words mean.'

'Well, it won't be long,' the librarian said, 'before you will have read everything I have. And what will you do then? It's such a pity that we don't have more books. It's all because of the war. Once we had so many there wasn't room for them on the shelves and we had to keep them in boxes in the cellar.'

'What happened to them?' I asked, puzzled. 'Didn't people return them?'

'Yes,' the librarian replied. 'People returned them all right, only too quickly once the Nazis started burning the ones they didn't like. I had to get rid of many of them. Now no one wants to read books any more.'

I was shocked. How could anyone not want to read books? And how could anyone want to burn them?

'But there are many here,' the librarian continued, 'that really aren't suitable for someone as young as you. If you are going to read this

240

quickly, I will have to have a word with your aunt.'

'Oh she won't mind,' I said, 'and anyway when I've read all the books I can always read them again.'

The librarian didn't look so sure and a few days later she took Aunt Zuzia to one side while I was busy looking for another book to borrow.

'Mrs Zielińska, a lot of these books aren't suitable for little girls. I really do think that it would be better if you or your husband checked what she's borrowing. Renata is quite insistent that you won't mind, but I just want to warn you. The selection isn't that great here any more and so I can't direct her towards more suitable literature for her age group.'

'Thank you,' Aunt Zuzia replied. 'Renata did tell me and I was a little concerned. But my husband, surprisingly, said to let her read what she wants and that she'll only understand what she is ready to understand. Not quite the response that I had expected, of course. Rather liberal for a man such as my husband.'

The two ladies laughed and I breathed a sigh of relief. I could read anything I liked. I silently thanked Uncle Julek a hundred times or more.

After that first visit to the library, we didn't return upstairs immediately.

'Let's go for a little walk,' Aunt Zuzia suggested. 'Let's go into town, I have your papers.' I was eager to explore, happy that I could, at last, be outside, walking around in the open air. Together Aunt Zuzia and I wandered through the streets like normal people, hurrying only when we caught sight of soldiers in the distance.

'This is where you lived, that apartment on the

241

first floor with the balcony,' Aunt Zuzia said as we stood outside the tall building in Jagiellońska Street. 'Do you remember?'

I looked at the windows above me. I had a faraway memory of a bell push on a wall, a blue chaise longue and a balcony full of plants. And then I remembered other things—the tall stove in the living room, the smell of Babcia's cooking and the blue peacock quilt.

'I used to come and visit you every single day,' Aunt Zuzia was saying. 'I would bring you a piece of melon or we would go together and buy it from the market. You loved it. Marynia then used to take you to the park and you always took your melon with you and ate it there. Do you remember the melon?'

Of course I remembered the melon. I looked at Aunt Zuzia to see if she knew what Marynia and I had done with those melon slices all that time ago, but there was nothing on her face to suggest that she had.

'Where is Marynia?' I said suddenly. 'I haven't seen her for ages. Can we visit her?'

'Marynia has had to go away,' Aunt Zuzia said quickly. 'You can't see her.'

'When will she be back? When can I see her?'

'Not for a long time, darling. I'll tell you when she comes back and you can see her then.'

'Where has she gone? Can I write to her? When she knows where I am she will come to see me. I know she will. She promised.'

Aunt Zuzia said nothing. Something wasn't quite right.

'You know where she is. I can tell. Has something happened to her? Please tell me.'

242

Aunt Zuzia sighed.

'Marynia's in prison,' Aunt Zuzia said. 'That's why she can't come and see you.'

'In prison? But why? Who put her there?'

'It's a long story but Marynia was caught by the Nazis trying to help a little Jewish boy. He had been left all alone by his mother. When they caught her the Germans put her in prison—she was lucky not to have been shot.'

The world seemed to stop. I started to shiver uncontrollably and it took all my strength to ask, 'Was the boy called Jan?'

'I don't know. Let's move on. I'll show you the *Rynek*, do you remember the market square where we bought the melon?'

'It *was* Jan. I know it was. And he wasn't left alone by his mother, he was thrown out by Maciej because his mother couldn't pay for him. When Marynia heard that, she promised me she would look for him. It's not her fault. It's mine. We must tell the Gestapo and get her out of prison. They will let her go if I tell them what really happened and that it's all my fault.'

I was so upset that suddenly I was shouting at the top of my voice and crying at the same time.

'Stop it. Stop it at once,' Aunt Zuzia hissed angrily, gripping my shoulders tightly. 'We're going home this minute and don't you dare utter another word or sound till we get there.'

She grabbed my wrist tightly and started pulling me back along the road from where we had come. Surprised at my aunt's harsh behaviour, I did as I was told, but I couldn't stop myself sobbing at the thought of Marynia locked up in a dark, damp prison all alone. Aunt Zuzia dragged me all the way and, as soon as we were back in the apartment, she couldn't stop crying as she tried to explain what would happen to me, to them, to Frederika and Marynia if I were to tell anyone about Jan. Uncle Julek who had come out of his consulting room to see what all the noise was about agreed with my aunt.

'You owe it to Marynia to keep your mouth shut,' he said. 'How do you think she will feel if the Nazis arrest you, or us, after all she has sacrificed? She will come out of prison one day, but you would be shot or worse and so would we because we are Jewish too. If you tell anyone, you will murder us all. You are a clever girl and I know you understand what we are saying. You've been through too much not to. Don't waste your precious life and ours. Marynia wouldn't thank you. It is not your responsibility that she decided to help the boy. It was her decision. She knew the risk she was taking and she was glad to do it. She will survive, I promise you.'

Uncle Julek was talking quietly, trying to make me feel better. His words soothed me and I began to calm down.

'I promise, Uncle Julek,' I said, 'I promise I will never mention Jan again, or Marynia, and I have never told anyone I am a Jew.'

But silently I promised myself that one day I would rescue Marynia. My father would get Marynia out of prison when he came back and then we would go and find Jan. And it wouldn't be long now before Tatuś was back—hadn't I heard Bożena tell my aunt that the war would soon be over? Soon everything would be all right again.

After this incident, Aunt Zuzia was very careful when she took me out in case other memories might upset me. It was obvious that Aunt Zuzia was happy to have me living with them but she was also frightened that something bad might happen to me, so she didn't let me out of her sight for a moment. For this reason, it took many days to explore Przemyśl; we only took short walks and we never went very far. Przemyśl had been heavily bombed and buildings had fallen down into piles of rubble that lay on the ground. I remembered some of the buildings that had survived the bombs—there was the Greek Orthodox church, with its columns and flights of steps, and the main market square. But all the cafés and most of the shops were shut.

But in a corner of the main square there was a small shop that was still open and every time we passed it there was a long, snake-like queue of people that went from the shop's front door right across the square.

'Why are there so many people queuing outside that shop?' I asked Aunt Zuzia on one of our trips.

'It's a bread shop,' she replied. 'The bread is better there than anywhere else.'

'Why don't the people come back when it is less busy?' I asked. 'Then they wouldn't have to stand outside in a queue.'

'There's not enough bread to go round and the Poles can only buy what the Nazis don't want. The soldiers get to buy whatever they want and however much they want. We can have what's left over.'

'But that's not fair. They should be sharing with the rest of us if there is not enough bread to go

245

round. Why doesn't the baker bake more?'

'It's not as easy as that,' Aunt Zuzia replied. 'There's not enough of anything any more.'

I never minded queuing for bread. The baker was so clever that he had made a wonderful display for the window. He had collected all the stale bits of leftover bread, small pieces of dough and crumbs, and using some water had moulded them together to make a small village with houses, cows, horses and even people. There were stalks of corn in a small field and on the roof of one of the cottages a stork nested on a cart-wheel base. Every bit of this magical model was a soft golden brown because, as Aunt Zuzia explained, he had first baked it hard and then glued it together.

'It's like the witch's cottage in "Hansel and Gretel" that is made of gingerbread and all sorts of lovely things to eat. It would be a shame to spoil this by nibbling bits off,' I exclaimed when I saw it for the first time.

'It wouldn't taste very nice because the baker told me that he added lots of salt to the mixture,' said Aunt Zuzia.

'Why did he do that? To stop greedy people having a nibble?'

'That might be part of the reason,' she laughed, 'but the real purpose is to stop it going mouldy. Salt is a preservative.'

I couldn't get enough of this wonderful model and we had to stop and examine it each time we passed, even when we weren't queuing for bread. I saw the village as it was, a place of comfort and peace, showing a happy and simple way of life. I invented people for every cottage and a name for every animal. Whenever we went in to buy bread, the baker, Mr Malewski, would talk about his village to me as if it was real. He was proud of his creation and delighted that I loved it so much too.

'You're so clever,' I told him one day, 'to think of using the crumbs and stale bits of bread instead of throwing them away. I bet you are the first person in the world to have done this.'

Mr Malewski laughed. 'I would be telling you a lie, little girl, if I said I was. Two or three hundred years ago French prisoners of war used to amuse themselves by turning bits of bread into wonderful models, far better than mine. And some of the models are still around today.'

'Has the war really lasted two or three hundred years?' I was flabbergasted. Maybe Frederika and Božena were wrong after all and it would never end—not in my lifetime anyway.

'No, not the same war, not the one we are in now. There have been lots of wars. People are always at war.'

'Why are we at war? Why are the Germans fighting us?' I wanted to know.

Mr Malewski laughed again but sadly this time. 'I wish I knew the answer to that one. Get your aunty to explain it to you. She's a clever lady.'

But Aunt Zuzia didn't explain. Every time I asked her questions about the war, about Germans or Jews, she quickly changed the subject.

'It's better not to talk about these things,' she would say. 'You never know who's listening.'

But I wanted answers to the questions that bubbled up inside. Questions that wouldn't go away: why were my mother and grandmother taken away? Where were they now? Why was Marynia in prison when all she wanted to do was help Jan?

247

Why had my father been away for so long and never written to me? Why did the Nazis hate Jews? But no one would help me and so I decided that I would have to be patient and wait until my father came home. He would answer my questions. I never for a moment doubted that he would.

The bakery wasn't the only shop to have stayed open on the square. A few doors down was a clothes shop that, Aunt Zuzia told me, before the war had been full of elegant and expensive dresses.

'All the richest ladies from miles around used to buy clothes here,' Aunt Zuzia told me as we stood hand in hand peering through the window into the darkness beyond.

'Did you buy your clothes here?' I asked.

'Yes, I did, but I also had a dressmaker. Ah, those were the days.' Aunt Zuzia sighed and glanced at the shabby coat she was wearing over a shapeless brown skirt.

'I think you still look beautiful and smart,' I said, and Aunt Zuzia smiled.

'And over there,' she pointed to the furthest corner of the square, 'was a wonderful coffee shop. My friends and I used to meet there every morning at eleven for coffee and cakes, and a good gossip. It was a very smart place called Wedel's and the cakes and pastries they sold were wonderful. Their speciality was *millefeuille*—puff pastry layered with chocolate and a dark glossy icing over the top. They put a curly "W" on the top of each slice.'

'It must have been lovely. I've never tasted chocolate—is it sweet?'

'You tasted chocolate when you were younger,' Aunt Zuzia reminded me. 'I remember buying you lots. But of course you've forgotten. You were so

248

small. You'll taste chocolate again one day, when the war's over.'

'Everyone keeps promising me things when the war's over. I wish it would hurry up and *be* over.'

'We all wish the same,' Aunt Zuzia said.

We crossed over the square and I glimpsed a statue of a man with a moustache dressed in a long cape and high boots and standing high up on a block of stone.

'Who's that?' I asked.

'That was one of our great kings. He lived a long time ago when Poland was a rich and strong country. Ah, here's the shop I want. Come on, let's go in.' Aunt Zuzia pushed open the door and walked into a stationery shop. She greeted the shopkeeper warmly. He smiled and looking at me started to fumble around under the counter. After much searching the shopkeeper finally produced what Aunt Zuzia had asked for and placed it on the counter.

'These are for you,' she told me. 'They are dolls to cut out. And look, there are lots of clothes for them to wear when you have cut them out too. I'll teach you how to do it carefully. I tried to get a proper doll for you, but there aren't any. But these will be fun to dress up.' I looked at the dolls and their outfits in delight. 'Now we must go home and cook supper for your uncle.'

'I don't want to go home yet,' I said. 'Can't we see some more shops?'

'No, we must get back. It's going to get dark soon and we're not allowed to be out in the streets after dark. We might get arrested.'

Uncle Julek was in the kitchen when we got back and he was looking cross.

'Where have you been all this time? You know how dangerous it is to make yourself conspicuous.'

'I was only showing Renata the town. She's never seen shops before. She loves Mr Malewski's bread model and so we had to stop and look at that and I also managed to find some paper dolls for her to play with.'

'Sometimes I really believe you're going soft in the head,' he snarled. 'Fancy risking everything for the sake of amusing a child. She's going to have to learn that life isn't all a big game and everything geared towards her.'

'I think she learned that a very long time ago,' Aunt Zuzia said crossly. 'What she needs to learn now is that life is not always unhappy, loveless and dangerous and I mean to do my best to give her a little normality. You ought to be ashamed of your attitude to the child. It's you who's a big spoiled baby unable to cope with what's happened.'

Uncle Julek did not reply. He got up from the table and walked out of the room slamming the door hard behind him.

*   *   *

Quickly I came to understand that I could do no wrong in the eyes of Aunt Zuzia. She gave me the best bits of food, never scolded me, waited on me hand and foot and protected me from Uncle Julek's sharp tongue. I enjoyed it. But the more she did for me, the more I began to demand and the more Uncle Julek would look at me crossly and either leave the room to go and hide in his consulting room (a place I was never allowed to enter) or start to behave in a childish way that annoyed Aunt

250

Zuzia. I didn't like my uncle and was afraid of him so I enjoyed seeing my aunt get cross with him. Then he started to sulk whenever Aunt Zuzia fussed over me, fighting with me over second helpings, complaining to Aunt Zuzia that she was spoiling me. But I didn't care. I just loved the attention.

Aunt Zuzia was a wonderful cook and even without a lot of different ingredients she managed to make a meal taste lovely. She would make delicious soup with water and a few vegetables, and even without eggs, butter and much sugar she managed to bake cakes. She always let me lick the bowl and this made Uncle Julek angry. Like the baker, she never wasted anything but, unlike most people, we were never hungry. Barek, the only person to visit Aunt Zuzia and Uncle Julek other than the odd patient, said that my aunt could create a feast from an old piece of leather—or even a simple potato.

Aunt Zuzia and Uncle Julek were very private. They never went out unless it was to do some shopping or Uncle Julek was called to see a patient. So that meant that I didn't see many people either. Therefore I would look forward to the visits from Barek, who was a very old friend of my aunt and uncle. He told me that he was their family lawyer before the war but he wasn't a Jew so when Aunt Zuzia and Uncle Julek had to 'disappear' he had moved into their apartment to try and keep it safe. I grew very fond of Barek with his smiling eyes and sticky-up grey hair; he always had time for me. He sat me on his knee and told me stories about life before the war and I would bombard him with questions about my father, my mother and Marynia whom he had known well. He'd tell

251

me tales about their lives, what they were like and how they looked. I wanted to know everything. Although Barek was also fond of me and spent time telling stories and answering my questions, Uncle Julek didn't seem to mind. It was only Aunt Zuzia's fussing that irritated him, and he asked her over and over again to stop.

'I'm just trying to protect her,' Aunt Zuzia protested in a low voice, after they argued. 'She has had so much unhappiness and I want her to have a normal life.'

'This life is not normal and it is certainly not normal to spoil the child,' Uncle Julek replied. 'She is totally wrapped up in herself, can't you see what you're doing?'

'You have changed, Julek,' Aunt Zuzia said, 'ever since the boys died. There's nothing we can do. We can't bring them back. Let me take care of Renata as I want. I know life isn't normal but we have to do the best we can. I love having her here. It takes my mind off all that has happened.'

Uncle Julek harrumphed and left the room.

CHAPTER FOURTEEN

July 1944

Things had begun to change. Now when we went out, people were talking more, they were more lively, and sometimes even smiled at one another. I decided to ask Aunt Zuzia why.

'Has something happened?'

Aunt Zuzia didn't reply but looked at Uncle

252

Julek across the table.

'They say the Russians are coming,' he said.

'The *Russians*?' I said. 'Why are they coming?'

'To save us,' said Aunt Zuzia. Then Uncle Julek told her to be quiet and not say anything more about the Russians.

Then I heard different sounds. The distant hum of aeroplanes and then thunder.

'The bombing has started,' Uncle Julek said to Barek, who now visited us more often. Barek nodded and his mouth as well as his eyes smiled in reply.

Not long after that Barek arrived at the apartment much earlier than usual.

'What a day! What a day!' He was trembling all over and panting because he had run all the way up the stairs. 'I never thought I would live to see it for myself.' He grabbed Aunt Zuzia, twirled her round the kitchen and hugged her, then he slapped Uncle Julek on the back and lifted me into the air. Tears began running down his cheeks.

'Renata has to be witness to this,' he cried. 'She is the next generation and it's her generation and the generations that follow that will want to know the truth. Let's take her and show her history in the making.'

'Barek, no,' said Aunt Zuzia. 'She's much too young and completely unused to hordes of people. She will be so frightened by the noise and the crowds and besides, she won't understand what is going on. It might even reawaken memories that are best forgotten and what if we lost her?'

'Barek's right,' Uncle Julek interrupted. 'This is a momentous occasion. Let him take her, if she wants to go. No harm can come to her. No one will take

253

any notice of her. She will be one face in a sea of people. Let her go and experience this for herself.'

So not understanding what was happening, I went out into the street with Barek, perched high on his shoulders with a marvellous view over the heads of everyone heading in the same direction. People were coming out of every house into the morning sun. I had never seen a place so alive, so full of people, old and young, children too. There was noise and laughter and then singing and shouting. People shook hands and hugged each other. A man came forward and he and Barek shook hands with great force.

'Who was that?' I asked Barek as the man turned away towards someone else.

'I have no idea,' Barek laughed as we were swept forward into the market square.

From high up on Barek's shoulders I looked around for the German soldiers in their grey-green uniform with their guns and dogs but I couldn't see a single one. Where were they? I couldn't see any of the horrible red swastikas in the windows or hanging from flagpoles. Instead people were waving a different red flag with a yellow hammer and curly moon thing and a star above. Barek pointed and laughed.

'That's a Russian flag,' he shouted and stamped on the tattered remains of a swastika that had been pulled from a window and trampled underfoot. 'The Russians are here.'

And in that moment, as if someone had waved a wand, the crowd stopped singing, shouting and hugging and stood still and silent. Then, a huge cheer began on one side of the square and rolled like a wave across the crowd, bounced off the buildings and away up the streets to those people standing at the windows who hadn't been brave enough to come out into the sunshine. Tears were mixed with happiness as the first of the Russians entered the square.

From this high up I could see the Russian soldiers. I couldn't believe my eyes. German soldiers were always so smart and neat. These Russians were shabby, tired and had beards. Their uniforms were strange—they wore round fur-lined caps with flaps over their ears and long green coats pulled in at the waist, even though it was summertime. They weren't marching like the Germans with their straight legs high in the air but in a messy line. But what surprised me more than anything was their faces—they were round and happy and smiling. Not a bit like the cold tight faces of the Germans.

As the Russian soldiers marched into the square they waved, then reached in their pockets and threw little packets at the crowd. People fought to catch them. I leaned down and shouted in Barek's ear, 'What are they throwing?'

'Chocolate!'

'I want some, too,' I shouted, stretching out my arms skywards.

None came my way.

Instead I watched the Russian soldiers march round the square in a great never-ending line with boots stamping all together. On and on they came, hundreds of them all smiling and throwing their little packets of chocolate. And then, when I thought that the line would never cease, came some strange animals I had never seen before except in one of the books I had borrowed from the library.

255

There was no mistaking what these animals were. They really were camels! They had long, long legs, knobbly knees and huge humps, and they rolled slowly through the market square, with their large eyes that looked in all directions and haughty, toothy smiles. They carried enormous packs on their backs and were led on long ropes by soldiers. The book said that camels lived in the desert, in faraway magical places like Egypt and Arabia. Perhaps the Russians had borrowed them? Seeing these animals here in Przemyśl made me realise that Barek was right and something great must be happening.

And then they were gone—the soldiers, the camels, the smiles and, worst of all, the chocolate. As the noise faded and the people started to go home, I felt very tired. I was also very upset that no chocolate had fallen into my hands. I caught sight of a man who had not yet unwrapped his bar. He looked up at me perched on the top of Barek's shoulders and then broke his bar in two. With a smile and a wink, he patted my leg and handed me one half.

Delighted, I took it from him, smiling to say thank you. I couldn't wait to taste it. I unwrapped it and bit into it gently. As the dark, sweet smoothness melted on my tongue, my taste buds came alive with the sensational flavour. Barek laughed at my astonishment and slowly we made our way home.

'That was a morning none of us will forget,' Barek said later as we drank coffee in the kitchen. 'You will tell your children and grandchildren about this wonderful day, Renata.'

'I will tell them about the camels and the chocolate,' I said. I knew exactly what had been

256

important about the morning even if Barek didn't.

*   *   *

After the Russian soldiers—people called them our saviours—came to Przemyśl, the whole town began to relax.

'We feel safer now the Germans have gone,' Aunt Zuzia explained.

Even Aunt Zuzia started to relax; she began to let me go downstairs to the library alone. All I had to do was go down the three flights of stairs, out through the front door, turn left and in through the door to the library. It wasn't very far but it made me feel grown-up and I enjoyed looking for books and talking to the librarian. She had read many of the books in the library too and we had long conversations about the books I'd read and then she would tell me the titles of others that she thought I would enjoy, steering me away from those that, according to her, were not right for my age by gently taking one out of my hands and replacing it with another.

'Are the Russians going to stay?' I asked.

'For a while, I think,' Aunt Zuzia replied. 'We don't want the Nazis coming back, do we?'

They did stay, some at least, but these soldiers were very different from the German ones. They were kind to children and had supplies of sweets and chocolates to give away.

Groups of women were meeting and talking on the street corners again.

'Just like before the war,' said Aunt Zuzia, 'even though there's still nowhere to meet for coffee and cakes.'

257

'And not enough food,' Uncle Julek sniffed.

Food was still rationed and everyone hung on to what they had—no one shared anything.

For a while after the Russian soldiers marched into Przemyśl everyone only said nice things about them. But then things changed again.

'The Russians drink too much, just like some of the Poles,' Uncle Julek complained. 'The Poles always come off worse.'

From my bed, I could hear slurry voices late at night in the street below, and often they were arguing. Fights started, sometimes ending in bloodshed, and Uncle Julek was called on once or twice to help. I could tell he wasn't happy about going.

One morning my aunt and I had got up early to make sure we reached the bakery queue before it was too long. We had bought our loaf and crossed back across the square towards home, enjoying the mid-morning sun on our faces. By the time we reached the apartment building my aunt was tired. We stopped for a moment on the front step for her to catch her breath and find her keys. Just then, from around the corner, stumbled a Russian soldier. He didn't look very well. His uniform was messy and dusty and his eyes were droopy and puffy. He didn't seem able to see anything: he kept bumping into things that weren't even in his path.

'Renata, come here,' called my aunt. 'He's drunk, let's get inside, quick.'

But the soldier had already caught sight of us and began shouting in Russian. We couldn't understand what he was saying and tried to ignore him. Aunt Zuzia dropped her keys. I watched her stoop to pick them up, then she dropped them again.

By now the Russian was close enough to be able to reach out and touch my curls. I froze as he started stroking my hair, murmuring in a soft voice. His voice cracked and he suddenly became tearful.

My aunt dropped her shopping and shouted, 'Leave her alone. Go away.' She waved her hands to shoo him away as if he were a fly.

The man looked at her and grinned, his wide yellow teeth showing through his thick lips—he seemed to think all her shouting and waving was very funny. He said something in Russian and then grabbed hold of my hand, pulling me towards him.

Aunt Zuzia panicked.

'Let her go! Let her go!' she screamed. 'Help, someone, anyone, help—'

But the soldier ignored her. As Aunt Zuzia continued to shout and scream, he calmly sat down on the steps to the house and sat me on his knee. He put his hand in his pocket and pulled out a packet. I recognised the colours of the wrapper and the strange gold letters and beamed in delight. He unwrapped the bar and handed it, the whole thing, over to me. Without a moment's hesitation I took it and bit into the chocolate. Oh was it glorious. It was even better than last time.

'Drop that chocolate! Renata, drop it on the floor at once! It's poisoned,' my aunt shouted and began hitting the man with her fists.

The soldier didn't understand, but his face suddenly lost its smile and he sneered at her. Putting me down on the step, he stood up and pushed me behind him. Reaching inside his overcoat, he took out a pistol and pointed it at Aunt Zuzia. With his other hand he began waving her away. He held the pistol at arm's length and beckoned towards the front door with it. My poor aunt had no choice but to open the door of the building and stumble inside, with tears streaming down her face.

I was so busy eating the chocolate that I didn't take much notice of what was happening. The soldier was my friend. He had given me chocolate. He was a very kind man and I couldn't understand why my aunt was making such a fuss. Of course the chocolate wasn't poisoned. The Russian, smiling at me and stroking my hair, pulled out *another* bar of chocolate from his pocket. I smiled at him and began to work my way through the second one.

When it became obvious my aunt wasn't coming out of the apartment building, he sank back down on the step and pulled me onto his lap again. He sighed and then began searching in his breast pocket. This time he produced some crumpled photographs and with one large, dirty hand flattened them on his knee so that I could see. They were of two children, a girl about my age with long blonde plaits and a round, smiling face and a very small boy with dark hair, holding a man's hand.

'*Moi dzieci*—my children,' the soldier said in very bad Polish.

'I have a father too,' I told him.

'*Tak, tak,*' he said, pulling out more chocolate.

Then all of a sudden he stood up, patted me on the head and, handing me the final bar, opened the front door and pushed me inside. The door swung shut behind me and I slowly climbed the steps, taking my time so that I could finish the chocolate before I reached the third floor. I was frightened that Aunt Zuzia would snatch it away from me. When I entered the apartment I could hear Aunt

Zuzia's anguished sobs coming from inside.

'Oh Julek, he has a pistol. Renata is still out there. What are we going to do? He might kill her.'

I hesitated and then pushed the kitchen door open and walked in. Uncle Julek was standing with his arms around Aunt Zuzia trying to calm her down.

'You are safe. Thank God,' she cried when she saw me.

She rushed over, hugged me, covering me with kisses. The concern I had seen on Uncle Julek's face disappeared and was replaced by his usual scowl.

'I told you you were making a fuss about nothing. Those pigs like small children too much to hurt them. That's about the only thing in their favour. Otherwise they're no better than the Nazis.'

'He was very nice,' I said. 'He gave me his chocolate and showed me photographs of his children. He has a boy and a girl. The girl has long plaits. I would like plaits like that too.'

*　　　*　　　*

As time passed I thought less and less about Aunt Adela and Zazula, Jorik and Jan. I was happy living with Aunt Zuzia and Uncle Julek. Sometimes after I'd been tucked up in bed, I would hear my aunt and uncle arguing but I couldn't make out what they were squabbling about. Sometimes I heard my name but I knew Aunt Zuzia would never want me to leave so I had nothing to worry about. But I also knew that she couldn't understand why Uncle Julek didn't love me like she did. But since the Russians had arrived Uncle Julek was less grumpy and was

261

being more friendly towards me, even playing cards and helping me with my reading and explaining the words I didn't understand. I began to enjoy these times together and didn't make my aunt choose between us so often.

Sometimes we got a letter from Božena, but more often we got one from Frederika. When a letter arrived, Aunt Zuzia would sit at the kitchen table and read it aloud. The letters always said that she was well, and so were her parents, and they all sent their love with special love and kisses for me. She was coming to see us just as soon as her work allowed but in the meantime she enclosed a little money to help with my keep. Aunt Zuzia always handed the money to Uncle Julek, who usually made some comment about it not being enough, which I thought was most ungrateful.

One day Barek appeared in the doorway of the kitchen while I was still eating my breakfast.

'Renata, I have asked your aunt if I can take you along to see a very important man who is visiting Przemyśl today,' he announced. 'It is another historic event. Zuzia has agreed so when you're finished we can go.'

We left the apartment as soon as I had swallowed my last mouthful of bread and joined the people making their way to the market square. The *Rynek* was not as crowded as the day the Russians arrived but it was still busy. Barek swung me up on to his shoulders and from there I could see a big, tall man wearing a peaked cap and military uniform standing at the base of a column. Music was playing and as he saluted, the people started to clap and cheer. I was disappointed. Was this it? I'd expected to see long lines of soldiers, hear the roar of the crowd and catch pretty packets of chocolate thrown into the crowd. But here we were watching just one man in uniform who wasn't as well dressed as the Nazis, and didn't look as friendly as the Russians.

'Remember that man,' Barek called up to me. 'Marshal Tito of Yugoslavia. He is very important. One day he will be famous and you will be able to tell your children and grandchildren you saw him.'

I had no idea who Marshal Tito was but, as I looked at him, I knew that I would not forget this dark-haired, tall man with his shiny uniform.

CHAPTER FIFTEEN

September 1944

One Saturday morning uncle Julek asked me if I wanted to accompany him on his rounds.

'Yes please,' I replied. I was always happy to be out in the fresh air and feel the warmth of the sun's rays. 'Are we going in a *fiacre*?'

I could never refuse the chance to sit in an open-topped carriage behind a trotting horse, listening to the clippety-clop of hooves on the paved streets, waving at people and feeling like a real princess from a fairy tale being driven to a magic kingdom. I loved it when children waved back at me.

'I need to go to the Zimińskis who live on the outskirts of town—it's about an hour's drive away. They are sending a *fiacre* for me. So if you want to come, get your coat. I can't keep the driver waiting.'

'Isn't it too cold for her to be sitting about

waiting for you?' Aunt Zuzia asked, wrapping me in one shawl after another until I looked just like the Egyptian mummy from a book I had just borrowed from the library. 'She might catch a cold or pneumonia.'

'Rubbish,' he replied testily. 'It will do the girl good to get some fresh air and get away from your ridiculous molly-coddling. How do you think she survived those years when you weren't there to wrap her up in cotton wool? She's as tough as old boots.'

That made me smile, but I didn't let Uncle Julek or Aunt Zuzia see. I didn't mind waiting in the *fiacre* while Uncle Julek went to see his patients. I had made friends with one of the drivers who always let me climb over the box and sit beside him. He told me all about his grandchildren and the old days before the war.

As soon as our carriage turned the corner and I could no longer see my waving aunt, I began to peel off the shawls, flinging them on the seat beside me. Uncle Julek watched but made no comment.

Uncle Julek began pointing out interesting parts of Przemyśl; some were huge, empty spaces but others still had the piles of rubble from the buildings that had been bombed. He showed me where the synagogue used to stand and I remembered how upset Mamusia and Babcia were when it was destroyed although I still couldn't really understand why.

'There,' Uncle Julek waved at a pile of rubble, 'was once a large building that . . .' On our journeys he liked to tell me what each building had been used for, who had owned it and all about the people who had once worked in it.

He was in a good mood that day, telling me stories about patients who had lived in the houses and about his friends, many of whom were now dead. He pointed out the hospital where his older son, Fredzio, had been a doctor before he moved to Warsaw.

'Do you remember Fredzio and Jerzyk?'

'I remember Cousin Fredzio,' I said. 'He was very tall.' I thought hard until I could see him clearly, his face close to mine. 'I remember being in a room with him once. He was lying down and I was standing next to him. I remember asking him how old he was and he said that he was twenty-eight and I said, "One day I will catch up with you and then I will be older than you." '

'And so you will,' said Uncle Julek quietly. 'He's not getting any older now.' He patted my hand. 'Both Fredzio and Jerzyk were lovely young men.' Uncle Julek stopped and when I glanced up at him I noticed a tear rolling down his cheek.

I stared at it in surprise and watched it run to the tip of his nose before he brushed it away quickly with his handkerchief. I put out my hand and took hold of his clasped firmly round his handkerchief. I felt the loose skin and the raised-up veins. I realised for the first time that he was an old man and gave his hand a squeeze. He turned his head away but kept his hand in mine. In that moment, I suddenly felt great sadness for him. I thought of Mamusia and I understood how he was feeling.

When we arrived at Mr and Mrs Ziminski's apartment Uncle Julek said, 'I may be quite a long time in there, so you must be patient. The driver will look after you.'

The driver smiled. 'She's welcome to join me up

here.'

The driver jumped down and, lifting me out of the *fiacre*, hoisted me up high and put me on the seat beside his own.

'Be careful with her,' Uncle Julek said.

'Don't worry, sir, I won't let her come to any harm,' he said. 'We have little ones at home too.'

He climbed back up beside me and handed me the reins. We sat there for a while whilst I pretended to be driving the carriage until he said, 'How about going for a little drive round the block? You can hold the reins.'

'Really?' I couldn't believe it. 'I would love to.'

He clicked his tongue and the horse set off at a walking pace. I felt very proud, sitting so high and holding the reins of such a beautiful horse.

'Pull on the right rein,' the driver said. 'Gently now.'

To my delight the horse responded and stepped to the right and around the corner. We went all the way round the block and on the way back the driver taught me how to make the horse trot, clasping his large, rough hands over mine and showing me what to do. We were going so fast and I was so high up. I could see the shiny cobbles on the street winking at me in the sunlight and I could feel the breeze in my hair. I felt free and wanted to go faster.

'Sorry,' the driver said, 'but the poor old fellow can't go any faster on these streets and we don't want him slipping and breaking a leg now, do we?'

We trotted on until we pulled up outside the house again. I felt so pleased with myself.

'Before the war I was a chauffeur to the couple your uncle is visiting right now. I wore a long coat, long gloves, hat and goggles. They had a big black car with shining brass lamps, a hood and leather seats, and I was in charge of it. I drove them everywhere they wanted to go and kept it clean and oiled.' His eyes shone with pride as he spoke.

Although I had seen soldiers' tanks and lorries, I'd never seen a motor car like that. The driver told me how he used to spend hours polishing the outside of the car to make it so shiny that you could see your reflection in it and then how he had to crank up a handle at the front to get the engine going. He told me that, after he got used to the smell from the engine, riding in a motor car was very exciting.

'Why don't you drive their car now?'

'There's no petrol. They still have the car but it's in a shed in the country. Without fuel, it's useless. But who knows, maybe one day when things improve it will come into its own again. Besides, this old fellow and I are old friends, aren't we?' He bent forward and patted the horse's rump affectionately.

'I'd love to see it,' I said.

'Maybe one day you will.'

I wanted to stay and talk to the driver for hours, but my uncle appeared.

'Renata, Mr and Mrs Zimiński would like to meet you,' he said. 'Are you presentable?' I showed him my hands. 'Yes, you'll do.'

The driver lifted me down and gave me a wink.

'They're lovely people,' he said. 'It's such a shame their little girl died.'

I looked up at him quickly wondering if I had heard him correctly but he had already turned back to his horse.

Mrs Zimińska was waiting in the open door of

267

her apartment on the top floor. She was tall and pretty with wavy blonde hair and big blue eyes that looked sad even though she was smiling when we came out of the lift. She bent down and kissed me.

'Lovely to meet you, darling,' she said. 'Come in and meet my husband. He is looking forward to seeing you. Your uncle has told us so much about you and what a good girl you are and what a hard time you have had and how brave you've been.'

I was surprised that my uncle had said nice things about me. I thought he thought that I was badly behaved and a nuisance.

Mrs Zimińska led us into a room full of lovely carved furniture. There was a man sitting in a large chair by the window. He had a rug over his knees and he didn't get up to greet us. Instead he stretched out his arms and smiled.

'Hello, Renata,' he said. 'We are so pleased to meet you at last. Your uncle has talked about you.'

I walked up to him and shyly shook hands.

'You are happy living with your uncle and aunt?' Mr Zimiński asked.

'Yes, thank you.'

'Do you miss your mother very much?'

'Only sometimes. But I'm not an orphan. I have a father who will come back when he's stopped fighting for Poland.' Then I remembered. 'He isn't fighting because he is a doctor. Doctors don't fight, they help ill people to get better.'

'What would you say if I told you that I knew your father and your mother too?'

'Did you?' I forgot to be shy. 'What were they like? Were they young like you?'

268

'Haven't you got any photos?' Mr Zimiński asked.

'No, but I wish I had.'

'Kalinka,' the man turned to his wife, 'fetch the red album from the cupboard in the study, would you?' Mr Zimiński looked at me. 'I'm not sitting here ordering my wife around because I'm lazy. I am stuck in this chair because my legs don't work any more. I'm a cripple.'

'Oh how awful.'

'Don't feel sorry for me. I am alive and your uncle looks after me wonderfully. He is the best doctor in the whole of Poland and we, like so many others, owe him a great deal. Has he told you about the orphan children?'

I shook my head. I had heard Aunt Zuzia mention the orphans to Bożena when I arrived but I hadn't thought that he was able to help them.

'Well, perhaps he will tell you one day,' Mr Zimiński added, looking at Uncle Julek who was smiling but didn't say anything. I thought that I would ask Aunt Zuzia about this when we got home. After a minute or two, Mrs Zimińska returned holding a large red book that she carefully placed on her husband's knees. It was a photograph album full of yellowing photos carefully fixed into see-through corners that were stuck onto the thick black paper. He turned over the pages.

'Here it is,' he said, very pleased. 'I knew we had one. Look, Renata, here's your mother.'

I saw the smiling face of a young lady who looked to me like a complete stranger. She had a round face and a lovely smile and a very straight nose. She had her hair swept sideways and was sitting, half turned towards the camera, with a patterned shawl draped around her shoulders. I looked closer and a strange feeling came over me. This was a picture of my mother and yet I couldn't remember her looking like that at all.

'Is this really a picture of my Mamusia?' I asked. 'I can't remember her looking like that. I remember her being very thin.'

Suddenly I felt terribly sad and tears welled up in my eyes. Why did I have to be Jewish and hated? If my parents had been Catholic, none of this would have happened. Life just wasn't fair. At that moment I hated being Jewish more than anything in the world. It didn't matter what I did—I would always be different.

'Your mother was such a lovely person.' Mr Ziminski tried to comfort me. 'I knew her well and I'll tell you a little secret.' He lowered his voice. 'When I was a very young man and she was a very young woman, long before she met your father and I met Kalinka, we fell in love. I had this photo taken of her. So Tosia is much younger in this photo than the mother you remember.'

I stared at him in surprise.

'But how could you have been in love with her?'

'We lived in the same town. We went to the same university and knew the same people.'

'But, but she was Jewish.'

'Renata, come here.' Mr Ziminski held out his arms and as I approached he leaned forward and drew me to him in a bear-like hug. 'Listen, my darling, you are becoming a big girl and you must remember what I'm going to say to you because it's the truth and very important. You must not grow up believing that it is wrong to be Jewish and that everyone hates Jews. Many people like me hate the

270

Nazis for what they did to the Jews. Hitler is an evil man and if there is any justice in this world he will get his comeuppance one of these days.'

'You are not alone in losing someone you loved.' Uncle Julek's voice came to us from where he was standing by the window. It croaked and he gave a little cough. 'Everyone has lost someone dear to them. Remember your aunt and I lost our two sons whom we loved very much. We understand how you feel, Renata. But remember too that we are blessed because we have you and you have us.'

Uncle Julek had surprised me for the second time that day and I knew that all the sadness I was feeling for my mother he was feeling for Fredzio and Jerzyk. I went over to my uncle, stood on tiptoe and gave him a kiss on the cheek. He grunted and turned away, but still half-turned towards the window he stretched out his hand behind him and gently patted my cheek.

'Renata, I want you to come with me,' Mrs Zimińska said. 'There are some things we would like to give you. They belonged to Maria, our daughter, who would have been the same age as you.'

'What happened to Maria?' I asked, remembering what the driver had said.

'She died when our house was bombed. She was killed when my husband was left crippled.'

'Oh, how dreadful,' I whispered. 'My cousin Zazula was shot in the street by Nazis and so was my aunt. Zazula was four years older than me and we used to play together all the time. I'm really sorry about Maria. Have you got a picture of her?'

Mrs Zimińska pointed to a photograph on the mantelpiece in which a little girl with dark curly hair was smiling. She was holding a doll dressed in a dark flowery dress and a light-coloured apron. She looked very happy.

'We like to remember her like that,' her mother said. 'Come with me to her room. There are some toys I am sure she would have been happy to pass on to you to enjoy. You can have them if you want. I know you will look after them and sometimes think of our Maria.'

She led me down the corridor and opened a door at the far end. As the door swung open I gazed at Maria's own fairyland. It was a beautiful pink room with a lacy bed; a bookcase full of books, a huge doll's house and over by the window a wonderful rocking horse with flared nostrils and a long golden mane.

I gasped with delight.

'We thought you might like to have the rocking horse and some of the books to take home, and you can come here as often as you like to play with the doll's house and read the rest of the books. Would you like that?'

I couldn't speak. I nodded my head up and down.

Mrs Zimińska smiled and kissed me again.

'That's settled then. Now come and have some cake. I baked it especially for you. You do like chocolate, don't you?'

CHAPTER SIXTEEN
September 1944–1945

'Now that we're told the war is nearly over, and the schools have reopened,' Uncle Julek said one morning, 'the sooner we enrol that child the better.'

For once Aunt Zuzia agreed with him. 'Children have missed out on so much education,' she said, 'and now everyone is trying to get their children into school. I will write to the headmistress of the Roman Catholic School and ask whether she can take you. It's always had such a good reputation and I am sure you will do well there.'

A few days later Aunt Zuzia came into the kitchen holding a letter. 'Read it aloud,' Uncle Julek and I said at the same time. He looked at me and we laughed.

'*Dear Mrs Zielińska,*' my aunt read. '*It is after a great deal of thought and consideration that I have decided to grant your request for your great-niece Renata to attend the school as a full-time day pupil. This was not an easy decision given that your great-niece is not Roman Catholic but of the Protestant faith—*'

'But, Aunt Zuzia, I'm not a Protestant,' I cried out. 'What is she talking about?'

'Renata,' replied Aunt Zuzia, 'do you think I would say I wanted my great-niece who is a Jewess to attend a Roman Catholic school? Think, my darling. And if I were to lie and say you were a Roman Catholic then they would wonder why you didn't know all the rituals and prayers and things

273

like that. No, Uncle Julek and I thought it best to say you were a Protestant so that at least you had a good chance of getting in and at the same time it would be an excuse for not knowing anything about Roman Catholicism. Let's see what else the headmistress says.

'*After consultation with the Board members we have decided that we can offer Renata a place on the condition that she attends, twice weekly, religious instruction in addition to daily morning prayer and, in time, seriously considers adopting the Catholic faith. I look forward to meeting you both on the first day of the new term. Yours sincerely, Mrs Malinowska, Headmistress*.

'That is wonderful news,' exclaimed Aunt Zuzia. 'Julek, aren't you pleased?'

Uncle Julek was looking worried.

'You must never, ever, tell anyone that you come from a Jewish background,' he said after reading the letter for himself. 'We can't take the risk. There is still so much ill-feeling, and I don't trust anyone.'

'And you mustn't say that your mother and grandmother were taken away by the Nazis,' Aunt Zuzia added. 'It's our secret and no one else must know.'

'Can I tell them that I'm not an orphan and that Tatuś is abroad with the Polish Army?' I asked.

'Yes, you can tell them that,' Uncle Julek said, 'but if anyone asks about your mother, you must say that she died. No more than that. Do *not* draw attention to yourself. Do you understand?'

I understood and I didn't mind one bit. My dearest wish had been granted. I was at last going to go to school. I would learn to read more new words and write. I was so excited. Then I thought

274

of Zazula and how much she had loved going to school and suddenly I felt very sad that she was no longer here and that we weren't going to be going to school together.

* * *

My first day at school arrived. I found myself outside a square grey building with three rows of windows and a large front door. Beside the front door was a sign painted in black on a white board: *Szkola prywatna dla Dziewczynek*.

'*Private School for Girls*' I read aloud. I knew at once that I would love this school. A girl, a few years older than me with her hair scraped back from her face and wearing a white apron over her dress, smiled at us as we stood in the entrance hall. Aunt Zuzia asked her where the Headmistress's office was and she showed us the way.

Mrs Malinowska was sitting behind a large desk reading through some papers. Her dark hair was swept up into a coil fastened with a huge comb. Without smiling, she offered three fingers in greeting to my aunt and nodded at me.

'Your aunt has informed me that you can read, Renata,' she said. 'That is good. Can you tell me what you have read this week?'

'I've read three books this week,' I replied proudly.

'Really? What were the titles?'

'*David Copperfield*, for the third time. *The Water-Babies* and . . .'

'But surely you haven't read all these in a week?' Mrs Malinowska looked surprised. 'They are difficult books and very grown-up for you.'

'No. Really, I loved them. I've also read—'

'In future,' Mrs Malinowska interrupted, 'you will read what your teacher recommends. We can't have you reading unsuitable books.'

'My husband,' Aunt Zuzia interrupted, 'feels that she will only understand what she is ready for and the rest won't do her any harm.'

Mrs Malinowska stared at Aunt Zuzia.

'Mrs Zielińska, we maintain a very high standard here and monitor our girls most carefully. We are already regaining the high reputation we had built up before this unfortunate war. You can rest assured that Renata will be in very experienced hands. I have put her in the second class where she will be fortunate enough to be under the tutelage of Mrs Dabrowska, a highly competent and experienced teacher.'

'Thank you,' Aunt Zuzia murmured. 'You are very kind. We really are most grateful.'

'Not at all.' Mrs Malinowska nodded her head as she pressed a shiny bell button set in the wall behind her desk.

'Now, Renata,' she said, turning back to us, 'one of your classmates will be along in a moment to take you to meet your new class and your teacher. I am sure you will settle in very quickly. But I see you haven't got an apron. All our pupils wear aprons, and your aunt will get you one for tomorrow, but in the meantime, and for one day only, you can borrow this one.'

She produced a folded white apron out of a drawer of her desk and helped me into it.

'There now,' she said, 'you will look the same as the others and feel more comfortable.'

'Thank you,' I breathed. I felt so excited in

my clean white apron and couldn't wait to start learning.

There was a gentle tap on the door.

'Come in,' Mrs Malinowska called.

A girl about the same age as me with the most beautiful shiny brown hair drawn back into a thick plait came in and smiled at me. She was dainty and the frilly apron she wore made her look like a girl that I'd seen in a picture book. I think I'm going to like her, I thought. I hope she will want to be my friend.

'This is Kasia,' Mrs Malinowska said. 'Kasia, this is Renata. I have asked Kasia to look after you because apparently you live very near each other, on the same street in fact, and I thought you might like to walk to school and back together.'

'Oh no,' Aunt Zuzia said, a bit shocked. 'There's no need, really, I will bring and collect Renata.'

'We encourage our girls to be independent,' Mrs Malinowska responded firmly. 'We are living in a very different world where it is important to be self-sufficient. I am sure that Kasia will be only too pleased to bring Renata home this afternoon.'

Kasia nodded.

Mrs Malinowska then turned to us. 'Now off you go to class, girls.'

Without remembering to say goodbye to Aunt Zuzia, I followed my new friend out into the corridor.

'I live at Number 16, Kolejowa Street. We can play together if you like. Where do you live?' Kasia asked, as we made our way quickly towards our classroom.

'Number 2. You can come and play with my dolls,' I said. 'I'm sure my aunt won't mind.'

'Nor will my mother. Why do you live with your aunt? Where is your mother?'

'She's dead, I think.'

'What a funny thing to say. Don't you know?'

'Yes I do know, but my father will be back one of these days.'

We had now reached the door of our classroom. Kasia led the way and twenty pairs of eyes turned and stared at me. I suddenly felt very shy.

'Hello, Renata. Welcome to Class 2. We are very pleased that you have joined us,' the teacher said, and smiled. 'I am Mrs Dabrowska and, girls, this is Renata who will be in our class as from today. I know you will make her very welcome.'

I smiled shyly and one or two of the girls smiled, but the rest just stared. I was much blonder than anybody else in the room and my hair, having grown quite long since I had left the orphanage, was tightly plaited like everyone else's, but I could feel the unruly curls already beginning to escape around my face. I was glad that I was wearing the borrowed apron because it helped to make me look like all the others.

'Renata, sit next to Kasia,' Mrs Dabrowska was saying. 'We are learning the alphabet at the moment,' and as we took our seats she turned to a girl in the front row.

'Iwona, will you explain to Renata what the alphabet is and why we have to learn it by heart.'

The girl obediently stood up but before she could open her mouth I stood up and said, 'But I already know the alphabet by heart. It's the letters that words are made up of and we have to know it so we can read. And I can read already.'

A little giggle went round the class. Mrs

278

Dabrowska glared and silence fell.

'So you can read?' Her voice was icy. 'And who taught you to read?'

'A lady called Jadwiga. She was a teacher.'

'Really. I hope she didn't teach you incorrectly. Reading is difficult to master and must be taught properly. So, tell me, Renata, what exactly can you read?'

'Anything.' I was so excited to be in a classroom and desperately wanted to impress my teacher. 'I belong to a library and the librarian says that she will soon run out of books for me and I will have to start reading them all over again. But I don't mind at all. I just *love* books. Don't you?'

The look on Mrs Dabrowska's face made me stop. She held up her hand.

'Little girls who show off,' she said, 'come to a sticky end.'

All the children in the room giggled and this time the teacher didn't try to stop them.

'I'm *not* showing off. I *can* read. I've just read *Oliver Twist* by Charles Dickens again. It's an English book but it's been translated into Polish. It's really sad about a little orphan boy called Oliver who . . .' I could feel my cheeks getting hot.

'Sit down and be quiet!' she ordered me.

Finally I understood. She opened her briefcase and pulled out a newspaper, and brought it over to me.

'Read us the first paragraph on the right,' she said, looking round the class with a big smile, 'so that we can all hear for ourselves how well you read. Unless of course you would prefer to stop this silly game right now.' She raised an eyebrow. 'You know as well as I do that little girls of your age cannot read, but they *are* old enough to know that it is wrong to tell lies.'

What a funny woman, I thought. She thinks I'm telling lies. No wonder she's cross. So I looked at the paper and began to read in a loud clear voice the paragraph Mrs Dabrowska had indicated. It was a report of a fight between a Pole and a Russian, both drunk. The Russian had pulled out a knife, but the Pole was strong and had killed the Russian with his bare hands. He was now in prison awaiting trial for murder.

Mrs Dabrowska came and looked over my shoulder as I read.

'Now read this,' she said, pointing to another part of the page. I did as I was told.

'So, you really can read,' she exclaimed, and the whole class began to clap.

'Quiet!' she shouted. 'I told you to sit down, Renata. I apologise for not believing you. Right, everyone. Silence. It's time for our history lesson. Now, Iwona, who was the first King of Poland?'

'You really can read,' Kasia whispered, 'that's amazing.'

It wasn't just Kasia who was impressed. Some of the other girls clustered round me at break time asking questions. I remembered what Uncle Julek and Aunt Zuzia had told me. I didn't mention my family but talked about books and how much I enjoyed stories, and I began to tell them the stories I had read. Every break time after that a huddle of girls would gather round me, their eyes wide, always wanting to hear more. I, of course, was only too pleased to tell them what I had read but I always stopped at the exciting bits.

'You will have to wait,' I would say. 'I will tell

you what happens next time.'

Learning wasn't what I'd expected. During the hours spent alone in Jadwiga's cottage or lying on my bed with the library books in my bedroom at Aunt Zuzia's, I'd wonder about the words I was reading. I'd ask Aunt Zuzia what the words meant and she would offer several more in return. I thought about the meaning of the words and how words and their meanings overlapped. Then I'd consider the meaning of the sentences and how, if I changed one word, the meaning would change. Stories became stories within stories. I took apart everything I read.

I thought that school would be the same. But it wasn't. The teacher stood in front of the class and talked to us and we sat and listened. She wrote on the board and sometimes we copied down what she had written into our exercise books. We kept our handwriting small so we didn't use up too much paper. And we weren't allowed to say anything. Then Mrs Dabrowska made us repeat our lesson, chanting it back like a song without a chorus, over and over again until we knew it off by heart and could repeat it without a single mistake. We were like parrots. Ever since I had left my home, I had been remembering things in my mind by repeating them over and over again so I was very good at learning this way.

Not everyone was impressed, though. Soon I began to hear the whispers. They watched as I walked towards them and sniggered after I'd passed by. I learned to take a deep breath and put my nose in the air and hope no one noticed how red my cheeks were. The more they sniggered behind their hands, the more exciting I made my stories—just to annoy them.

'She thinks she knows it all,' I heard one girl say.

'She's so stuck up,' said another, 'with all her stories and showing off that she can repeat everything without making a mistake.'

'She's no better than the rest of us, but she thinks she is,' complained a third.

Then I began to worry that I had drawn attention to myself and Uncle Julek and Aunt Zuzia would be cross with me, and one day even Kasia was unusually quiet as we walked home.

'What's the matter?' I asked, trying to link arms with my friend.

She pushed me roughly away.

'Nothing's the matter,' Kasia snorted.

'Yes there is. Why are you angry with me?'

'I'm not. Only you're a show-off. They're right.'

'I'm not a show-off. They are only jealous because I'm cleverer than them.'

'There you go again. You're showing off now.'

I tried to change the subject, desperate for things to return to normal.

'Come home with me and see if Aunt Zuzia has made anything nice for us to eat,' I suggested.

Kasia relented and was about to run off up the street ahead of me to ask her mother when I grabbed her by the arm.

'You say I show off, but you're always showing off that you have a mother when you know I haven't. So that makes us the same. You're just as bad as me.'

Kasia stopped and turned round to look at me.

'Oh Renata, I'm sorry. I never thought of that. I don't *mean* to keep reminding you about your mother.'

'And I don't *mean* to be a show-off,' I said. 'It's just that I find it easy and I don't know why no one else does.' I looked down at my feet.

'It's just that we try so hard to learn everything off by heart and it seems so unfair.'

'It seems so unfair that all of you have mothers and mine's dead,' I said.

'I wish you had one too,' said Kasia, 'but your aunt's ever so nice and one day your father *will* turn up. Come on, let's not quarrel—you're my best friend.'

'And so are you,' I said, and arm in arm we skipped happily up the street, our argument forgotten.

*   *   *

'What did you learn at school today?' asked Uncle Julek each day as I came through the front door.

'Today I learned that Jesus loves everyone,' I said one afternoon. 'If Jesus loves everyone then he must be such a kind person. I don't think I could love *everyone*. Could you love everyone?'

'Definitely not,' Uncle Julek replied. 'Ridiculous thing to say.'

'But it's true,' I said. 'Father Pawel told me. He said God loved the world so much that he sent his son Jesus to save everyone so Jesus *must* love everyone if he wants to save them. Do you love Jesus?'

Uncle Julek chose not to answer.

As the days went on and I learned more about this wonderful man who loved everyone, I decided that I would love Jesus back. But how could I love Jesus if I had never met him and how could he love me in return?

I decided to ask Father Pawel.

'Oh my child,' he said, 'Jesus knows you for He is watching you all the time. He sees everything you do and knows everything you feel. You just need to accept Him into your heart and your heart will be full of love and you will love Him. But this is not enough. You need to become a Catholic for only by being Catholic can you be sure that He loves you and you will then have eternal life.'

I thought about this all day and realised that all the girls in my class were loved by Jesus and would be going to Heaven and I so wanted to be loved and I desperately wanted to be the same as my classmates. So that evening when I returned home, I told Uncle Julek and Aunt Zuzia that I wanted to become a Roman Catholic so Jesus would love me for ever and I would go to Heaven when I died.

'Absolutely not!' Uncle Julek spluttered into his tea.

'Renata!' said Aunt Zuzia in an unusually shrill voice.

'But why not?' I asked.

'Because you are not becoming a Catholic,' said Uncle Julek, 'and that's the end of it.'

No matter how much I tried I could not get Uncle Julek or Aunt Zuzia to agree, even though I talked about it every day.

'I want to be a Roman Catholic like all the other girls. Why won't you let me go to church and take Holy Communion? They get a wafer to eat and some lovely sweet wine to drink. Why can't I?'

'Renata, you cannot become a Catholic until your father comes home. He can make the decision for you.'

'But why can't I decide for myself?' I demanded, stamping my foot. 'I'm a big girl now. I can decide for myself. And where is he, anyway?'

Uncle Julek began shouting. 'If we hear any more of this nonsense you'll get a hard smack and go to bed without supper.' He stomped out of the kitchen leaving Aunt Zuzia to hug me to her chest and apologise for his harsh words.

I decided to get Father Pawel on my side. I could tell he felt sorry for me because when I talked to him he would shake his head and look at me with such pity in his eyes. He told me the only way I could be saved was to become a Catholic. He spent every lesson making everyone feel sorry for me.

'This child,' he said to the class, 'cannot enter the Kingdom of Heaven because of her father. Her father is a *Protestant*. If her father *really* loved her then the last thing he would want would be to *prevent* his daughter from being saved—'

I sat there with my hands in my lap, looking down and wishing I had a father who *really* loved me and that I could be saved for eternity.

'Wouldn't he be so happy, so delighted to find out on his return that his beloved daughter had saved herself from eternal damnation? That his daughter had made the one decision that would guarantee eternal life? What father would not be blessed for letting his child return to the fold? The Almighty is a Father and He knows only too well what it is like to have his Child saved—'

I was cross with my uncle and aunt who said that I was too young to make a decision about becoming a Catholic. I wasn't too young, I was seven, and I knew what I wanted. And then it came to me—I could make the decision for myself.

So, I told Father Pawel a lie—a lie that I told myself I could confess later, when I had become a Catholic. Then Father Pawel would forgive my sin but I would still have a place in Heaven at the side of the Almighty. I told Father Pawel that my aunt and uncle had decided that I could, after all, become a Catholic.

He was delighted when I told him. Tears sprang into his eyes. 'This is my work, my life,' he said, 'to save the sinners and children and bring them to the fold. It's nothing less than the Lord Himself would have wished. It is expected of me no less. Does the Bible not say there will be more joy in Heaven over one sinner who repents than over ninety-nine just persons who need no repentance? The same is true for those coming to the fold of faith.'

When he told me this, something heavy lifted itself from my heart.

Aunt Zuzia was pleased that I had become such good friends with Kasia and she was even more happy when Kasia started inviting me to play at her house every Sunday morning. Just after breakfast my aunt kissed me at the door of the apartment and waved as I walked up the street alone to visit Kasia.

What I didn't tell my aunt was that Kasia and I didn't really play with each other for as soon as I arrived I would go hand in hand with her and her parents to church and take Communion from Father Pawel. Every week Father Pawel made me feel very special because he said a blessing for the little child he had personally saved from damnation. Every Sunday lunchtime I returned home to Aunt Zuzia feeling normal and happy and safe with my new life of deceit.

'It's Mrs Dabrowska's birthday on Saturday,' I announced to my aunt. 'I want you to make her a birthday cake.'

'A cake?' said Aunt Zuzia. 'But Renata, darling, you know how difficult it is to get even the basic ingredients. I don't think I can make a cake for your teacher. Why don't you recite a poem or something?'

'The others will be doing that. Anyway she's always telling us how much she loves sweet things and how easy it was to get them before the war and she hasn't tasted cake for ages.'

Somehow Aunt Zuzia managed to make a coffee cake which, despite the lack of butter and shortage of other ingredients, was light and fluffy and rose to a magnificent size. Aunt Zuzia then coated it with a thin layer of chocolate icing and arranged it carefully on one of her very best plates.

As she fixed a single candle right in the middle she said, 'Now, Renata, here's the cake for Mrs Dabrowska but under no circumstances do you leave the plate behind. It's part of my best dinner service and you *must* bring it home with you.'

I objected but for once Aunt Zuzia was adamant.

'I most certainly want the plate back. The cake is a more than generous present. Besides, Mrs Dabrowska will divide the cake amongst you all and the plate will be empty.'

On Saturday the whole class met in the street outside Mrs Dabrowska's house and compared gifts. There was no doubt that my present was the best by far. Everyone gasped when they saw the lovely cake and Kasia with eyes shining said, 'Oh

Renata, your aunt makes the most wonderful things to eat, she is so clever. Mrs Dabrowska will simply love the cake.'

Puffed up with pride I knocked loudly on the door and led the line of classmates inside.

Mrs Dabrowska sat in her tiny sitting room smiling as she watched the little procession come in. We went up one by one to recite the little poems or greetings that we had prepared, then curtsied and presented her with our gifts. In return she complimented every one of us. 'Oh how lovely . . . how wonderful . . . you must have practised so hard . . . what a surprise . . . I never expected anything . . .' and so on until she had accepted each gift with a gracious smile as the girl pecked her waiting cheek and then stood back to make room for the next one.

When it was my turn, I held out the cake for her to hold whilst I delivered my birthday wishes. Mrs Dabrowska's eyes were gleaming and she couldn't take them off the cake even when I kissed her. She then rose from her chair and disappeared with the cake and my aunt's precious plate into the kitchen. The girls all looked at one another, somewhat surprised by her exit.

'Oh don't worry,' I said in a hushed voice. 'She's gone to cut the cake so that we can all have a piece. Aunt Zuzia said she would.'

Then we waited expectantly for our teacher's return. When she emerged her hands were quite empty. There was no sign of either the cake or the plate.

'Thank you, girls,' she said, 'you have been so kind, so generous. Now I have things to do so you may go now.'

And she stepped towards the door and opened it wide. The girls looked at me expectantly. I didn't know what to do but as Mrs Dabrowska was staring straight at me I began walking towards the open door and out into the street. We stood briefly on the pavement, surprised and disappointed.

'But I thought you said we'd have some cake,' Iwona said.

I didn't say anything. I couldn't believe that we hadn't been offered a single crumb of that delicious cake. I turned and, pulling Kasia by the hand, walked away from the disappointed crowd.

'Where's my plate?' were Aunt Zuzia's first words as we entered the apartment.

'I couldn't ask for it,' I said. 'She took the cake into the kitchen. It would have been rude to ask.'

'Did she give you all a piece?'

Kasia and I shook our heads.

I had never seen Aunt Zuzia so cross before.

'Of all the greedy, ungrateful people,' she shouted. 'It took me ages to work out how to make that cake, and she didn't share it out. Then I shall go and collect the plate from her myself.'

'Please don't, Aunt Zuzia. She'll think we're mean and everyone will know and they will be horrible to me.'

'Don't be so ridiculous. If anyone deserves to be called mean and greedy, it's your teacher. I simply don't know how she can behave like that, taking it into the kitchen and not sharing a scrap. Did she at least offer you something else to eat or drink?'

'No. She thanked us all and said she was sorry she couldn't invite us to stay but she had things to do. You won't go and ask for the plate back, will you?'

'Yes, Renata, I will. She should have given it to you when you asked for it.'

'But I didn't ask.'

'Then you're a very naughty girl. I told you to bring it back. Now unless you ask her for it on Monday I shall come up to the school and ask Mrs Dabrowska for it myself.'

This was the first time that I had failed to win an argument with my aunt and I knew that I had no choice but to pluck up the courage and ask Mrs Dabrowska for the plate myself. I spent the rest of the day tormented by worry, which I secretly shared with the priest at confession the next day. But Father Pawel told me that it was not a sin and I could ask for the plate back.

Although this greatly relieved my mind, it only occurred to me after I had finally recovered the plate that perhaps it was a far greater sin to be secretly 'stealing' bread and wine from the church and deceiving my aunt every Sunday than to ask for the plate back.

*   *   *

There were many days when I did go and play with Kasia and coming home one afternoon after school I let myself into the flat and called out, 'Kasia's asked me to tea. I said you wouldn't mind. Is that all right?'

Usually Aunt Zuzia would come out of the kitchen, hug me, tell me to behave myself nicely at Kasia's and let me go. But today, she rushed into the hall, grabbed me and hugged me tight.

'Where have you been? You should have been home ten minutes ago.'

'I came straight home. Kasia's invited me to tea. I said I'd tell you and go straight back.'

'You must go to her house and explain that you can't come today.' Aunt Zuzia was acting very strangely. 'Run and apologise. Say something has happened and that you are very sorry but you must come straight back home.'

'But why? What's happened?'

'I'll tell you as soon as you're back. Or rather, Uncle Julek will. He's taken the afternoon off especially to tell you, so come back immediately.'

'I hate you,' I shouted, stamping my foot, frustrated that she wasn't budging. 'You're being so mean. You never want me to have any fun.'

'Darling—' Aunt Zuzia began.

Just then Uncle Julek appeared in the kitchen doorway.

'Go and do what your aunt says, *immediately!*' he roared.

Coming back, I was expecting my uncle and aunt to be very angry with me but instead I found Aunt Zuzia waiting for me smiling but with tears pouring down her cheeks. She gave me a big hug, calling out, 'She's back.'

Uncle Julek was sitting at the kitchen table reading. He didn't look up.

'Tell her, Julek.'

'Don't rush me, Zuzia,' Uncle Julek said, then looking at me, 'We've had a letter today all the way from England. It's from your father ... He's safe and well.'

'My father? Tatuś is coming home?' I cried. 'At last. Now he's finished in Europe he can come and live with us again. Now everyone has to believe me when I say I'm not an orphan. When's he coming?

Does he ask about me in the letter?'

'Yes, but he's not coming home. He wants you to go to Scotland, to join him as soon as possible.'

I was startled. What did they mean? Go to Scotland? Leave my friends? My school? Start all over again somewhere else?

'But I would far rather he came here, so all my friends could see him and he could talk to Father Pawel about letting me become a Catholic so that I won't be damned when I die. You could look after him too. He can have my bedroom.'

'I would far rather he came here too—' Aunt Zuzia began, but she stopped when Uncle Julek waved his hand at her.

'Impossible,' he said. 'You are to go to Britain to join him just as soon as it can be arranged. I will contact Frederika immediately and she will make all the arrangements. She knows the right people.'

I grabbed my aunt's hands and danced her around the kitchen.

'I'm going to England to see my Tatuś,' I sang out. 'You wait till I tell Kasia and the others. Can I go and tell her now?'

'No,' said Aunt Zuzia.

'Yes,' said Uncle Julek. 'Go and tell your friend, but come back at once. Your aunt, of course, will not let you out of her sight from now on.'

I rushed into the hall but hearing a loud sob come from my aunt I peeped back through the crack in the door. I saw Uncle Julek get up from his chair and go over to where Aunt Zuzia was sitting, crying into her handkerchief. He bent down and put his arms around her.

'I shall miss her so much,' Aunt Zuzia sobbed. 'She's the only thing in my life. There'll be no point in living after she leaves.'

'It's me you married, not her, remember,' he said gently, trying to make her smile. 'Yes, we will miss her, but we are too old for her. She needs her father and we must thank God that Erwin's still alive and that his letters have finally got through.'

'He's got Renata back and we are left with nothing. Jerzyk and Fredzio have both been taken away from us and now we've got to give up Renata too. I can't go through all this again.'

'Of course you can, you silly hysterical woman. Pull yourself together and be happy for the child. It will be hard enough for her to go and live in a foreign country without you making it worse.'

'I know. I'll try.' Aunt Zuzia wept into her apron.

'Good,' he said. 'Now how about some sort of a celebration tea for us all? Renata will be back at any moment.'

And on hearing that, I flew down the stairs to tell Kasia my wonderful news.

CHAPTER SEVENTEEN

October 1945–March 1946

My dearest darling Renata, my father wrote. *I still can't believe I have found you after all this time. I can't wait to see you again—to hug you and kiss you* ... and at the end he would sign off, *Until we meet. Your ever-loving Tatuś.*

His letters came full of happiness and plans. I heard from my father nearly every day now.

I showed the letters to Kasia.

'It doesn't matter so much that you don't have a mother any more,' she said, 'because you have a father. Not everyone in the class has a father. In fact a lot of them died in the war.'

Kasia's words made me feel so much better. I wasn't different from the other girls any more. I still had one parent and, even though I wasn't living with him, it didn't matter because he was alive and soon we would be together again. I read and reread his letters. With each letter, my father and my new life became clearer. He wrote in detail about his friends who were all *so very anxious to meet me*, especially Mr Horowicz and his young wife Audrey who had heard how much I liked to read and were eager to meet this mysterious 'lost' daughter from Poland.

He wrote about the special plans he had made for my arrival.

You will have to travel by aeroplane across Poland and then take a ship across the sea that separates Poland from England. After your arrival we will stay in London, the capital of this wonderful country where policemen are friendly, will always help you, and don't carry guns . . .

'That's impossible,' I said to Aunt Zuzia. 'Policemen always carry guns.'

'The Gestapo did, that's for sure,' Aunt Zuzia replied, laughing. 'But not all policemen do.'

Then we will head north through England to Scotland . . .

'Where's Scotland?' I said.

We opened the atlas from the library and looked through the pages until we found a map with a pink blob labelled England and a blue blob, Scotland, stuck on top.

'I didn't know Scotland was a different country,' I said. 'I thought all of this was England.' I pointed to the island that looked like a funny old lady with a big skirt and tall hat, holding a basket.

'That island is England and Scotland and Wales all together,' Uncle Julek informed me. 'It's a long and complicated history.'

I was amazed. This little pink blob seemed so small that it was hard to believe that it could have won a war against the mighty Germany.

We will travel on a train and the journey will be a long one. But don't worry, my sweetheart, it won't be like the wagons you travelled in with Frederika. Here the engines pull carriages with two rows of padded seats that face each other. Each carriage can hold up to eight people and their luggage quite comfortably. In fact our cases sit in racks above our heads . . .

'On trains in England,' I told a wide-eyed Kasia, 'even the luggage has somewhere to sit.'

We laughed at the thought of all the bags and boxes and chickens and rabbits sitting in seats above our heads.

From the window (each carriage has its own window that opens) we will be able to see all the towns and the fields rushing past. The church spires . . .

'Are they Catholic in England?' I asked Uncle Julek hopefully.

'No,' he replied. 'Mostly Church of England. Now, let's not go into this again. As I said before it is your father's decision now.'

And people going to and from their work in cars or on bicycles . . .

So these people still drove cars. Maybe like the cars that had disappeared from Poland and were now just stories just as the *fiacre* driver had told me.

295

We will see hills becoming higher and higher as we head north and finally in the Lake District, just before we reach the border with Scotland, the hills become mountains . . .

'The Lake District. But that's where John and Titty live,' I exclaimed.

You will love Scotland, my father wrote, *I live in a castle, a fairy-tale castle just like the ones in Mamusia's stories that you loved so much.*

'Aunt Zuzia, he lives in a castle,' I cried.

'He actually lives next door to a castle,' said Uncle Julek. 'He works in the grounds of a castle, Dupplin Castle. They set up a Polish hospital there during the war and your father's been working there as a doctor for a couple of years now.'

Even better, I thought, I will be able to look at a real castle every morning when I wake and every night before I go to sleep.

The castle is very old and turreted and belongs to Lord Forteviot. Inside there are thick tapestries and hunting trophies (heads of stags) hang on stone walls, and on the floor in front of one of the fires lies a tiger rug complete with head and claws. In glass cases you can see huge fish that have been caught in local lochs and rivers and every room is filled with very old beautifully carved furniture . . . and here the men wear skirts and carry daggers in their long knee-high socks . . .

This was unbelievable but my father had included a picture of a fierce-looking man with a beard, wearing a checked skirt, knee socks and a beret.

'Look, the men wear skirts!' I exclaimed.

I showed the picture to Uncle Julek who snorted loudly and told me the skirts were called kilts.

'And the women wear the trousers,' Aunt Zuzia said laughing, and for a moment I wondered whether they were all playing a big joke on me or whether it really was true all that my father had written.

And you will be able to play in the grounds of the castle, walk through the rose garden, watch the red squirrels leaping from tree to tree, smell the pine trees and swim in the loch. It is such a wonderfully quiet place, so tranquil. It's the ideal place for the soldiers to get well again . . .

I tried to imagine what this beautiful Scotland looked like with its mountains and deer, forests and squirrels, rivers and lakes—called lochs—and enormous fish that leapt from the water. It sounded like a story book. But in the end I gave up and resorted to leafing through the books on the library shelves to find what I was looking for. I could only find a few pen-and-ink sketches that didn't help much.

'I can't wait to go and live with Tatuś in Scotland,' I said, about a hundred times a day.

One day my uncle said, 'Renata, make sure you tell your aunt how much you love her and how much you will miss her. It will make her so happy.'

'But I do love her . . . ever so much,' I said. 'How can I tell her that I will miss her? I don't know if I will.'

'Assume that you will,' he said in a crisp voice.

In one letter Tatuś included a small photograph of himself in military uniform, looking tall and distinguished. The photo was a bit blurry so it was difficult to see his face clearly, but he was smiling. I was so proud of the photo that I showed it to all my friends. I read his letters again and again and thought of little else except the wonderful new country far away over the sea and the magical time I would have when I finally got there.

One day I turned to Aunt Zuzia. 'Does Tatuś know about Mamusia and Babcia? Does he know that they were taken away and they are dead? Does he know that he will never see them again? Does he know that you and Uncle Julek and Frederika are the only ones left alive in our family?'

Aunt Zuzia stopped what she was doing and turned to face me.

'He does,' she said. 'We have told him everything. He has been distraught but he has you and that makes up for everything.'

Every week Aunt Zuzia helped me write a letter to my father.

'I don't know what to say,' I said. 'I have told him everything already. If only I could talk to him. Perhaps I'll wait until I get to England and then we can talk all the time. I'll tell him everything then.'

'But you like getting letters from your father, don't you?' Aunt Zuzia asked.

'Oh yes.'

'Well he likes getting them from you too. He hasn't seen you for so many years and he wants to know all about you.'

'What shall I write about? Shall I tell him about the orphanage and how much I hated it?'

'No, I don't think that is a good idea.'

'But he does know about it, doesn't he?' I said. 'You told me you've told him everything.'

'Yes, but all that is in the past, so why make him unhappy? Better to write and tell him how much you love him and how happy you are at school.'

'I've told him everything about school and

anyway I don't know if I do love him,' I retorted. 'I don't really remember him. Perhaps I won't love him, so isn't it better to wait till I see him? Father Pawel would be very upset if I was to tell a lie.'

Uncle Julek chuckled out loud.

'That girl's got more brains than I give her credit for,' he remarked, but Aunt Zuzia would not let it go.

'Of course you love your father and you are going to tell him so. I will dictate what you must write.'

So my stiff little notes were sent off weekly. I wasn't sure what my father would think. Even though I wrote the letters the words weren't,

One of Renata's letters written to her father from Przemys´l, found amongst her father's belongings many years later

299

really my own and I worried that Tatuś would see straight through the not-quite-truths that I had written.

It was not only me who received letters. Uncle Julek poured over endless communications.

'They are from Frederika, mainly,' Aunt Zuzia explained. 'They're to do with the arrangements for you to leave Poland and get to England. Thankfully Frederika knows who to contact. It makes it a bit easier but there is still an awful lot of paperwork.'

As the weeks turned into months I began to worry that I would never get to England. Perhaps another promise would be broken. Perhaps my fairy-tale ending wasn't going to happen after all and I wouldn't be living happily ever after. To begin with my schoolfriends had envied my good fortune and were always eager for me to read out loud the latest letter from my father. But now they were beginning to grow tired of my talk of this huge adventure that might never take place. So I began to tell them exaggerated tales of this wonderful new place called Scotland and, as I made up more and more stories, soon everyone wanted to listen.

At home, Aunt Zuzia was growing sadder and sadder. Every time a letter came, Aunt Zuzia and I read it together and every time my aunt would start to cry and cling to me.

'Oh my darling,' she sobbed. 'I love you so much. I am going to miss you more than you know. Will you miss me too? My darling, tell me you will.'

I began to feel sorry for my aunt. I knew what it was like to be separated from the ones you loved. I could still feel the terror of being separated from Mamusia and Babcia, Aunt Adela and Zazula; of not being able to do anything, of being left behind and not knowing. I hugged and kissed Aunt Zuzia a lot, telling her, 'I love you, of course I love you. I will come back and visit and I will write every day.'

But as time went on I found it more and more difficult to keep this up. All I could think about was starting my new life in this fairy-tale land and I felt so happy and excited that it was difficult to pretend to be sad, and why should I? Then I began to find it hard to look at Aunt Zuzia as her eyes were always puffy and red and this made her look tired and old. Sometimes when she thought no one was looking, I would see her weeping into her apron. One day when I watched her crying, I thought to myself that I didn't think I was going to miss her at all and the sooner I went, the better. But then I felt guilty and tried hard to pretend that the separation was going to be as painful for me as it was going to be for her.

Uncle Julek could see that I was pretending; he didn't say anything but the more I pretended the more worried I became because lying was sinning in the eyes of God as Father Pawel reminded us every week: 'Lying is one of the *deadliest* sins,' he shouted every Sunday from the pulpit, his voice rising and filling the church.

I began to feel his stare on me and, as I lowered my head, I would see the eyes of Jesus watching me and knowing the sin that lay heavy in my heart. I carried this feeling around with me all week until the following Sunday. Then, with a lighter step, I would join Kasia and her parents as they walked to church where I could confess everything and be absolved of my sin—until the arrival of the next letter which would spark another wave of guilt and I would have to pick up my lie and carry it wherever I went, all over again.

Finally the letter from Frederika that finalised the date for my departure arrived, 20 March 1946.

Kasia wanted to know all about the arrangements.

'Where are you going to live? Is the castle as big as Sleeping Beauty's? How are you going to get to England?'

I answered her as best I could and what I didn't know I invented. I said that I would be travelling with my cousin Frederika, she was going to take me to my father. We were going on the big ship full of children.

'Tell us about the ship,' said my friends in chorus. 'We have never seen a ship before.'

And neither had I, nor the sea for that matter, except in pictures, but I let my imagination run wild. 'My ship is huge,' I told them, thinking of Kitty's sailing boat, 'much bigger than *Swallow* of course but like *Swallow* it is powered only by wind.'

'How?' asked Iwona, wide-eyed.

'The white sail has to be hoisted up and down twice a day. The ship is blown by the wind.'

'How does it stay upright?' Kasia wanted to know.

I had to think fast.

'The children all have to be weighed before we set sail and then divided into two equal groups. These groups take it in turns so that, while one group is sleeping or eating, the other group will have to rush from one side of the ship to the other to make sure the ship stays upright.'

'It all sounds very dangerous,' Iwona remarked.

'Oh it is,' I said. 'You have to be carefully selected to go on that ship. You have to pass a special test. I passed it with flying colours.'

Iwona was wide-eyed. 'What did you have to do?'

'I can't tell you because it's a secret test and I had to swear to tell no one,' I replied solemnly, carefully crossing my fingers behind my back to save myself from carrying around more guilt for the rest of the week.

*   *   *

A few days before my date of departure Kasia's mother came to visit Aunt Zuzia to ask if she could arrange a goodbye party for me.

Because of the food shortages they both agreed that everyone should make something. Aunt Zuzia baked a splendid cake covered with chocolate with my name in pink inscribed on top. It was so big that there was enough for everyone to have a slice. I proudly walked alongside Aunt Zuzia and Uncle Julek to Kasia's house. Everyone was full of praise for my aunt and her cake. It was a work of art, and it tasted delicious. My aunt was so pleased that for once she forgot to cry and her puffiness went down and her face took on a soft pink glow. She looked very pretty and much more like my old aunt. The other parents had also brought wonderful things to eat such as potato *placki*, and pancakes filled with sweet cream cheese and a delicious cold soup made from plums.

Everyone made a huge fuss of me and I felt so important and grown-up.

'This is from us,' Kasia said, holding out her hand. 'It's for when you get to England, so you have something to play with.'

I took the little package and inside was a new paper doll with lots of clothes to cut out. I was so pleased—the doll had long fair plaits coiled round her head in exactly the way I had always wanted mine to look. In Scotland I would have time to tie my hair up like that, I thought. One of the outfits was a Polish national costume with the wide skirt and the bright ribbons at the shoulders.

'I hope you won't forget us, especially me,' Kasia added sadly when I held the costume up for everyone to see.

'I will never forget you,' I said solemnly.

The grown-ups also gave me a present: my very own suitcase with my initials painted on the outside.

'You will be able to pack all your clothes in here and your possessions and everyone will know who it belongs to,' said Kasia's mother.

'Very important if you lose sight of it on the aeroplane,' added Aunt Zuzia.

'Or when you are on the ship and you have to leave it to run from side to side,' called out Iwona and the grown-ups looked at her in amusement.

Then some of the mothers began to make little speeches. Aunt Zuzia was, once again, overcome by emotion and started sobbing.

'For heaven's sake,' grumbled Uncle Julek. 'Not here. Please.'

But Aunt Zuzia couldn't stop so he bundled her from the room. I hardly noticed them leaving; I was too happy and excited—I was queen of the party and loving every moment.

*   *   *

Those final hours before Frederika arrived went on for ever and ever. Aunt Zuzia packed, unpacked and repacked my suitcase and didn't stop giving me instructions about what I must and must not do. All the time she was remembering something important that had to go into the suitcase and then, having packed that carefully away, she thought of another even more important item and started all over again.

'But, Aunt Zuzia, I must take my books,' I said, watching her remove all of Maria's books, which Mrs Zimińska had given me, and putting them on the table by my bed.

'They won't be of any use in Scotland,' said Aunt Zuzia. 'You will get plenty of new ones in English. And anyway your case will be far too heavy.'

Aunt Zuzia had bought me a new coat that I would wear on the journey and I kept trying it on and looking in the mirror. Did it fit properly? Did the blue tweed look nice on me? I must ask Kasia, I thought, and so added it to my list of things to do. My list grew longer every day. I had to say goodbye to all my friends at school and to my teachers and of course to Father Pawel. I had to thank him again for saving me from eternal damnation. Then there was the librarian downstairs, the man at the bread shop and dear Barek.

When there was no one else to say goodbye to, I tried to reread as many of my old friends, my wonderful Polish books, as I could before having to leave them behind.

'It won't be for ever,' Aunt Zuzia told me. 'You will come to see us often and who knows, maybe we will be able to visit you too.'

'You *must* come and visit me,' I told her,

'because I will be far too busy to come all the way back here. There will be so many new things for me to do. That's what Tatuś told me. And he knows.'

'We are getting a little tired of hearing you talk only of yourself and what you will be doing,' Uncle Julek said suddenly. 'It might be nice to hear you ask your aunt what she will be doing and how she will manage to cope with not having you to look after. She has been very good to you, you know.'

Both Aunt Zuzia and I looked at him in astonishment. Suddenly I felt terrible. I was ashamed of myself and embarrassed that Uncle Julek had finally spoken out loud the fact that I wasn't at all sad to be leaving my aunt.

I gave Aunt Zuzia a huge hug.

'I really *will* miss you,' I said and this time I meant it. 'You must come to Scotland to see us soon.'

Then seeing the tears well up in my aunt's eyes, I took a deep breath and turned to Uncle Julek.

'What will happen to my rocking horse? He's too big for me to take. Should I give him to Kasia?'

'No, I think we must leave that decision to Mr and Mrs Ziminski. They may want to give it to someone themselves. I shall ask next time I see them.'

'I would like to visit them before I go. They have been so nice to me.'

'I'm afraid there isn't time, but why don't you write a little thank-you letter and I will deliver it.'

I groaned. More than anything I hated writing letters. I never knew what to say. Nevertheless, I sat down at once and with my tongue sticking out of the corner of my mouth and without any further prompting wrote a nice little note to Mr and Mrs

Ziminski to tell them how much I had loved the rocking horse and how I would miss him and hoped he would go to a good home. Uncle Julek was pleased with my effort.

'I see you can write a good letter when you put your mind to it,' he said, 'so why do we have the weekly fuss when you have to write to your father?'

'That's different,' I replied. 'I don't know him. I never know what to say.'

*   *   *

The big day finally arrived. I lay in bed woken up by the early morning noises in the street below. Now that it was time to leave, I found myself wishing that it *wasn't*. Facing the window, snuggled under my blue quilt, I was sad that this was the last time that I would wake up in this room. The last time I would see the watery sunlight dancing off my rocking horse's golden mane. I was really and truly leaving my aunt, uncle, friends and school. I was going to a foreign land to live with a father who was a stranger. I wouldn't be able to understand what anyone said to me. I would have to learn to read and write all over again, I would have to start at a new school without any friends. How would I be able to talk to them? How would they understand me?

Suddenly I longed for Aunt Zuzia to come into the room, arms outstretched ready for a cuddle, and say, 'I'm sorry, darling, but there has been a change of plan. You aren't going after all. It's for the best.'

For once, I wanted to be met by bad news.

Or perhaps a letter had arrived to say that my father had changed his plans and was coming back to Poland, after all. Then we could all live happily ever after, here in this flat in Przemyśl. I would give up the bedroom I so loved and go and sleep on a mattress in the sitting room. Anything would be better than heading into the unknown again. Maybe it wasn't too late. Frederika would understand how I felt and she could go without me. She could explain the situation to my father and he would say that it didn't matter and would pack his belongings and come straight back to Poland.

But I knew that it was too late. Frederika had arrived safely late the evening before, long after I'd gone to bed. I hadn't heard her arriving, but when I got up to go to the toilet in the middle of the night I tripped over a huge suitcase standing in the narrow hall.

There was a knock and the door opened. Frederika stood in the doorway in her nightdress, her red hair tumbling over her shoulders. I leaped out of bed and rushed to hug my favourite person.

'I'm so happy you've come. I've missed you so much,' I said.

'I've missed you too, my darling, and now we're going to be together for more than a week. Won't that be lovely?'

'Yes, but couldn't we all stay here together?' I looked at her. 'I've decided that I don't want to go to Scotland. I think we should tell Tatuś to come back here instead.'

Frederika laughed and stroked my hair. 'We can't do that. All the arrangements have been made. Your father is so looking forward to your arrival. We couldn't disappoint him now.'

'Why can't he come here instead?'

'It's too complicated to explain, sweetheart. He

just can't. It wouldn't be safe, so you must go to him. Besides, I have worked very hard to make all the arrangements and I wouldn't be very pleased if they had to be cancelled.' She looked at me with a cross expression on her face before it broke into a smile. 'Now you must get up and have breakfast. Aunty Zuzy has prepared a feast and you must do it justice or you will upset her. She is very unhappy that you are going and she thinks you don't care. So, you must tell her how much you'll miss her and promise to write to her very often.'

'I *shall* miss her,' I said, 'very much,' and I did mean it. With all my heart I realised how loving and kind my aunt had been to me. 'I suppose she will miss me a lot because she has also lost Fredzio and Jerzyk. I think she *needs* to have someone to look after. Do you miss Fredzio?'

'Very much,' said Frederika, stroking my hair. 'But I have you and my parents and Zuzia and Julek to look after and that keeps me busy.'

'What about my father? Will you have to look after him too?'

Frederika laughed. 'No, of course not. My job is to take you to him so *he* can look after *you*.'

'Yes I know that, but will you stay with us?'

'No, I can't. I have to go to Norway. We shall meet him in England and then I shall go on. Neither of you will want me around. Now get dressed as quickly as you can and don't keep breakfast waiting or we will miss the aeroplane.'

CHAPTER EIGHTEEN

20–28 March 1946. Przemyśl to London via Gdyńia

Uncle Julek, Aunt Zuzia, Frederika and I stood shivering on the runway, a long, straight road that led to nowhere. It was bitter and cold. The wind howled across the airfield and there was icy snow on the scraggy, yellow grass. Everyone looked sad and miserable including all the other children wrapped in mufflers and coats, stamping their feet to keep warm. Some were alone with no one to wave them off, others were in groups with teachers. I was one of the lucky ones with a group of my own. But soon it would be time to leave my family and join everyone else milling around the wooden hut on Przemyśl airfield.

I didn't realise there would be so many children leaving with me.

'There will be far more at Gdyńia,' Frederika told me.

'How many?'

'Thousands probably,' she replied.

'Can a thousand children fit on one ship?' I was stunned.

'Probably not,' said Uncle Julek, 'but there will be more than one boat sailing to England.'

I felt both happy and miserable. This time it was me who was crying while Aunt Zuzia did her best to keep cheerful and make me feel better.

'Don't cry, darling, you are a very lucky girl. Just think of the wonderful life you are going to have with your father.' But I think she said it not only to make me feel better but herself as well.

The Russian military aeroplane stood at the end of the runway, a great grey beast hugging the ground, its huge wings stretching out on either side. I had never seen an aeroplane on the ground before, only heard their roar as they passed overhead before the sirens and the mad rush to the cellar. I'd never had time to study them high up in the sky and, looking at this monster, I found it hard to believe that it could fly through the air like a bird. I couldn't imagine its wings flapping. Was it safe? Aeroplanes were used for carrying bombs and destroying cities and people. Could my father really want me to go on such a terrifying monster?

'Is it safe?' I asked my uncle. 'It looks so big and heavy. How does it stay up in the sky?'

'Of course it's safe,' he said. 'I'd love to fly in an aeroplane. I never have and probably never will.'

'When you come and visit me, you will,' I said, but no one replied.

We had all run out of things to say. I clung tightly to my aunt and looked around at my fellow travellers. Most of them seemed to be of a similar age to me and looked as nervous as I felt.

I noticed a boy standing on his own not far from our little group. He looked very small and lonely. He was staring down at the ground then raised his arm and wiped the corner of his eye with his sleeve. As he did so I noticed the huge hole in the elbow of his jacket. He reminded me of Jan and I thought perhaps it was him. Since no one had said anything for a good few minutes I let go of Aunt Zuzia's arm and walked over to him.

'Hello,' I said. 'Are you going to England?'

The boy turned around. It wasn't Jan. He was older and his hair curlier than Jan's. I felt disappointed.

'No,' he answered with a sniff. 'I am going to Palestine.'

'Where are your parents?'

'I don't have any,' he said, his eyes still fixed on the ground. 'I am an orphan. I am going to be adopted.'

I then noticed that one of his shoes also had a hole through which I could see the pointed end of his uncut toenail. His trousers were too short and his coat was very thin. I could see by the way he was shivering that he really was very cold.

'What's your name?' I asked.

'Tomasz.' He finally looked up at me and I could see his sad grey eyes. 'Are you going to Palestine too?'

'No, England. My father is there. I am going out to join him.'

'You're lucky,' Tomasz said. 'What about your mother?'

'She's dead. She died ages ago. The Nazis took her.'

'Both my parents died in a concentration camp too. So you're sort of half an orphan?'

'I suppose so. Come and meet my aunt and uncle,' I said.

'I like being on my own. I'm fine,' Tomasz said. 'I'll see you on the aeroplane.'

Somehow I couldn't bring myself to tell him that I wasn't travelling alone. He would find out soon enough. I gave him a little smile and walked back to rejoin my family.

'Who was that little boy?' Aunt Zuzia asked.

312

'He's an orphan and he's going to Palestine to be adopted.'

'How nice.'

I looked at my aunt in astonishment. 'What's *nice* about that?' I said. 'He's all alone. I asked him to come and talk to you but he refused. I feel sorry for him.'

Aunt Zuzia opened her mouth to reply but stopped when she saw a woman in uniform approaching us.

'Time to board the aeroplane. Only passengers allowed beyond this point. Please say your goodbyes here.'

*   *   *

My heart leapt, thudding in my chest. This was it. We were off. From then on everything became a blur—a confusion of kisses, tears and loud sobs. Aunt Zuzia hugging me, Uncle Julek patting my head. I heard myself say goodbye and thank you over and over again but that wasn't enough. My words let me down. I couldn't say what I felt, I couldn't tell them how grateful I was to them for looking after me, for loving me and caring for me. I didn't know where to begin. I wished I could go back and do it all over again but this time properly.

Now Frederika was taking my hand and pulling me away. I turned back to my aunt to give her a final kiss, then to my uncle to give him a hug. He hugged me and smiled, a real one that went all the way from his lips to his eyes. I felt my eyes well with tears once again. I couldn't go, I couldn't leave them. Uncle Julek planted a kiss on the top of my head and then I found myself walking, half dragged

313

by Frederika, across the vast windy tarmac towards the plane.

I started to panic and I turned, waving frantically, walking backwards so as not to miss one tiny moment of seeing them. Aunt Zuzia was waving back. And then I saw my uncle take her arm and begin to lead her away in the opposite direction. She turned to follow him but she looked broken and bent, like Mamusia when she left the room for that last time. Then Aunt Zuzia stopped and tried to find me again, to have one last look. I waved and waved but she was looking in the wrong direction. Now Uncle Julek was pulling her forward again, keeping his gaze firmly fixed on the way ahead. Then they were gone—my aunt, my uncle, my safety, my happiness, my life as I knew it, had disappeared. For ever.

A huge cloud of loneliness swept over me. I was leaving it all behind for a life that I didn't know, and at this moment didn't want, and I was to live with a stranger again. I had told all these wonderful stories to my friends, but that is all they were— stories from my imagination. I felt dizzy and clung to Frederika, big, fat tears rolling slowly down my cheeks.

'Here we are,' Frederika said cheerfully.

We were close to the aeroplane and it was enormous. A gigantic metal bird with a gaping black hole in its side. There were steps leading up, which I realised must be the way in, and several men were standing around. They all looked important in their uniforms. One of them was very tall wearing a Russian uniform with a fur flap cap. This was the pilot. The other men were too busy to notice us, peering at the wheels and the underside

314

of that great bird.

I looked back the way I'd come, hoping for a final glimpse of my aunt and uncle, but all I saw was a seemingly endless stream of children coming towards us. I searched for Tomasz's pale face in the crowd, but couldn't find it.

'You need to board,' said the woman, who had reappeared.

The pilot smiled at me as I began to climb the steps, higher and higher. I felt like the Pied Piper, leading a long line of children.

'Please take this.' Someone handed me a brown paper bag as I entered the aircraft.

'What's this for?' I asked Frederika. 'It's empty.'

'It's in case you feel sick,' Frederika said.

As my eyes adjusted to the dim light, I saw rows of hard wooden benches running down each side of the cabin beneath little round windows. I took a seat next to Frederika and watched the other children do the same. As more and more children filed in, the narrow seats filled up until we were all squashed in together. The door was closed and locked. For a moment we all sat there staring at each other, not knowing where to look or what to say and then there was the most almighty roar. The engines started, and then there followed an even greater roar as I felt the plane suddenly move, slowly at first and then gradually faster and faster, gathering speed.

I was terrified. We were all going to die!

It wasn't possible for such a heavy beast to stay up in the sky. I knew that because every time I threw something up in the air it always came down, very quickly. Gravity—that's what my teachers had called it. Then my heart went into

315

my mouth and the front of the aeroplane rose up and we were flying. Up and up, higher and higher into the sky. I closed my eyes and prayed. Thank goodness I was now a Catholic. I had been saved just in time. I waited for the horrible crash to tell us it was all over. There was a terrible bumping and the aeroplane began to shake so violently that I thought it was going to shatter into a million pieces like the mirror in *The Snow Queen*. But it didn't. Instead, the aeroplane levelled and the bumping and shaking went away leaving only the roar of the engines.

'Are you all right?' Frederika shouted.

'Yes,' I replied. 'Are we back on the ground?'

'No, we are high up in the sky. Look.'

I twisted round in my seat and looked through the window. All I could see was fluffy white clouds below us and the deep blue sky above. All of a sudden I felt violently sick. I hastily opened my paper bag and vomited. As I came up for air, I noticed, thankfully, that I wasn't the only person with my head over their paper bag.

After a couple of hours of sitting on the wooden benches, my bottom had become numb. I wanted to stretch my legs. I wanted Frederika to tell me a story but the noise of the engines was too loud and we were too tightly packed in to allow me to move. Then the front of the aeroplane began to go down and we passed smoothly through the clouds as they parted for us on either side. As I saw the ground racing towards me I felt an almighty jolt. Children screamed as they lurched into the person sitting next to them. The plane shook and from somewhere beneath us came squeals and a rush of air. Frederika gripped my hand and smiled reassuringly at me.

'It's all right,' she shouted. 'Don't worry. We're quite safe.'

When we had come to a standstill and the door had been opened again, I felt the cool air on my face and began to feel a bit better. I never wanted to set foot on an aeroplane again. I followed Frederika out into the fresh air. As I waited to go down the steps onto the tarmac I watched the pile of luggage grow higher and higher as it magically spilled out of the back of the aeroplane and onto the ground. I pulled on Frederika's arm.

'We'll never find our bags,' I wailed. 'My lovely little case. I'll never find it!'

'You don't have to,' Frederika replied. 'They will take it to the docks for us and we will collect it when we board the boat.'

So we left our bags and boxes and were taken by lorry from the aerodrome to the harbour and by the time we reached the docks I still hadn't recovered from the shock of landing. We were led into a crowded hall where we stayed for several hours. When I felt less sick, I ate some of the food that Frederika had managed to save me; a couple of sandwiches given to us by the lady.

The hall was large and grey with dirty windows. On the wall facing me was a long, narrow board painted white. As I gazed at it, I heard music and to my astonishment a black-and-white image appeared on the board. It was a picture of men in evening suits and white shirts and black ties playing musical instruments. And then the picture started to move. It was as if I was looking through the wall into a room beyond, except that everything was in black-and-white and shades of grey. The men were

317

smiling as their long fingers plucked at strings, their hands moved bows up and down; others with round cheeks blew into trumpets. I couldn't understand it but stood transported by the magic, feasting on the moving images, dancing in my imagination to the wonderful tunes.

*　　*　　*

It was time to board the ship. We were led outside and there I saw it for the first time, a massive ship sitting in the water with the thickest ropes I had ever seen to stop it from floating away. I thought it must be bigger than the home of the biggest giant on earth. There were no sails and it wasn't made of wood. I had been so wrong. I was glad that my friends weren't here and that we weren't going to be weighed and divided into groups before getting on.

As the hundreds of us children collected our cases from the huge pile on the dock, we formed a line and as darkness fell we went on board. I was so glad that my case had my name painted on the outside as otherwise I knew I would never have found it. Frederika helped me to lug the heavy case up on deck and then she went back to get her own bags. She reappeared a minute later empty-handed but followed closely by two young sailors who had offered to help her.

'Thank you *so* much,' Frederika said, giving them one of her winning smiles.

Frederika led the way to our cabin along the maze of narrow corridors where we had to stand back against the wall if we met anyone coming in the opposite direction. We squeezed past boxes and cases left outside the cabin doors. Finally she produced some keys from her handbag and unlocked a door that looked just like all the doors we had passed. She stood back to let me go in first.

'Oh look,' I said, delighted.

The room was large and in one corner was a washbasin. Set against the walls were three beds, one of which was above the second, and the third stood on its own beneath a round window through which I could glimpse the sea. I was surprised to find that the best bunk bed, the one with the view out of the porthole, already had luggage on it.

'Someone's left their luggage behind!'

'We have to share our cabin,' Frederika said.

'Who with?' I said unhappily.

'With a little girl called Anka. She is travelling alone and will be going all the way to America to live with relatives. She is eight, like you,' explained Frederika. 'She's probably very lonely and you must be kind to her.'

Frederika could see that I wasn't happy with the idea of having to share a cabin with a stranger and said, 'It'll be nice for you to have someone of your own age to play with when you get tired of me.'

I didn't say anything.

'Come on,' said Frederika, trying to cheer me up. 'You and I will have great fun on these bunks. We can take turns at sleeping on top.'

When Anka appeared at last she was pale and miserable and hardly said a word. I thought that she must be very frightened, all on her own, surrounded by so many people.

'Isn't this exciting?' I said. 'We are going to be living on this big ship for a week. We can have so much fun—there are so many places to hide. We

319

can play the best hide and seek ever.' Still she said nothing. 'Would you like to go for a walk?'

Anka wouldn't reply. Frederika tried to comfort her and talk to her, but she wouldn't say a thing. I decided that she wasn't going to be much fun after all and so began unpacking my suitcase.

'I know,' said Frederika, looking at her watch. 'I think we'll all feel better if we have something to eat. Shall we go and find some food?'

Anka nodded her head politely.

We made our way up to the huge dining room and found it bursting with children. We were given soup and pancakes filled with cheese and mashed potato, and then Frederika announced that it was time for bed.

I woke in the night and for a few moments I didn't know where I was or what was happening. I was being tossed up and down and flung violently from side to side. I could hear cracking sounds, water bashing against the sides of the boat, the wind howling and through the porthole came a weak watery grey light that made the inside of the cabin look scary.

'Frederika, what's happening? Where are we? I want Aunt Zuzia.'

There was no answer. I saw Frederika's outline bent over the washbasin where she was being sick. From the other side of the room I could hear Anka moaning in her bed. I jumped out of my bunk and, grabbing onto the furniture for support, struggled over to Anka's bed trying not to bump into Frederika. Close up I could see Anka's cheeks were a bright scarlet colour and she was covered in big red spots. Her eyes were wide open and stared straight at me, but she didn't seem to recognise

320

or see me at all. Frightened, I made my way back to Frederika who was sitting on the edge of her bunk looking like a ghost. The dim light made her red hair darker and the whiteness of her face even whiter with her freckles standing out like spots.

'I'm sorry, Renata,' she gasped. 'Are you all right? I must lie down. I feel terrible.'

She collapsed on her bed with a groan and closed her eyes.

I moved over to Anka's bed, but Anka seemed to be fast asleep. She was breathing heavily and her cheeks were still fiery. I didn't want to wake her and I couldn't bother Frederika so there seemed little else to do but go back to bed myself. I lay in my bunk enjoying the swaying and rocking and very soon fell fast asleep.

When I woke again the light inside the cabin was brighter but the boat was still tossing and heaving and both Anka and Frederika were awake.

'I'm hungry,' I said. 'Shall we go and get some breakfast?'

'I can't face food,' Frederika said. 'You go and get some if you like.'

'Do you want to come, Anka?' I asked cheerfully, but Anka turned her head and was sick over the side of her bunk. Frederika forced herself out of her bunk to see to the mess. I thought that this was a good time to go in search of food.

In the dining room three waiters were talking, holding on to the furniture as the ship continued to heave beneath our feet. They seemed pleased to see me.

'Please, take a seat,' they said, waving to an empty dining hall that today seemed vast as no one was there but me.

321

I chose a seat next to the window where I could watch the angry sea lunging towards the ship that dipped down to meet it before being thrown high into the sky, the waves crashing over the window. The lurching and rolling made me feel hungrier than ever and the waiters proceeded to wait on me hand and foot.

'What an appetite that child has,' I heard one waiter say to another as he spooned yet more food onto my plate.

From that morning on, I enjoyed huge breakfasts, alone, every day.

Since the dining room was deserted after breakfast I decided to explore and find some good hiding places for when Anka was feeling better. I made my way along the narrow corridors and up some stairs along more corridors until I came to a door that blocked my path. I tried the handle but the door remained shut. I tried again, pushing against it with all my might, and it swung open. I found myself outside on the deck, the wind was howling, whipping my hair against my cheeks, making my eyes smart, tugging at my clothes. Spray from the sea hit my face with its stinging force. I felt exhilarated. I ran back to our cabin to tell Frederika and Anka but they were too ill to care.

For two days no one walked on deck except the sailors and me. No one used the public rooms and only a sprinkling of people ventured into the dining room. I soon grew tired of my own company and of waiting for Anka to get better, so I decided to talk to the sailors.

'Where are you from?' I shouted to one I met on deck. He too was enjoying being thrashed by the storm.

'Russia,' he shouted back.

I smiled up at him thinking of the friendly Russian soldiers and their bars of chocolate in Przemyśl.

'I am surprised you aren't sick like everyone else,' he commented.

'I don't feel sick. I love the ship going up and down like this,' I said. 'But it is a bit lonely with no one to talk to or play with.'

The sailor smiled down at me and put his hand into his pocket and produced a small package. I recognised it instantly.

'Chocolate!'

From then on I always smiled sweetly at the sailors and asked them questions. It turned out that they all carried packets of chocolate. As I tore off the colourful wrappers and enjoyed their contents, they would stroke my fair hair and talk to me about their children.

After three long days the storm died and gradually the ship came to life with passengers again. Frederika was much better and she gave me all her attention. We were never apart. Poor Anka was now completely covered in spots.

The ship's doctor came to see her.

'This is serious,' he said, peering at the spots then into her mouth. 'It's chicken pox, it's contagious. She will have to come with me to the clinic where we can keep an eye on her.'

So poor little Anka, too ill to care, was moved out of our cabin and I never saw her again.

Not long after this, the ship stopped in a Scandinavian port and we were told this was the first and only time in the week-long journey that the boat would dock.

'Shall we go ashore and take a look around?' Frederika asked me. 'It will be good to be on dry land again.'

I could tell she was excited so we made our way up the hill from the docks towards the inviting lights of the town. We had a whole evening to explore the streets and shops lit up by hundreds of warm yellow lights that drew us, like moths, to gaze in the windows. The clothes were so lovely—in more colours and patterns than I had ever seen before.

'This is wonderful,' Frederika sighed. 'Quite the most wonderful place on earth.'

As I watched Frederika examine everything in detail, I saw her passion come alive. Murmurs of joy and amazement at the fineness of the cloth and the elaborate stitching went on and on. Then I spotted a pair of green shoes with very thin pointed heels, and I began to giggle.

'Look, Frederika,' I exclaimed. 'How can anyone walk in these?'

'Oh, they are *gorgeous*! What a pity this shop's closed. Otherwise I would have bought them—if I had the money that is,' she sighed.

The journey passed quickly; I was loving every moment, so much so that I hadn't given Aunt Zuzia or my father a single thought. But on the night before we were due to dock in England, I was terribly worried and nervous and I began asking Frederika a million questions. For some reason Frederika was also nervous; she only answered my questions briefly.

'Do you think Tatuś will recognise me?' I asked.

'Of course,' Frederika replied.

'But he hasn't seen me since I was a baby, so how will he?'

'Aunt Zuzia has sent him a photograph. Don't you remember?'

'Yes, but that was horrible. I couldn't sit still while the man had his head under that hood—he looked so funny, and anyway the photograph didn't look anything like me.'

But Frederika would not answer and eventually I gave up and went in search of chocolate.

CHAPTER NINETEEN

29 March 1946. London

Through the porthole above Anka's bunk I could see sunlight twinkling on the water. The sky was a brilliant orange. But inside the cabin, we were arguing. Frederika insisted I wear several layers of woollen clothes.

'But it's so hot,' I complained. 'And I should know. I've been out for a walk on deck. The sun's out and one of the sailors told me it's going to be really hot. There's a heat wave.'

'It can't possibly be *really* hot. It's only March,' Frederika said crossly, trying to stuff my arm into yet another cardigan sleeve. 'I don't want you arriving to meet your father with pneumonia or worse. Just do as you're told and stop being such a baby.'

'I'm not a baby. I'm boiling hot. Why aren't you wearing hundreds of layers?'

'Because I'm not a little girl about to meet her

father after five years. Just do as you're told,' she said.

I didn't understand. I had never heard Frederika speak so angrily and I looked at her in surprise. Her hair had fallen across her face in our struggle, but I could see small red spots. Her face was red and blotchy—just like Anka's.

'Frederika,' I said, 'you look ill, just like Anka. Do you have chicken pox?'

'I don't feel very well,' Frederika replied wearily, 'but you mustn't say a word of this to anyone in case they don't allow me to leave the ship.'

'But what will we do if the spots on your face get bigger? Will we have to go back to Poland without seeing Tatuś?'

Now I was worried. After all this, the thought of having to turn round and go back without seeing my father was simply too much to bear. I didn't for one moment imagine that I would be allowed to leave the ship without Frederika.

'Don't be silly,' Frederika laughed. 'Of course I won't be going back. Anyway I have a plan, I shall wear my hat with a veil and no one will notice—just as long as you don't go saying anything and drawing it to their attention. Promise me?'

'I promise.'

Without further protest I stuck my arm into the sleeve of yet another cardigan.

I thought Frederika looked lovely even if she was ill. She was wearing a green dress which made her brown eyes look more like shiny chestnuts against her fair (but blotchy) skin. Her rich dark red hair gleamed in the sunlight; and she had a little green pillbox hat perched at an angle on her head. Frederika took a deep breath and looked at

326

herself in the cabin mirror one last time. Then she nodded at me and lowered the veil to hide most of her face. I thought this made her look beautiful and mysterious. Then with a small smile she stretched out her hand towards me and together we walked towards the cabin door.

We joined the other passengers on deck as the ship sailed slowly up a wide river with ancient, rundown warehouses bordering the banks on either side.

'This is the River Thames,' Frederika told me, 'the most important river in England.'

It certainly looked very important. I had never seen so many boats going up and down one stretch of water before. Long thin barges, carrying steel and coal, chugged past in either direction. There were even police boats going up and down very fast, making the waves roll towards the shore tossing smaller boats up and down.

The people on the other boats waved as they passed and we waved back. The sun was already hot and my layers of clothes felt unbearable. I gradually peeled off the cardigans and left them in a pile at my feet. Frederika said nothing; she seemed entranced by the scene before her; the faraway look in her eye had returned. I wondered what she was thinking.

As I followed Frederika's gaze, I saw straight ahead in the distance a huge bridge. As we sailed closer I noticed that there was a tall house at each end. The bridge seemed quite low. Our ship would only just pass beneath it, I thought. As we got nearer I realised, with horror, that what I'd thought was the bridge was not the bridge at all. Far below it, just above the water, was a second bridge. There was absolutely no way a tall ship like ours would fit underneath—and we were heading straight towards it. The ship wasn't slowing down. I began to panic. I imagined the houses at each end with their pointy spires and pretty windows tumbling into the water and the beautiful bridge destroyed.

I squeezed my eyes in fright and held my breath.

But there was no crash, no screams from passengers on board and when, after a few moments, I opened my eyes, I saw—to my amazement—that the lower level of the bridge had parted. The two halves were slowly rising and, like two giant arms, they waved to us.

Welcome to London!

The ship passed through. All noise on deck had stopped and everyone turned to watch the giant arms, having waved us through, slowly lower themselves. Then our chatter and laughter erupted, far louder than before. No one could believe such an astonishing bridge.

'Tower Bridge,' breathed Frederika quietly. 'Renata, that was Tower Bridge.'

Just beyond Tower Bridge our boat slowed down, churning up the brown waters of the Thames before coming to a standstill alongside a dock. Thick ropes were thrown and caught as the sailors jumped into action. They fastened the ropes to the enormous bollards that stood in a straight row along the harbour wall.

When they were ready the sailors helped us and our luggage down the gangways and into small boats that took it in turns to take groups of us further up the river.

'Why are we going on little boats?' I asked Frederika who was trying to keep the veil from blowing about in the breeze.

'That's why,' said Frederika and she pointed to a low bridge that barely seemed to skim the water's surface ahead of us.

Further up the river I spied a magical fairy castle with golden towers and spires glowing in the sunshine. It was covered in windows and a huge clock stood tall over everything; its face watching over London.

'The Palace of Westminster. That is where the government of Great Britain meets and works and makes all the laws for the land,' said Frederika.

I was in awe—this is where the *government* met?

'So where does the King live?' I asked.

'He lives in Buckingham Palace. I expect your father will show you it before you leave London,' Frederika replied.

'Oh, but I thought the King must live *there*,' I said, pointing to the Houses of Parliament. 'He could lie in bed and look at the clock out of his window. I think it's far too grand for the government.'

I could now clearly see the faces of the people standing and waving from the dock. They were happy faces, pleased to see us, and everyone was eager for us to come ashore. They were so different from the pale, tight, sad faces I had left behind. As the other children on the boat pushed and jostled to get closer to the side to wave to the crowds, an almighty cheer rose into the air, upwards and upwards, until it surrounded us. I felt then that we couldn't have had a better welcome anywhere in the world. But all the while I was scanning the people in front of me for the one that I was sure I would recognise. When I saw no familiar face, panic set in.

I grabbed Frederika's arm.

'Renata, that's about the fourth time you have nearly wrenched my arm off. What is it this time?' Frederika sounded cross as she tried to steady herself.

'How will Tatuś be able to recognise us? Suppose he takes somebody else home instead? What will we do? We can't possibly find him in this crowd.'

'You are a terrible worrier,' Frederika said, shaking herself free. 'Of course he will recognise us. Don't forget he knew me long before the war. I haven't changed *that* much.'

She was adjusting her hat as she spoke and then drew out a small powder compact from her bag and carefully powdered her nose and cheeks trying yet again to mask the blotchiness of her face.

With a loud clanking the gangplanks were moved into position and the ropes tied. At the end of each gangplank there were men in uniform who looked at all our papers to check if we were allowed to get off the boat. When they said you could go, you had to make your way over to another group of officials who had registers, and were waiting to lead the children to the next stage of their journey, either to a place where they would be met by someone, or a meeting place for groups travelling on to another town or country.

I thought of Tomasz. I hadn't seen him on board and I knew that I wouldn't see him again. I hoped he was going to be safe and looked after and happy in his new life. I hoped I was going to be too.

Frederika and I stood in silence watching the file of children and few remaining adults slowly make their way ashore. She wasn't in a hurry and I couldn't think of anything to say. Frederika said nothing either but stood quietly at my side. Watching. Waiting.

When at last it was our turn to make our way down the gangplank I found I was clutching my documents so tightly that they were becoming damp and creased in my hands. My heart was in my mouth as I tried to flatten the crumpled papers. Frederika checked the veil covering her flushed face one last time and led the way off the boat.

At the end of the gangplank we were met by a tall man in a military uniform talking to one of the passengers. As we approached, Frederika uttered a little cry and her grip lightened on my shoulders. The man looked swiftly up back and then down again before his head snapped up for a second time. He ignored the boy he had been talking to and held out his arms towards us. I recognised him immediately from the photograph he had sent. My father with his broad shoulders and dark hair that had gone grey around his ears. I could remember those dark eyes and lovely smile. But best of all he recognised me. Dazed, I saw him take a few paces towards us, then felt his hands around my waist and he was lifting me high into the air. Just as he had done so many years ago back home in our apartment in Przemyśl. Up into the sunlight, into the deep blue sky. Up and up, towards the clouds— and heaven.

Then he was hugging me with a love that I knew had kept him looking for me all these years. I could feel his deep intakes of breath and the clenching in his jaw, the slight roughness of his face and the wetness on his cheeks. After a while he put me down and turned to Frederika, who had been standing quietly watching us. Still she didn't say a word and my father embraced her politely. Then suddenly he hugged us both, again and again, with tears streaming down his cheeks that he made no effort to brush away. We laughed and cried, all three of us together, as the people behind us on the gangplank and the officials on the dock watched and smiled.

'Hello, Tatuś,' I said. 'Here we are at last. This is Frederika. I think you know her. She is very nice and I think that if you are planning to marry again you ought to marry her.'

Frederika gasped and looked horrified.

'Renata, how could you?' she said, looking at me angrily from under her veil. I immediately regretted my words and felt very embarrassed.

My father said nothing but looked at Frederika for a long time. Then he turned to me and said very gravely, 'Thank you for your advice, young lady. We will have to talk about it later on because now I am going to have to send you both in a taxi to the hotel where I have booked rooms for us all.'

'Why do we have to go alone? Aren't you coming with us?' I asked in a small voice, worried that I had upset him already and desperately not wanting to be separated from him again now that we had found each other at last.

'Don't look so worried,' my father replied, stroking my hair and caressing my cheek with his thumb. 'I have to check that all the children on these boats are healthy. But I shan't be too long, I promise.'

We drove away with our luggage piled high in the back of a big black London taxi. I had never been in a car before and as I climbed inside I thought back to what the *fiacre* driver had told me. This car had leather seats, it was black and rather dusty, not polished and shiny. There was no hood but a solid roof. The driver didn't wear a long coat with long gloves and goggles but ordinary clothes with a flat cap and a stub of a cigarette hung off his bottom lip.

I relaxed into the deep seats as the car drew away from the quay. Frederika sat beside me, still rather quiet, and I thought she must be feeling ill. I looked at the scenes racing past the window outside. It was Sunday. We drove past enormous white houses with gleaming windows and the remains of black railings. We sped past parks and open spaces. Men and women were walking along the pavements, holding hands with small children or pushing babies in prams.

Then all of a sudden the taxi driver stopped. He opened his door and got out. We watched as he made his way across the road to a flower stall full of golden daffodils. They were arranged in buckets on a cart and were bright and cheerful. They looked the way I felt. The taxi driver spoke briefly with the flower seller and fumbled in his pocket before returning to the taxi. He opened the door nearest to Frederika and held out his bouquet to her.

'Beautiful flowers for a beautiful lady,' he said.

Frederika was completely taken by surprise. I saw her jaw drop and a flush start at her neck and rise slowly up towards her hair.

'Thank you,' was all she could manage in English.

'What did he say, Frederika?' I asked.

'Oh nothing, darling,' she replied, obviously embarrassed.

'Tell me! Tell me!'

Frederika looked at me and laughed and then she repeated what the man had said.

'How nice,' I smiled, 'and completely true of course.'

As Frederika laid her bouquet on her lap so that she could wipe some smut from her eye (or so she said), the taxi driver started up the engine again and began whistling, which he continued to do all the way to the hotel.

My father had reserved two rooms at a Park Lane hotel. The taxi driver helped us upstairs with our bags and Frederika gave him one of her wonderful smiles and said, 'Thank you,' again in her broken English. He went away whistling. I walked across the thick carpet to the bedroom window and stared out.

'Frederika, come and have a look,' I called out. 'There is a man down there who has hung up all of his paintings on the railings. Isn't it strange? What will he do if it rains?'

'What, on a day like this?' Frederika laughed, removing her pillbox hat and laying it on the bed.

She was right, there wasn't a cloud in the sky and it was hard to imagine on this balmy sunny day that it ever rained in England.

'In London it is the custom for artists to hang paintings on rails. They are for sale.'

I was impressed. My cousin knew a lot about this new country. I turned to ask how she knew about these things when something caught my eye and made me stop. When I turned back to face Frederika I noticed one single bed and . . . a cot. A baby's cot with wooden sides that could be lowered and raised; surely it wasn't for me. My eight-and-a-half-year-old pride was mortally wounded. I could

334

not believe my eyes—not only was the cot far too small for me, but the insult was unbearable. Did my father imagine I was still a *baby*?

'Look at that cot!' I cried.

Frederika looked up and for a moment said nothing. Then seeing how upset I was said, 'Don't worry about it, darling.'

She could not have said a worse thing. Was she expecting me to sleep in a cot too? Who did she think I was?

'How dare he!' I screamed. 'I am *not* a baby. I want to go back to Poland. I want my Aunt Zuzia. I am *not* staying here. Take me back, please take me back.' I stamped my foot and all the love I had felt for this new country, the waving bridge, the whistling taxi driver, the smiling people all disappeared and I wanted to be back in the comfort and security of people who knew me.

Frederika sat on the bed and said nothing. She allowed me to shout and cry until I was exhausted, then quietly she took me by the hand and gently drew me down on the bed beside her.

'Listen to me, Renata,' she said quietly, 'your father has not seen you for more than six years. In all that time he has thought about you all day and every day. He has held a picture in his mind of the baby he had to leave behind. This picture has helped him to survive the loneliness and unhappiness of all those years, not knowing what had happened to you, your mother, your grandmother, everyone. He simply forgot that you would have grown bigger. He prepared the cot for the daughter he remembered.'

'But—'

'But,' Frederika interrupted, 'the years have

passed and now you are a big girl and, as soon as he gets here, he will realise for himself the mistake he has made. Don't make it hard for him. He did it out of love for you.'

And suddenly I was no longer cross. All the frustration and anger I had been feeling towards my father just disappeared and was replaced by another feeling, just as strong and just as intense: that of pure love. We had found each other at last and my future with darling Tatuś lay stretched out before me in this wonderful land where I knew we would live happily ever after.

AUTHOR'S NOTE

This book is an account of my early years spent in Poland under the occupation, first of Nazi Germany and then of the Soviet Union. This photograph of my mother, who died together with my grandmother in Auschwitz, was the spur that prompted me to write this memoir when I unexpectedly came upon it some years ago.

Those years were terrible for millions of ordinary people, many of whom, such as my mother and grandmother, did not survive. But I did survive. My love of stories, both those that were told to me, and later those I read for myself, afforded me a place where I could retreat from the horrors of everyday life, where I could retain a perspective on what was happening, and from where I nurtured my unshakeable belief in the happy-ever-after.

For many years following my ordeal I took comfort from the people who loved and cared for me, in a happy, safe family environment both in Poland and later in Britain. This helped to heal the painful wounds and enabled me to enjoy the ordinary, normal things other girls of my age were doing. I went to school and became totally British. I fell in love with my new country where policemen were unarmed and friendly, and one could stand on a soap box in the middle of London and shout criticisms of the government without fear of retribution.

With the passing of the years I thought less and less about my horrific childhood experience until finally I believed it was past history and forgotten. After all it had left no mark on my attitude, my reactions or indeed my relationships with family and friends. That was until the day when I heard an interview on the radio with a Holocaust survivor who had been deeply affected by her experiences and how, in turn, these experiences had affected her family. I commented to my two daughters how strange it was that I had suffered no such after-effects. They laughed and showed me that I had indeed been affected by my experiences, but they loved me just as I was.

Many friends with whom I have shared my story over the years have encouraged me to write it down. I tried, but the first publisher told me that it wasn't violent enough. A second publisher asked why had I written it as fiction and not as a memoir. I couldn't at that time write it as a memoir and my story was locked away in a drawer for many years.

Two years ago I was reunited with my

goddaughter, Imogen van Bergen, and we decided to revisit the manuscript together. Using the editorial comments of my good friend, Graham Mays, we began again. This last year Imogen and I have worked tirelessly, rewriting the manuscript as seen through the eyes of a child. Then, through a series of coincidences that included a lunch, a sale of a house and a chain of friends including Dinah Reynolds and Rebecca Carter, this memoir reached the desk of Jemima Hunt (of The Writer's Practice), who, acting as my agent, suggested further improvements (duly taken on board), and finally brought it to the attention of Alexandra Pringle of Bloomsbury Publishing. The rest is history.

I would like to express my sincere thanks to Imogen to whom I owe a huge debt. I am very grateful for her determination, support, enthusiasm, commitment and encouragement. We have worked so well together. I thank Graham Mays for his hours of work organising an earlier draft of my manuscript. Thanks too to Alexandra Pringle, Gillian Stern, Alexa von Hirschberg, Tess Viljoen, Mary Tomlinson, Laura Brooke and all the members of the Bloomsbury team who guided me through the marketing and production processes with patience and enthusiasm. And finally to my friends, too many to mention by name, who have all listened to my story, and urged me over the years to put pen to paper.

I dedicate this book to those who have literally enabled me to live my life. To the dead: my mother and grandmother killed in Nazi concentration camps; my beloved father who died in England in 1989; and all those who helped to keep me safe in Poland and whose names I have changed in this account. But also to the living: to Dady who, as Frederika and subsequently my loving second mother, has played such a large part in my survival and in my life since; and to my younger brother, Alex. Above all to Bruce, my husband of fifty-two years, and our daughters, Sarah and Kay, all three unfailing pillars of love, patience and strength. Thank you all.

A NOTE ON THE AUTHOR

Renata Calverley was born in Poland in 1937. She
has an Honours Degree in English Literature and
American Studies from Nottingham University,
a Post Graduate Certificate in Education from
the London University Institute of Education
and a Diploma in Creative Writing. A retired
deputy head of a Sixth Form, she taught English
for thirty-seven years, including twenty-five years
at Aylesbury High School. On retirement she
worked with GAP Activity Project for ten years as a
project manager successively in Canada, Japan and
Poland. Renata Calverley is an accomplished public
speaker, regularly recounting her experiences to
societies and interested parties across the UK. She
lives in Oxford with her husband.